PRAISE FOR
GLOVE SHY

Janet Hurley's stunning memoir *Glove Shy* is an unflinching portrait of her Hudson River Valley family, centered on her older brother Brian, a boxing phenomenon trained by two-time World Heavyweight Champion Floyd Patterson. Brian's arc becomes part Icarus, part Hamlet, and his triumphs and tragedies leave no one close to him untouched. As Hurley herself struggles to escape the long shadows and snares of her brother's near-fame and grim misfortunes, an intertwining tale emerges: one of his tragic flaws and almost inevitable demise, and of her troubled yet powerful and loving indomitable spirit. *Glove Shy* is fast-paced, emotionally rugged, and just as poignantly moving as can be.

> –**Bland Simpson**, author of *North Carolina: Land of Water, Land of Sky, Little Rivers* and *Waterway Tales: A Carolinian's Eastern Streams* and an inductee of the North Carolina Literary Hall of Fame

In *Glove Shy*, Janet Hurley tells the deeply moving story of her love for her brother, Brian, a talented amateur boxer who struggles with addiction and depression. Along the way, she offers up a poignant group portrait of the renowned Huguenot Boxing Club, a unique world overseen by the enigmatic former World Heavyweight Champion Floyd Patterson. Throughout this harrowing memoir of remorse and reckoning, Hurley offers a clear-eyed account of her life with Brian; she also takes us with her on a journey to make sense of her brother's tragic death. That she manages not to pull any punches, and that she shines a light on the subtle workings of race, class, and family in America, only makes her accomplishment all the more impressive. A knockout of a book.

> – **Sebastian Matthews**, author of *Beyond Repair: Living in a Fractured State, Life and Times of American Crow, The Beginner's Guide to a Head On Collision* and *In My Father's Footsteps*

The searingly sad story of a younger sister watching her brother—a gifted boxer—fighting powerful addictions. Her helplessness and frustration, along with the ring-smart power of her prose, all hit the reader like an overhand right to the face. Finish reading this book, then take a standing eight-count, blink your shattered vision back into focus, try to stop your eyes from watering.

– **Jim DeFilippi**, author of *Forty Steps to Old Sparky* and *The Mules of Monte Cassino*

Janet Hurley's *Glove Shy* is indeed a "grace of reckoning."

Exquisitely written, this tale of sibling love, talent, character and addiction chronicles the pain, the scars and the secrets that slowly tear a family apart. And like in a boxing match, Brian Hurley's brilliant insights are the opening bell that announces each round. The narrative bears witness of his tortured journey as a gifted young boxer, mentored and trained by the great Floyd Patterson to be a future champ. It's a story of his life of promise and of pain, both a blessing and a curse to him and to the many who love him. For anyone who loves the sweet science, the ancient sport of boxing, this books brims with the sweat and years of discipline it takes to reach those pure "moments of possibility" that frame the human story. Says fellow boxer Andy Schott to the author: "If we're all here on earth for two blinks ... and Brian was here for just one, isn't that still worth something?" In a haunting memoir whose reticence weighs and measures for value and relevance each emotion and each word, Janet has made sure that her brother's single blink matters in ways not counted by the victories, but by the words we leave; by the endurance of love and the fidelity of the human spirit.

–**Rachel Manley**, author of *Drumblair: Memories of a Jamaican Childhood*, *Slipstream: A Daughter Remembers*, *Horses in Her Hair: A Grandaughter's Story* and *In My Father's Shade*

GLOVE SHY
A SISTER'S RECKONING

JANET HURLEY

LYSTRA BOOKS
& Literary Services

ISBN 979-8-9850083-5-7 paperback
ISBN 979-8-9850083-6-4 ebook
Library of Congress Control Number: 2023904972

Grateful acknowledgement is made to Andrew Schott, Harold Issen, Jamie Rhein and Michael Kelsh for permission to reprint excerpts from emails, letters and song lyrics.

Excerpts of writing by Brian Hurley, Sonia Hurley and William Hurley reprinted with permission by Janet Hurley.

Unless otherwise credited, all photographs are from the collection of Janet Hurley.

Excerpt from *Young Men and Fire* by Norman Maclean reprinted with permission of the University of Chicago Press. © 1992 by the University of Chicago. All rights reserved.

Media excerpts reprinted courtesy of *The Record* (Middletown, NY), *The Freeman* (Kingston, NY), *New York Daily News*, *The Poughkeepsie Journal* (NY) and *Hudson Valley Magazine* (Today Media, Wilmington, DE).

The publisher or author has obtained the permission of rights holders whenever possible. Should the publisher have been unable to locate a rights holder, notwithstanding good-faith efforts, it requests that any contact information concerning such rights holders be forwarded, so that they may be contacted for future editions.

Author's photo by Eliza Bell Photography.

Book design by Kelly Prelipp Lojk.

Published by
Lystra Books & Literary Services, LLC
391 Lystra Estates Drive
Chapel Hill, NC 27527
lystrabooks@gmail.com

For Maren and Liam
and, of course, David

Even so, there may somewhere be an ending to this story, although it might take a storyteller's faith to proceed on a quest to find it and on the way to retain the belief that it might both be true and fit together dramatically. A story that honors the dead realistically partly atones for their sufferings, and so instead of leaving us in moral bewilderment, adds dimensions to our acuteness in watching the universe's four elements at work—sky, earth, fire and young men.

–Norman Maclean, *Young Men and Fire*,
University of Chicago Press

Author's Note

[2022]

In 2003, I signed up for a creative nonfiction class—thinking I would write about topics, events, history, or the unusual worlds and obsessions of people I didn't know. Instead, I wrote short pieces about my relationship with my brother and my childhood infatuation with his boxing. By 2004, I'd made a commitment to a memoir. I worked on the manuscript for seven years, wholeheartedly through a master of fine arts program, then intermittently as energy, heart and brain space would allow. Eventually, priorities of family, community and work ventures prevailed. I rarely opened any of the files in my *Glove Shy* folder until I just didn't at all. I returned to the manuscript in 2021. I had new awareness, perspective, information and, still, some of the old questions.

As guideposts for readers, and when possible, I assigned years to numbered chapter headings and to titled sections. The latter serve both to move the narrative forward and illuminate my inquiries, my reflections, and my reckonings. These reckonings were with what happened or didn't and my own missteps and mistakes—or with the tension arising when memories and facts didn't align or proved elusive. To ground and shape the narrative, I refer to journals, letters, emails, interviews, press clippings, biographies, autobiographies, photos, public documents and artifacts.

But this book isn't just a collection of memories and facts, it's about all that is greater than the sum of its parts: story, personal truth, reckoning, healing and love. To serve this, I reconstructed some scenes I wasn't present for based on family stories, what was told to me in interviews and my own familiarity with place and people's speech patterns and gestures. I've endeavored to let the reader know who or what the sources are. I changed some of the names of the people included.

This is my story. My sisters are present, of course, but not fully—out of respect for their memories and their narratives.

//////////////////////////

Part 1

//////////////////////////

The squared circle creates a fantasy world of sorts. All outside reality becomes inconsequential; your horizons extend no further than the ropes that confine you. Your mind's workings are reduced to the sweetness of primal instinct. Your two objectives are so awesomely simple and clear-cut: survival and victory. The fight seems to combine all that is life and caters to those possessive of attributes distinguishing monks and infants. To extend oneself towards and past the breaking point of conscious endurance realizes a satisfaction unbecoming any other action.

– Brian Hurley, "The Other Side of the Ropes,"
The Huguenot Herald, New Paltz, New York,
June 23, 1976

Heavy Bag

[2009]

I'm cooking dinner with my husband, David, when I hear it. *Thap…thap…thap-thap-thap-thap…thap.* I glance over my shoulder to see the basement door slightly cracked, the light from the top of the stairs illuminating a narrow wedge of the kitchen floor.

THAP, thap, THAP, thap, THAP, thap-thap-thap-thap.

Our ten-year-old son, Liam, is hitting the heavy bag, the sound now in concert with my heartbeat. If he were older, with more weight behind his blows, I might be hearing thud, thud, thud. Maybe even punctuated with those airy-raspy sounds that come from exhaling through the nose, the sounds every boxer makes when throwing a punch. Sounds that resonate from my childhood, from a basement in a ranch-style house in upstate New York, where my older brother, Brian, attacked this same heavy bag, fervent, at first, with ambition.

Maren, our thirteen-year-old daughter, a dancer and a dazzle in Liam's eye, stomps to our basement door, swings it wide and yells, "Liam, you are being so loud!"

I hear a mild "OK, OK" and then *thump-thump-thump-thump* as he runs up the basement steps. I'm not surprised that he acquiesced so easily. I know how it is.

I followed my brother everywhere when we were children. Brian was four years older, and he let me tag along on his daily excursions with a resigned, but not unkind, patience and occasional brilliant moments of favor. We lived in New Paltz, a small town in between the cliff-faced Shawangunk Mountains and the Hudson River. Our neighborhood was not unlike the one I live in now: long established, middle class, no two houses alike. My family home was on a street that ran out of streetlights by the time it spilled down the hill and pooled into a cul-de-sac of sorts. We didn't have a view of the mountains. But we had woods, acres of them. There was a grapevine that we swung on, pushing off from a large, gray boulder that hosted settlements of long-legged moss. And we had a brook, where Brian pursued huge, sly carp with a rod and reel, rarely catching anything. I know this is true for many siblings, one adoring and the other allowing it. I also know that some actually move abreast and share a path—which is *my* most fervent ambition for my children. And why I've spent so many years retracing my brother's steps and choices and my own.

Brian and Janet dressed for Sunday school, circa 1966.

Chapter One

[1966–1971]

First, there were the ants. And then, my mother's face sliding off.

I was only four, maybe five. Brian was eight—maybe nine—and home from school with one of his many ear infections. I had instructions from my mother not to bother him, but he'd called to me. "Jan." Raspy. "Jan." Urgent. I eased into his room and right into his enormous green eyes, blackened with pupils. They pinned me to the door until Brian blinked and pointed a shaking finger. Down. I couldn't bear to look, to see what was there. So, I looked at him instead. He was half under the cover but still wore a blue terry cloth bathrobe, his hair a jumble of reddish-brown cowlicks and frizz. His skin, normally white in that bluish way of the Irish, had the look of peeled onion, somewhat translucent, with freckles like a delicate net holding it all together.

"No, Jan, not me," he whispered. "Not me. They're on the floor. Get them. They're on the floor."

He'd fooled me so many times, made me look, made me jump, convinced me to hand over my allowance for a child's equivalent of swampland. But still, I glanced down. Nothing. Maybe I shook my head because he yelled, "No, you're missing them. The ants. Please get the ants."

They must have been in his voice because when I looked down, I saw them. I lifted a foot and stomped.

"Over there," he swung his arm like a crane. "There, there."

I stomped again, and then again, and then felt the panic, felt the sinister tickles of the ants, sure they were tiny and carnivorous and in the millions, sure that they would cover us both with so many stings we would die before my mother came in to check Brian's temperature. And that's how she found me, trying to cover the floor as fast as I could with my ant-smashing dance.

She might have explained that Brian was delirious with fever and having a reaction to penicillin—but my memory skips that, takes me right to lunch, when Brian was able to get out of bed and sit at the dining room table, spooning broth back and forth while I peeled the crusts off a baloney sandwich. Just as I took a bite, Brian leaned forward over his bowl and whispered, "Did you see Mom's face?"

Again, the eyes. Now even wider behind his black-rimmed glasses. I stopped chewing. He glanced over his shoulder at the kitchen where my mother washed dishes. "You can't see it now," he turned back to me, voice as hushed as a spy. "But when she came into my bedroom, her face slid off. It was all bloody, and there was all this pus. Her face, it was...it was hanging from her chin." He slumped back in his seat, let his spoon drop into the bowl with a clank that made me swallow a glob of bread and deli-meat all at once. "I don't know what to do," he said. "I don't know what we're going to do until Dad gets home."

I had just seen my mother's face when she set the sandwich in front of me. I knew—*knew*—that her face was fine. But that knowledge fled under the assault of this image and the intensity of Brian's whisper. Ants were nothing compared to the molten mess he'd just stuck in my head, nothing compared to pus and blood and a faceless mother. And even worse—the lash of Brian's wondering. What are we going to do?

It cut deep.

I always followed Brian's lead.

What are we going to do?

When I was six, maybe seven, and Brian was ten or eleven, he called me into his room to show me a silvery angelfish, partially wrapped in a wet paper towel, lying under his microscope. His room bubbled and hummed around us with small fish tanks where angelfish, tetras, guppies and gouramies darted peaceably in and out of faux vegetation. Brian knew all the facts about every fish and was part of a tropical fish club based at a local shop, where he sold the fry that his fish produced, or traded with other members. He loved the furred and feathered, too, and talked about being a vet one day. He and his friend, Alex, who lived next door, formed a zoological club, which I wasn't invited to join. They set out Havahart traps so they could study reluctant and sometimes snarly raccoons or opossum. Brian had put a microscope on his Christmas list to do more research, he said. He and Alex spent hours peering down at slides, refusing my entreaties to just have a peek.

Now, I climbed quickly up on a chair, impressed, as always, that I had been summoned. I listened carefully to Brian's instructions about where to put my eye and how to focus. And then I was looking into endless translucence. With blue. I took my eye off the scope and bent down to look closely at the fish. "It's got blue on it."

"What? What are you talking about?" Brian slid it out and popped it back in the tank. It darted about the water as if to say, thank God that nonsense is over. As it flicked by, Brian frowned, "It looks like it has a fungus on it."

He scooped out another with a net, wrapped it in a bit of wet paper towel and slid it under the microscope.

"Man," he muttered. "This one, too." Then he glanced down at the roll of paper towels. There it was, on the end, a smear of blue ink across the edge of all the sheets. "Oh no. I hope it won't hurt them. I'm glad you noticed that." The acknowledgment flushed through my body as I jumped off the chair.

When I was seven and Brian was eleven, our neighbor Tommy—older and bigger Tommy—decided to start a business with a drink machine his father brought home from his job at Woolworth's. He recruited Brian to help. It was folly, really. A lemonade stand at the bottom of a dead-end hill.

I helped them set up. Tommy hadn't really invited me, but he tolerated me as Brian's shadow, and I made sure to do everything he asked just right. Tommy was our equivalent of the neighborhood don—giving orders, demanding loyalty. He was a solid boy, not very tall, with a distinctive walk. He pushed off his toes, swung his arms and kept his chin up, dirty blonde hair tangling with his eyelashes. Being invited to play with him meant an opportunity to get into his good graces or fall into exile. Or worse. So, when he asked me to go inside and get glasses, real glasses, not the Dixie cups every other kid used at their summer stands, I just did what I was told. He said I'd get a quarter for washing them at the end of the day.

By that time, we'd sold one or two glasses of the faux lemonade to immediate neighbors and drank the rest of it ourselves.

Tommy looked in our cardboard cash box. "Shit."

I got down to business. "Do I still get my quarter?" I ignored Brian's attempt to shush me.

Tommy stood and put his arms around the drink machine. "If you wash the glasses, you get the quarter." With a grunt, he staggered back up the drive, the extension cord dragging between his legs. "Use the hose," he called over his shoulder.

Brian helped me carry the eight glasses to the front walk where we lined them up, dull with lemon film in the late afternoon sun. I squeezed in behind the boxwoods, found the hose and nozzle and tugged it out to the glasses. It caught on a branch, and from the sidewalk, I grabbed tight with two hands and gave the biggest jerk I could. The hose looped out and hit the glasses with a lash and crash that left me staring.

Tommy was beside me in an instant. "You're fired! Go home. Go on! Git!"

I threw the nozzle to the ground and sobbed as I turned and ran as fast as I could across the street. When I reached my front-porch steps I felt safe enough to sit down and look back at the scene of my disgrace.

Brian stood very still in Tommy's drive; the edge of the card table lifted in his hands. His shoulders were slumped and his head lowered, as if he knew what was coming and might avoid it if he were quiet enough.

"Brian," I screamed, "run!"

But a moment later, he and Tommy were a pinwheel of ferocity, rolling about on the grass, grabbing each other's hair, punching. The front door of Tommy's house opened with a bang. His mother hauled her son off my brother and held him with both arms as he kicked and swore. Brian escaped across the yard, jumping the ditch as my mother came out on the front porch. He pushed me to the side as he went up the stairs, and my mother greeted him in a way that suggested she wasn't surprised by the turn of events. She guided him inside, leaving me to hug my stomach and watch as Tommy's mother cleaned up the broken glass.

The next morning, Brian looked at me as we ate oatmeal together, his face puffy and smeared with blues and purples. "We are going to have the stand open today," he said. "And you can't come."

When Tommy was in eighth grade, his father brought home mats and gloves and helped his son build a crude ring in their rec room. One by one, boys with cracking voices climbed through the ropes and took a now-sanctioned pounding from

Tommy. It must have been gratifying for Brian when the basement bouts began, welcoming all comers, and he could see that he wasn't the only one to take a beating. Though he was one of the few who kept coming back.

This became part of Brian's usual story, to say that he sought out Floyd Patterson, former World Heavyweight Boxing Champion and the founder of the Huguenot Boxing Club, after years of taking punches from the neighborhood tough guy. Brian said this in interviews, on television, in the local paper, in national magazines. He even said this to me, as I interviewed him for a book report I was doing on a novel called *The Contender*. I know for sure that Brian was fifteen and I was eleven. He was in the halcyon days of his amateur boxing career. He told the neighborhood tough guy story on tape as if I hadn't witnessed it.

Chapter Two

[1972]

Question

Climbing into the ring
the dust of resin rising
can you become the victor?

—Brian Hurley, senior English class journal, 1976

My father flipped through the channels and played with the antennae to get the reception just right. I lay on the floor, sphinxlike, resting my chin on the heels of my palms and reaching my fingers up under my glasses to pull at the corners of my eyes. "C'mon," I said, frustrated. "It's gonna start."

It was the second matchup of Floyd Patterson and Muhammad Ali, who was seven years younger and weighed thirty more pounds. Floyd was thirty-seven and had been fighting since he was thirteen. Brian and my father had been talking about the fight for weeks, worrying about it really. Not me. I was too young to understand what words like "stamina" and "comeback" meant. This was Floyd Patterson. He was a celebrity who actually lived in our small hometown of New Paltz. He'd been the youngest man to win the world heavyweight championship, the only man to win the title twice. I just knew he'd do it a third time, even though he'd lost to Ali before. Back then, Ali had called him an Uncle Tom, according to Brian.

I didn't know what that meant exactly, but it was obviously something bad. Floyd had always called Ali "Cassius Clay" even though Ali said it was a slave name. That was bad too. My mom said that it was all part of the "hype" and things were better between them now. How did she know? I wondered.

Now, Brian sat in one of our blue-green swivel chairs, gliding to the right and then to the left while jiggling his foot. "Shut up," he said to me. "Dad's gonna get it right in a minute."

"Brian, please." My mother sat on the couch with my six-year-old sister, Nora. Mom was still in a dress, though she had been home for hours from her job as the director of a substance-abuse prevention program for the nearby Poughkeepsie public schools, just too busy to do anything but take off her heels and put on a pair of green felt and faux lamb's wool slippers. She stretched slender legs out in front of her with a sigh. I could still see a slight stain of red lipstick feathering from her top lip. It was the only makeup she ever wore or needed. Her eyes were the same green as Brian's, but her hair was dark gray, cut short and stylish.

"Just all of you, be quiet," my father muttered. His heavy, black-rimmed glasses were down on the tip of his nose so that he could see the connection between the television and antennae better, stopping to take a drag on his cigarette, then resting it back in the ashtray on top of the TV so that he could adjust again.

It was rare for us to be watching a heavyweight fight together; that was usually something just my father and brother did. Tonight, my older sister, Julie, was out of the house. A sophomore in high school, she might have been at cheerleading practice or at her best friend's, up the street. My father, Coach Bill Hurley, was the athletic director of Kingston Schools Consolidated, just thirty minutes north, and his life revolved around sports, particularly football. He grew up in Yonkers, toward New York City, in an Irish Catholic family, with a dad who was a trolley car conductor and a mom who was a switchboard operator. He and his brother were the first to go to college, through football scholarships. His was to Alfred University, where he planned to major as a ceramics engineer. Though he transferred to the state university at Cortland for a degree in physical education, he viewed sports through that engineer's problem-solving lens. And he watched as much football, along with boxing, as he could, to my mother's perennial annoyance.

My father fixed the reception and gingerly sat down, ready to jump up at any minute. The fight was in Madison Square Garden, and the crowd looked enormous. Once the fight started, it seemed to be going OK, with Ali dancing around and Floyd connecting with his famous leaping left hooks from time to time. I felt cheered by the infrequent exclamations of Brian and my father—"Yeah, that's it," or "Ali didn't like that!"—and tried to ignore the small murmurs of "oh dear" that came from my mother whenever Floyd was hit, which was a lot in the sixth round.

Coach Bill Hurley, center, conferring with colleagues about a play on the football field.

Much to my dismay, the Ali-Patterson fight was stopped in the seventh round, and Floyd climbed through the ropes and down the steps with an eye swollen shut, never to declare retirement but never to return to the ring. Instead, he returned to New Paltz. Maybe that's when he took another good look at that barn on his farm-turned-estate and decided to turn it into a gym where he could work with young fighters.

Chicken Farm

[2005]

The windshield wipers squeal for want of bolder rain, but it's a slight winter mist they attend to, just enough to tease my vision as I drive. I slow and make the gradual merge right, onto Springtown Road, which runs parallel to the Wallkill River on the western side of New Paltz. When I was a kid, this road and the rest of the "flats," as we called them, flooded every spring. After the water receded, the soil was dark and eager for the crops that were soon planted, corn mostly, and pumpkins. For folks who lived on the mountain, the floods meant a long drive around to jobs at the state university or across another river, the Hudson, to IBM, or as merchants in the small downtown area. The town was safe from the water, settled on a rise by Huguenots, who wisely took the advice of the native Esopus people and built their stone houses within view, but not within grasp, of the river. I grew up with children who bore the names of the original twelve patentees of that settlement, and when I was in high school, some of my girlfriends donned bonnets and long skirts to lead tourists through the old houses.

There's no danger of flood now on Springtown Road. I look up to my left and see the old stone and white buttress of a house. It's long and low, with a row of windows across the front that suggests a sunroom. The groupings of trees on the property are leafless scribbles against the blank of gray January sky. A faint remnant of snow smudges across the lower lawn. I turn into the long driveway that leads up to the house, to the outbuildings, to the barn that evolved into a gym. I'm not worried that anyone will want to go in or go out. I know that Floyd Patterson and his wife, Janet, are reclusive. I have written to them and asked them to talk with me but received no reply. I don't intend to invade their privacy and have promised I won't call more than once while in town. After that call went unreturned, I had decided to drive out, take a look, just see what comes up for me.

I remember Floyd talking about how he fell in love with the country in the mid-Hudson Valley when he was just a boy. His mother, Annabelle Patterson, sent him upstate from New York City after years of truancy and run-ins with the police and juvenile courts, where no one cared to find out what was really going on for a Black boy from Bed-Stuy. Annabelle hoped that the Wiltwyck School for Boys, funded mostly through the efforts of Eleanor Roosevelt, who lived across the river, would keep him out of trouble, teach him to read and write, help him with the debilitating shyness that had kept him so isolated. It did that and more.

Floyd won awards for academics, developed a friendship with Roosevelt that lasted until her death and made his way into a ring for school-sponsored boxing—where he was cheered as he won. Living at Wiltwyck also instilled an appreciation of the woods and fields that guided him all those years later to buy the large home just outside of the main village of New Paltz. Though reporters always referred to it as an estate, originally, it was a farm. Belonging to the Krauders. Chicken farmers.

I can barely see the barn now, through the trees. I wonder what I would find if I were able to go in. Would the ring still be up? The heavy bags? Maybe it is just a storage place now, for the clutter one means to sort through but never does. I check my rearview and side mirrors, take a last look up the driveway and turn the car around to head back into town.

Chapter Three

[1973]

> Floyd is not a large man, not for a KO artist in the
> heaviest divisions. He stands under six foot but has
> broad muscular shoulders. When he walks there is a
> certain sway or swagger that exudes confidence. It
> is a walk that says he is in no hurry, that he is a man
> of accomplishment.
>
> —Brian Hurley, "Character Portrait: My Impressions
>   and Learnings of Floyd Patterson," 1983

The long asphalt drive lined with hedges led the way up to
the boxing club. Brian and his good friend Fred stood at the
bottom of the hill. They had walked the mile or so from town,
Brian eager, Fred not so sure. He was a slender boy, with dark
hair and eyes, not as confident in his stride as Brian, surer of
his artistic talents than athletics. Brian was fifteen. His black
glasses, usually taped with a Band-Aid on the side, had recently been replaced by contacts. A dark curly mass of hair sprang
from a head that had sported a father-engineered buzz cut
through his middle school years. He could run a tongue over
teeth that had just emerged from the tyranny of braces.

"Why is Floyd gonna let us in the gym?" Fred asked. "We're
wrestlers, not fighters. My mother wouldn't even let me go out
for football with you."

Brian shrugged. "There's a lot we already bring to it," he said.
"I've been thinking about boxing since Tommy had his ring.

Wrestling is cool but..." He considered the hedges. "Look, we'll say we can cut his hedges and then ask to see the gym."

Fred laughed. "You're kidding, right? I don't know how to cut hedges."

But Brian had already started up the drive. "We'll figure it out."

At the top of the drive, the boys hesitated. They didn't know whether to knock on the door of the old barn they knew housed the gym or knock on the door of the big wood-and-stone house. Floyd solved their dilemma by coming out of the house. He stopped when he saw the boys. He was early in his retirement from boxing, still a powerful man who wore T-shirts that stretched across his shoulders. His skin, dark and lustrous, bore few scars from his twenty-year pro career. He smiled at the boys and ran a huge hand over his close-cropped hair. It came to a knob over the center of his forehead, like the prow of a boat.

"What can I do for you?" he asked. His voice was low and relaxed.

Brian and Fred were silent in their unabashed adoration. Finally, Brian said, "Do you need some yard work? We saw your hedges and wondered if you needed some trimming?"

Floyd looked at the two for a long moment. "You ever trimmed hedges before?"

Brian nodded. "Yes, sir, I helped my dad."

"Uh-huh, well." Floyd paused and in that moment Brian's life could have gone one way or the other. "I'll get the trimmer."

Later, the three of them stood together to consider a driveway lined with jagged green teeth.

"I thought you boys knew how to do this," Floyd said.

"I never said that," Fred burst out. "We just wanted to see the gym."

Floyd nodded. "You could have just asked, instead of ruining my hedges."

Brian glared at Fred. After a moment, Floyd said, "All right, all right, well, put that thing down and come in."

The gym was not what they imagined. It was still in the process of being converted from its former identity. There were three floors; they entered on the middle loft area. Looking over the half-wall to the bottom floor, Fred and Brian saw the ring. It was a twenty-by-twenty-foot square with three rope sides that were dingy and tired in the middle. Old sparring gloves, headgear and protective cups hung from hooks on the wall. Brian breathed it all in: dust, sweat, leather.

Floyd motioned for the two to follow. On the third floor, Brian was immediately thrilled to see three heavy bags hanging from the giant old barn beams. An old speed bag, a sit-up board, a mirror, not much else. He stepped next to a bucket and glanced down to see several leather jump ropes soaking in water to increase their heft and manageability.

Floyd nodded toward the lockers that cornered a single bench. "Guys that come up here stick their stuff there. But we got a shower down on the bottom floor." The sound of the door opening on to the loft caused the three of them to turn. Floyd took a step back toward the stairs. "Who is it?"

Fred whispered in Brian's ear, "There's not much here. It's kind of a dump."

But Brian couldn't get enough. He leaned over to pick up a jump rope to let it drip back into the bucket. What he and Fred and even Floyd didn't know was that the gym would always look weary and sparse, but out of it would come several New York State champions, a member of the United States Boxing Team, a World Super Bantamweight Champion and a World Super Featherweight Champion.

They heard someone running up the stairs, and a small man joined them, wearing a T-shirt and jeans with a carpenter's belt hanging on his hips. He was white, with brown curly hair and frank blue eyes. He looked a bit like a leprechaun.

"Floyd, whaddaya want me to do with that last paneling we took off?"

Floyd shrugged. "Just stack it in the back there somewhere for the time being." He motioned to the boys. "This is…"

"Brian and Fred," my brother supplied.

"Jimmy, but everyone calls me Longo," the man said and nodded at them without offering a hand.

"They want to see the gym," Floyd said. He turned toward the stairs. "I need to go. They can look around."

After he left, Longo turned to the boys. "You wanna see the gym?"

"I wanna box," Brian said. Fred said nothing.

Longo looked around for a long moment. "We been working on this for a while. Me and some other guys. We thought we'd just come up to train and have some fun. Floyd needed some help getting the gym in shape so we kinda traded, you know, helpin' him and he helps us out. We gotta few fights under our belts now. The other guys, they'll be here a little later." He grinned at them. "Floyd know you wanna box?"

Brian shook his head. Fred said, "We told him we'd cut the hedges, and we did a really bad job. I don't think he's much for keeping us around."

"Holy shit!" Longo said. "I saw that when I pulled in just now. You guys are the wackadoos that cut those?" He shook his head and laughed. "What the hell were you thinkin'?" After a moment he said into the silence, "Well, if you're brave enough to come back tomorrow at five o'clock, I bet Floyd will let you in."

It was only Brian who came back the next day, and Longo was right. Floyd let him in.

Longo

[2004]

It's a small apartment. It suits Longo. He still looks like a lep-rechaun. A much-older-Florida-variety leprechaun. I haven't seen him in at least fifteen years, and as he lets me in the door, I give him a hug, though it isn't as if we were ever close. We sit at his kitchen table, which takes half of the space and can only seat two people. I'm a bit nervous, though Longo has been nothing but enthusiastic from the day I first called him at his shoe repair shop on the east coast of Florida.

I remember seeing Longo fight only once. He'd entered the ring wearing trunks, a T-shirt and a pair of rust and green argyle socks, sagging on one ankle. He'd won his fight handily, but in the following years, I mostly knew him as an assistant trainer/manager of sorts at the Huguenot Boxing Club.

As I fiddle with my tape recorder, I glance up to find him watching my every movement, like a bright-eyed bird. He's at least fifty-five, and his face seems to have spread a bit as if to make room for the years, hair still brown and curling but thin toward the back. His scrub of beard and mustache is most-ly gray. No longer wiry, Longo is now just small and thick, though still in shape, and wearing a pair of sweatpants and a jacket with a T-shirt underneath. Just as I turn on the tape recorder, he says, "Wait a minute."

He leans back and crumples a beer can in one hand while opening the refrigerator with the other to take out another. It's a practiced movement and the empty is discarded somewhere, just gone, when he swivels back and settles in to tell stories about the Huguenot Boxing Club, Floyd and Brian. Longo is a first-rate raconteur, and it's not just the beer talking. He falls quiet when I stop him to load another tape into the recorder.

He suddenly asks, "What's your mom think about all of this?"

"I haven't told her. I need to write it all out and then show her."

"Well, look at it this way: she's already lived through Brian dying. There ain't nothin' that'll be more painful than that."

"You're probably right," I say. I can tell that he isn't satisfied with the word *probably*. Neither am I.

Jimmy Longo, right, and Floyd Patterson, at a match bout.
COURTESY OF THE JIMMY LONGO COLLECTION

Chapter Four

[1973]

> Programs must deal with people and helping them to see themselves as worthy individuals who are able to cope with life's daily problems without the need to escape through the use of drugs. The young child who matures having some of these skills and attitudes and resolving problems as he grows is an unlikely candidate for drug abuse.
>
> – Testimony of Sonia Hurley, Coordinator of Drug Abuse Prevention Program, at the Poughkeepsie Public Hearing before the Temporary State Commission to Evaluate the Drug Laws, November 8, 1973

One evening, as I set the table, my parents were sitting in the living room, with martinis, as they often did at the end of the day. Their murmuring was low, and I wasn't really paying attention.

"Yes!" my mother suddenly exclaimed. "That is what I told Hatch. He just doesn't listen. And he's got the superintendent fooled. We've put in over two years building this program, focusing on families, and he thinks he just can change everything after being there a couple of months. How many years did it take me to even get this going?"

More low murmurs from my dad.

"I know that!" My mom stood up suddenly. "But I just don't know, Bill, how we are going to deal with this. The staff morale just keeps going down, and it feels like we made promises to the state for the funding they gave us." Her voice was tight and forceful. "It's just wrong."

I had no idea what any of this meant. Not really. Other than something was going wrong with my mother's job, which had something to do with drug abuse, which had something to do with people who were down on their luck.

Through the next couple of weeks, my mother was tense and irritable when she came home from work. One night, she sat down with the typewriter and banged away on it, muttering to herself as she made mistakes and had to correct with white tape.

A day or so later, when she got up to help us get ready for school, she was wearing slacks and her blue sneakers, not the dress and pumps and lipstick she usually appeared in. She was pale and distracted. When I came home that afternoon, she was taking a nap.

That night, my father made us hot dogs and canned baked beans. Which is when I knew something was really wrong. "Your mom decided she needed to quit her job," he told us. "She didn't want to. So just be patient with her."

I looked around the table at my brother and sisters. Who wasn't being patient?

The Poughkeepsie Journal carried an article a couple of days later, which detailed why my mother resigned as coordinator of the Drug Abuse Prevention Program of the Poughkeepsie schools. A Mr. Hatch had revamped the program she and her staff had worked on for over two years without talking with any of them. Even though the program was funded and commended by state legislators as being the type of drug prevention project that should be replicated. And Mr. Hatch was in charge of Federal Programs, whatever they were. I guessed it meant he went out of bounds.

"I feel very badly about resigning because it is one program that is probably ahead of its time," my mother was quoted.

"Other programs tend to concentrate on scare tactics. We had a mental health program that allowed children in early elementary school to learn to cope with the problems of everyday living."

For a while, it seemed every time I picked up the phone, it was someone from the program calling my mother to offer support. She sat on the kitchen stool, holding the receiver with one hand, a cigarette in the other, and chuckling wryly as she said, "Thank you, I really appreciate you" over and over.

Apparently, the staff of the program—two psychologists, a social worker and a school guidance counselor—wrote to the school superintendent and asked him to convince my mother to reconsider her resignation. They offered many examples of her leadership. Maybe to honor this, or maybe because she really wanted to reconsider her resignation, my mother went to a meeting with the school superintendent and Mr. Hatch. But nothing was resolved.

My mom was forty-seven when all of this happened. She'd wanted a career and was the only one in her family to get an education beyond high school. After graduating from Cortland State Teachers College in New York, she'd gone to the University of North Carolina for a Master of Public Health Administration in the late 1940s .

My grandfather came from outside of London, where he'd apprenticed as a farrier and then took a job on ships transporting fruit. After arriving in the States, he worked as a railroad dining-car conductor and as a chauffeur. He married my grandmother, Hannah, who had come to the States from Sweden to be a nanny when she was seventeen. I never knew my grandmother. She died while my mother was pregnant with me. But I heard lots of stories about her, about her penchant for wearing pants and smoking cigarettes when women just didn't, at least not publicly. I also heard a lot of stories about a great-grandfather in Sweden who'd been a socialist labor organizer. And about Sweden, which my mother had visited during the summers with my grandmother, and all the ways in which it took care of its citizens. Which led me to an argument in my seventh-grade social studies class about socialism when I didn't even know the name for it. I remember a bemused smile on my teacher's face as he asked other students to respond.

My mother seemed busier than ever now that she didn't head across the river to work with the Substance Abuse Prevention Program. She took on the role of president of the New Paltz Parks and Recreation Association, leading the effort to build a new community pool. She was the co-founder of a family resource center, a preschool for the families who worked as migrant farm labor and, with others, started a thrift shop to support the local library. She was more active than ever with the League of Women Voters and fought against overdevelopment. She was an FDR Democrat, and like Floyd Patterson, an Eleanor Roosevelt devotee. My mother quoted her often, including "Nothing has ever been achieved by the person who says, 'It can't be done.'"

Chapter Five

[1973]

Finally, your name is called, paired with another, enmeshed for the evening. You sense more than hear the crowd as you move forward. Your frame and muscles are a bit stiff, so you bounce, jiggle and shadowbox to get the rhythm that will decide the fight.

–Brian Hurley, "The Other Side of the Ropes,"
The Huguenot Herald, New Paltz, New York,
June 23, 1976

I was eleven the first time I went with my parents to see Brian fight. I expected a large, clean gymnasium, but found myself choosing a metal folding chair through a haze of smoke in some small armory near Albany. I sat down next to my father and mother and studied the program. Typewritten and mimeographed, the program misspelled most of the names of Floyd's fighters. But not Brian's. I was relieved and felt strangely proud, as if this conferred something special on him.

"There's Floyd." My mom nodded her head as she shrugged off her coat. She had a tightness to her movements, as if unwilling to really settle in and be a part of the crowd and the night's events.

Floyd made his way to us, sometimes stopping to sign autographs or to talk with someone who might have been a trainer or a promoter or just a fan. Finally, he reached my parents and put a hand on my father's shoulder as he leaned over. Next to Floyd, my father looked small, though they were close to the same height.

Floyd told us that Brian would be fighting a kid from Troy. "Supposedly just has two fights, but probably has more. Probably as many as Brian, though I said Brian had two fights too. I don't think he'll be any problem." Floyd looked around the crowded room and raised a hand to acknowledge someone.

"Yeah, well, thanks, Champ." My father was old school; I'd never hear him address Floyd as anything but Champ in the years to come. Now he said, "How's he doing? Should I go back and see him?"

Floyd shrugged. "Sure, sure." He glanced briefly at me without registering my presence, and then smiled at my mother. "My wife and little girls are here tonight too." He nodded toward a slender dark red-haired white woman a couple rows away. She was settling into her seat, with a child on either side.

"They're beautiful children," my mother said. "Maybe after the fight we can meet them."

But Floyd was already leaving with my father and said absently, "Sure, sure."

I peered through the crowd, fascinated with Floyd's daughters. They looked a lot younger than me. I wondered what it was like to have your father be so famous.

My mother leaned her head close to mine and said in a low voice, "I think one is...Jenny? The other is Jeanie? Or something like that. But guess what, his wife's name is Janet."

"Really?" I was immediately smitten with her.

The crowd grew as fight time drew near, and my mother and I had to move our legs to let people squeeze by, arms laden with beer or soda, chips, hot dogs. All kinds of people. If I had expected men who could have been extras in *On the Waterfront*, they were there. But there were also men who could have starred as defending counsel on *Perry Mason*, still in their suits and ties. I stared at women who surely had worked on their hair and faces and clothes for hours, just to cross their legs in a smelly, smokey place where no one would see their red high heels. But right next to them were women who wore sensible shoes, like my mother. There were a few small boys who snaked in and out of the rows of chairs and some older kids, like me.

My father sat down. "They'll be starting in a minute here," he said, pushing his glasses back up his nose. "Brian's nervous, but he's good."

The house lights suddenly went down, and those over the ring came up to illuminate a casually dressed man with a microphone. He wasn't the tuxedoed announcer I had expected, but he did have the requisite drama in his voice.

"Welcome to the National Guard Armory of Latham, New York, where local boys from Troy, Schenectady, Cohoes, Albany and New Paltz will meet each other in three-round amateur bouts."

The ring announcer finished introducing the judges and, after we stood for the national anthem, gestured for the audience to take a seat, then took a deep breath for the next announcement. "And here tonight with the Huguenot Boxing Club, former World Heavyweight Champion..." He paused as the applause started. "...the youngest man ever to win the heavyweight championship, the only man to win the World Heavyweight Championship twice—FFFFLLL-LOOOOOOYYYYDDDD PATTERSON."

Floyd stepped through the ropes and turned slowly, his hand raised as if to fend off the cheers. I glanced around, wondering if the people sitting around me had noticed Floyd talking with my parents.

Brian was seventh on the card, right after the fifteen-minute intermission, which stretched to half an hour, then forty minutes, with announcements and a fifty-fifty raffle. I felt a little sick from all the smoke, tired of rubbing my eyes, nervous.

Finally, I saw Brian heading to the ring, throwing punches into the air as he walked behind Floyd. As he clambered through the ropes, I saw his opponent, already in his corner. A tall kid, he had long, white arms that looked like chameleon tongues, like they might stretch to twice the length of his height. As the referee checked his gloves and cup and mouthpiece, the kid looked over the striped shoulder to Brian.

The referee leaned into the boy's ear, as if he was whispering sweet nothings. But I knew it wasn't sweet, it wasn't nothing, and Brian would hear the same thing: "Obey my commands at all times and protect yourself at all times." Brian had whispered this in my ear on more than one occasion, usually just before he switched the television channel.

After the referee gave Brian his commands, Floyd leaned in close himself, maybe to say good luck. Then he stepped off the ring apron, came down the stairs with his back to the audience and stationed himself on a chair at the bottom.

Living with Brian had been hazardous over the previous six months. We never knew as we came around a corner if he would be shadowboxing, using the reflection of a window or the bathroom mirror or maybe even the toaster. I'd laughed at him more than once when I caught him practicing his stance in the reflection of the sliding glass doors that led out to the patio, his right hand held up close to the right cheek, left hand under the other eye just a little lower, knees bent slightly, head down, elbows in tight to his body.

And now, I finally saw what all that was about. Brian brought that stance right into the ring, hands in proper position, as if he had unpacked it from his gym bag along with his trunks. The fight started slow. The opponent threw the first punch, but Brian didn't seem to register the blow. Instead, he looked comfortable, with full control of his body, something the other fighter lacked.

He moved in and then back from the other guy, and then, just toward the end of the round, Brian threw a series of short punches. A few to the body and a couple to the face and one that obviously hurt his opponent because he took a step back. My father shifted in his seat as the bell rang and looked at me. "That gave him the round." He looked at my mother. She had watched only the last ten seconds, pulling her hands down from her face. This would never change.

Just before the start of the second round, a teenage girl climbed into the ring. Luminously white through the haze, she wore a one-piece, low-cut purple bathing suit, stiletto heels and a smear of red lipstick that made her appear as if she had been punched in the mouth. She tossed limp, tea-colored hair over her shoulder and then raised a sign over her head that was imprinted with a large "2," which she paraded around the ring. I decided she was like Carol Merrill on *Let's Make a Deal*, having no real function other than looking sexy.

I looked over to the corner where Floyd leaned into Brian, told him something that made Brian nod, and then the warning whistle sounded, telling Floyd that he had to exit the ring.

The bell rang and the boxers met. It was obvious that their trainers had urged them to get in there and do some damage. Brian's opponent threw a few punches that seemed pretty accurate, and just when I was about to close my eyes on a drive toward Brian's face, I didn't. The blow missed. There were a few exchanges and then Brian stepped back. He popped a shot to the kid's face. Then he dipped and sent another to the kid's body. The other boxer moved as if he were blocking that shot. When Brian saw that, he went to the left and hit the guy twice in the head with that short punch. He leaned to the right, and the other boxer leaned a bit with him as if he knew where Brian was going and could block it. But he didn't know.

Brian's left hand hit the kid from Troy, square and hard. The boy turned away and, covering his face with his gloves, came to stand at the ropes, right in front of us. I could see the sweat dripping onto his gloves, hear the air being sucked in around his mouth guard. Behind him, the referee hesitated. But the kid stayed at the edge of the ring, head down, shielding his nose. I tried to see around him, to find Brian, but that's when the ref stepped closer, blocking my view, and called the fight.

My father slapped his program on his thigh and jumped to his feet, along with the rest of the crowd. I stood next to him, peering through the arms of the people in front of me. After a moment, the kid from Troy moved back toward his corner, and I could see Floyd taking out Brian's mouth guard. The ref motioned him to the center of the ring. In the lights, Brian's skin shone paler than usual, almost bloodless except for the few pink splotches just beginning to emerge. He blew hard from his nose, sweating, restless, his head lowered. The clapping and cheers swirled around me, into me, making me feel taller, filling me with a promise that made me pump my fist in the air, something I had never done in my life. When the crowd finally settled and we all sat down, I glanced at my mother, who'd never joined the celebration. She just seemed relieved that it was over.

We waited for Brian outside the locker room. He came out with his gym bag in one hand, his dark hair wet and curled around his ears. He grinned at the three of us, his face only a little swollen on one side. I reached up a finger. "Does it hurt?"

"Nah," he said with good nature, but he moved his head back slightly so that I couldn't reach the bruise.

"That was damn good," my father said. "Damn good."

Brian, age 15, at a match bout, where various clubs bring their fighters, i.e., not a tournament.

Book Report

[1974, 2005]

It's still in print. A good thing, because I've lost my copy of *The Contender* somewhere along the thirty-odd years since I read it in the seventh grade. I'm still impressed. The protagonist, Alfred Brooks, is Black, from Harlem and had dropped out of high school. He lives with his aunt and cousins in a one-room flat, lifting boxes at a local grocer, trying to stay away from the drugs and crime that have claimed his best friend.

The story fits Floyd's early life of poverty and few options, not Brian's. Like Floyd, Alfred finds a white trainer who runs a gym to guide him. But Alfred doesn't rise to fame and wealth. Instead, he realizes that he doesn't have the "heart" to be a fighter, no matter how good his technique, and he "retires" to get his GED and pursue his dreams another way. And of course, in the end you know he'll be behind the resurrection of his friend, still strung out on heroin but willing to face the consequences.

For a time, Alfred and Brian shared the one thing that mattered most. The dream. Of being an Olympic gold medalist, maybe even a world champion. I decided to interview Brian as part of my book report, and he was willing.

I kept the taupe-colored cassette that I submitted to my teacher—on the B side is a recording of the song "A Horse with No Name"—wrapped in a plastic bag, and I worry about its fragility. But that's not why I rarely play it. Still high in

our throats, Brian's voice and mine are too much like genies—
Brian's just having made the descent, still not quite full—and
they fill a room with what-if wishes.

When I transcribe the conversation, some thirty years after
it was taped, I can picture Brian as he lounges across my twin
bed and I kneel next to it, tape recorder on the bedspread, my
list of questions written on a yellow legal pad. I am surprised,
again, at how formal Brian sounds, how serious—at the time,
I thought he needed to loosen up and was a bit irritated. But
now I wonder if he wasn't holding his normal humor in check,
trying to match my demeanor, not demean my efforts.

Janet: How long have you been boxing?

Brian: Well, all together it's been about three years. A year
          since I've been going to Floyd Patterson's house and
          training at the gym.

Janet: How did you get interested in it?

Brian: Well, the kid across the street boxed and, uh, one day
          he invited me over to box with him and for about the
          first few months he really tore me apart. But I stuck
          with it and eventually went up to Patterson's house.

Janet: How many fights have you had?

Brian: I've had fifteen fights, won ten of 'em, and I won five of
          'em by a knockout.

Janet: How does it feel to have Floyd Patterson as your man-
          ager and trainer?

Brian: Well, Floyd has to be about the best manager and
          trainer for amateurs available on the East Coast. This
          is a definite advantage in fighting in the tournaments
          and dual meets around the area.

Janet: How did it feel to fight in the Golden Gloves?

Brian: Well, it's a lot more organized than most matches that
          I am involved with. I fight much better under the type

of pressure which is present in a tournament of that sort.

Janet: What did it feel like to fight in Madison Square Garden?

Brian: Well, there's a lot more people there and your adrenalin gets going a lot more than it usually would in a normal fight. 'Cause you have more like 3,000 people than usual, maybe 1,500 or so that would be at your normal interclub boxing match, so I usually fight better with a lot of people around.

Janet: What did you think when you saw yourself on TV?

Brian: Well, I think it showed a lot about my style.

Janet: How do you get to go to the Olympics?

Brian: There are a series of eliminations, starting out with the Golden Gloves. And if you win the open class, which means you have had fights in the amateurs, you go on to the Easterns, and if you win the Easterns then you go on to a tournament in Chicago where you fight the West Coast champions. And if you win there, you can go on to the Pan American Games and then to the Olympic Trials. And if you win there, then you can go on to the Olympics. So altogether you have about thirty fights to get into the Olympics."

Janet: How many hours a day do you train?

Brian: I usually work out about three hours a day, seven days a week.

Janet: What do you think is your best shot?

Brian: Well, actually my best shot is a combination, but if I had to say what punch was my best punch, I would have to say that it was a left hook. As that is the type of punch where the fighter does not see the punch coming and is not able to prepare his mind for the impact of the punch and it results in a lot of knockouts.

Janet: Has this helped you in your fights?

Brian: Yeah, I've knocked out several people or I've TKO'd several people with a left hook.

Janet: Who are some of the famous fighters that you have met?

Brian: Some of the fighters I've met: I've met Jersey Joe Walcott, who was a heavyweight champion back around in the 1950s; I've met Kid Gavilan, who was a welterweight champion from Cuba; Willie Pep, who was a lightweight champion; I've met Jimmy Dupree, who many people may not know but Jimmy Dupree is a middleweight; I've met Chuck Wepner, who recently lost to Mohammed Ali. I've met Joe Frazier and Duane Bobick and Tony Zale, Rocky Graciano and … that's about it.

Janet: What do you think your chances are of becoming a pro heavyweight boxer?

Brian: Well, this all depends on how well you do in the amateurs. If you do well in the amateurs, boxing can become very lucrative financially because if you win in the Olympics or do well in the Olympics you are automatically million-dollar merchandise. If you go into the professional divisions without a reputation, you really have to work a lot harder, to get to where, take a lot more steps to where an amateur fighter with a good record would be. So, it depends on how well I do in the amateurs.

Janet: Would you be willing to work that hard and to stick to it all those years?

Brian: Boxing, as I said, is very rich in money, fame, and it's a very rewarding sport, although it is also tough. But if you don't take any risks, you don't get any benefits. It's worth a shot; it depends on how I do in the next few years.

Janet: Would you have liked to go out for other sports, or it doesn't matter that you have to give up a lot of things to go on with boxing?

Brian: Well, I did go out for sports, at least football and wrestling, and I find that boxing is a much more demanding, much more rewarding sport than football or wrestling. And I find it is also my individual effort that is involved in boxing, whereas in football and wrestling you are pushed by the coach, and you don't get as much self-satisfaction as you do in boxing.

Janet: How does it feel to actually fight Floyd Patterson, to spar with him?

Brian: Well, at first it was rather strange, and a lot of kids that go up there don't even want to hit him. After a while you get used to hitting him, and there's absolutely no way you could hurt him because I have seen men much bigger than Patterson when he would drop his hands to say something and they, not knowing, hauled off and hit him and it didn't even affect him at all. He wouldn't even pause in the middle of a sentence without him really even noticing being hit. So, boxing Patterson is kind of like boxing a moving heavy bag.

Janet: Do you want to go into the 1980 Olympics?

Brian: Well I figure this [next] year if I do well in the New York Golden Gloves and I continue from there, I would like to go into the 1976 Olympics, but this is rather unrealistic as many of the fighters in the Olympics have had 250 or so fights, and by that time I would only have maybe forty or so fights. So, this probably will not result in the next year, so I'll see how I do in the four years afterwards. And if I do well then, I guess I'll go into the 1980 Olympics.

Janet: That's good. I hope you do well.

I did hope, so much, he would do well.

Chapter Six

[1974]

Ever wonder if Bill Hurley, Kingston High Athletic Director, ever dreams about having a World Boxing Champion in the family someday?

−Charles Tiano, "Sportside," *The Sunday Kingston Freeman*, February 8, 1976

The dining room was the hub of our home, with a long, dark pine trestle table and six chairs. This was where all visitors first sat when they came in, where we read newspapers, made papier mâché volcanoes and dioramas, played Monopoly and card games, and lingered after dinner with dessert and stories. My mother implored us to use a magazine under our homework papers as we wrote, but we rarely did. The ghosts of letters and numbers were discernible in the grain of the wood, and bumps could be felt under the fingertips like our own special Braille.

And now, Floyd sat at our table, much like a giant in a troll's house; his shoulders and biceps looked like they were shrink-wrapped in his white T-shirt. He tipped a handful of M&Ms into his huge palm from my father's always-full candy jar.

"Thanks again for doing this." He crunched the M&Ms for a minute and then swallowed. "It's a big favor to ask, I know."

None of us thought we were doing Floyd a favor. I looked out to where the photographer was setting up in the family room. He was sturdy and blonde, dressed in slacks and a turtleneck. He looked too fussy to be a friend of Floyd's. But they'd met in Sweden, and now he was here to do a story for a magazine on a "typical American family." My mother thought it would be fun to have her cousins in Sweden read the article and had agreed immediately to the request.

My father shook his head. "Don't mention it. We're happy to do it." He was dressed in the sports coat and tie he'd worn to work. Julie and I wore skirts that were part of our everyday school wardrobe. But Nora, who always preferred jeans and being outside, looked out of sorts in her dark blue dress with a little white collar. She sat next to me at the table, swinging her black patent leathers, kicking the crossbeam under the table lightly but persistently.

"Stop!" I whispered and grabbed her hand. My father gave us the look he gave his football players if they ever dared to goof around in practice. He rarely employed it here at home, and when he did, we rarely paid attention. After a moment I heard it again: swish, clunk, swish, clunk.

My mother came into the dining room, lovely in a silvery gray dress that offset her hair, pearls at her neck. As she walked by, she grabbed the knit hat off Brian's head. He was sitting next to Floyd and wearing his usual pin-striped button-down, jeans and sneakers.

"Hey!"

My mother gave my father the look that meant, *Back me up.* He shook his head at Brian. The hat stayed off.

Floyd grinned at my brother. "Mothers know best."

Brian ducked his head, a blush sneaking up from his collar to find his jawbone.

My father cleared his throat. "How's business in Sweden, Champ?"

"It's good, good. I have a couple more places opening up next month. We'll see."

Floyd had partnered with a Swedish businessman to open a fast-food restaurant in Uppsala, selling Floyd Burgers. I could never quite figure out why the Swedes liked Floyd so much. When Swedish fighter Ingemar Johannson took away Floyd's heavyweight title, he'd returned home to great celebrity. But then Floyd took his title back by knocking him out and making history. In a third rematch, Floyd beat him again, easily. You'd think that the Swedish people would be sick of Floyd beating up on their man. Sometime between the second and third fight, Floyd visited Sweden, was greeted graciously by the king, and was amazed by the lack of racial division. Of course, at that time, the early sixties, and in that place, white divided by white was still white. When he returned to the country after the third fight, I imagined the Swedes just shrugged and said, *Ya! OK already, Floyd. You're good!* They welcomed him with open arms. He and Ingemar became friends. Floyd admired the Swedish fighter's easy personality, so different from his own shy way with the media. And now, here we were with this Swedish photographer, trying to be as typically American as we could, in our dresses and sports coats and heels.

The photographer finished with his preparations and gestured to my parents. His English was good, if heavily accented. "Mr. and Mrs. Hurley, I would like to start with pictures of you here in this room. Very sunny, very pleasant." He smiled at them. "I'll get the children in a moment." As he gestured, like a maitre'd in a fine restaurant, he said, "Your home. I like it very much. It could be in Sweden."

"Thank you." My mother glanced about with a smile. She and my father had designed our house, built in 1961. From the street, it looked like a typical ranch, all wood, some stained red, the rest white. But the floor plan was unusual in its day with a great room that stretched the house into a t-shape. Huge picture windows looked over a stone patio just outside the back door and into the woods beyond. The far wall of the living room was made of stone, with a fireplace set off center. My mother loved to tell the story of how she had to convince the stone mason that off center was really what she wanted.

My parents followed the photographer into the family room, which was just off our dining room, visible through sliding glass doors. He pulled over a chair for my mother and asked my father to stand behind her. He then stepped back, put a finger to his lips and pondered. "Not so formal, I think," he finally said. "Mr. Hurley, please, if you would hold this."

He picked up one of my mother's potted plants and handed it to him. It was large, a geranium, flashing red, leafy enough to hide my father's tie. My father held the pot like a football. The plant waggled over my mother's head.

"No, no, no," The photographer said. "How about you are *giving* this plant to your wife."

My father bent a bit and held out the plant to my mother, who had to turn awkwardly to receive it.

"Good, good," the photographer said. "Smile, tenderly, yes, tenderly at each other."

Coach Hurley, who had probably never even said the word *tender* unless it described a steak, smiled self-consciously. My mother smiled back at him as if he were a small child.

"Yes, yes, I got it," the photographer said.

I had to giggle. I snuck a look at Brian and then Floyd. He had rocked back in his chair; his hands were behind his head. I couldn't be sure, but I thought he was sleeping. Nora giggled too. Brian grinned at me and lifted his finger up to his lips. Floyd startled awake and let the chair come down on all four legs, his hands slapping on the table. Not loudly, but enough to make us swallow our laughter; Brian's eyes widened into a warning to keep quiet. Then Floyd smiled at us. Brian smiled. Julie smiled. Nora smiled. I smiled again.

Floyd reached for the M&M jar. "Photo shoots can get pretty boring." He sounded bemused.

We all nodded, as if photo shoots were a common event in our lives.

The photographer stayed about two hours. After posing all of us in equally stilted tableaus and promising prints and copies of the magazine, he left with Floyd. My mother wrote to a cousin in Sweden, "Be on the lookout for this!" But we didn't hear anything from the photographer. My parents reminded Brian every couple of months, "Ask Floyd if that article ever came out."

Brian would dutifully inquire, and Floyd would shrug. "Maybe they didn't run it," he finally said. "That happens."

Chapter Seven

My father was like many owners of ranch houses in the seventies. When he finished out our basement as a recreation room, he used the dark paneling, blue-green wall-to-wall carpeting and fluorescent lights that were ubiquitous in that era. He built lots of shelving, including a trophy case for all of Brian's, and even created a home gym—where Brian could work on a speed bag or his heavy bag.

My father loved projects like this and learned all his carpentry skills from books. He disappeared into his wood shop for hours, sometimes with a project in mind, sometimes just puttering about, putting tools in their place, he said. After hours of screeching a table saw or smacking a hammer, he came upstairs smelling of sweat, cigarette smoke and sawdust. And something else, though, when I was small, I noticed the easiness, a sentimentality that wafted about him more than a smell of alcohol. I never questioned the green and brown bottles tucked away behind the cans of varnish.

Sometimes he would come upstairs for dinner after the third or fourth call, and my mother would put an electric skillet of Spanish rice or a casserole dish on the table, not looking at him, compressing her lips as if there was something heavy in her mouth that she had to keep in.

Both my parents liked to have a drink, or drinks and a cigarette, or more. When they went out to eat, they had cocktails and after-dinner liqueurs. On rare evenings, their friends Jude and Wally came to the house before they all went out to dinner. I was allowed to sit with them if I was quiet, and I saw them hold glasses of amber in one hand while they scooped globs of clam dip onto a potato chip with the other. The conversation usually got more pointed as glasses were refilled, more intricate, and though I could feel the keen edge to the words, I often just didn't understand what was being debated, only that my mother would get more annoyed and sarcastic and my dad more jovial.

As the athletic director of a large public school system, my father was at many of the evening games and matches, coming home after Nora and I were in bed, sometimes after Julie, Brian and my mom were in bed, closing the front door a little too loudly. I didn't think much about this. I knew the coaches were his friends, and they liked to go out after a game for drinks, to relive a win or examine a loss.

And then, one evening, when I was nine or ten, after a loud argument between my parents that was clearly about his drinking, my mother told my father to leave. I stood near the front door as he carried out piles of clothes to his Volkswagen, wishing Brian and Julie were home from wherever they were. My mother sat in the living room at one end of the couch, unmoving, not crying. Her legs were crossed, with her hands on her lap, as if she were politely listening to a guest. She gazed straight in front of her, as if she were studying her reflection in the big picture windows.

"Where are you going?" I asked my father, but all he would say was, "Shush, don't wake up Nora." He was gone by the time Julie and Brian came home. When I told them what happened, Julie immediately began to cry. Brian's face seemed to close in on itself. He went in his room and closed the door.

It was all very confusing to me. My father wasn't a bum. He didn't yell. He didn't hit any of us. He wore a suit and tie to work, and he worked hard. And not just at his job as athletic director. He was a lieutenant colonel in the US Army Reserves, after serving in both World War II and Korea, and attended monthly meetings and an annual training every summer in New Jersey. His picture was often in the local paper with an article about a Kingston High team earning a championship or a commendation he'd received as a reservist.

As it turned out, my dad didn't stay away for even a night, coming back home at 2:00 a.m. and going to work the next morning.

But no one talked about what happened. As if he were on some sort of probation, my father pulled his clothes out of the Volkswagen and left them piled up on the basement couch for weeks. We played around them and walked past them like they were heaps of disgrace that we couldn't bear to touch or talk about. And one day they were gone, back in the closet and drawers.

In the weeks and months that followed, I sensed an agreement had been made between my parents. I figured out the terms through hypervigilant scrutiny, terms that became just the way things were. No more cocktail hours, no more going out after games with the coaches and coming home after too many drinks. No more than one martini if they went out to dinner, no more than one after-dinner drink. No more dip and drinks with friends at the house. My dad didn't go to Alcoholics Anonymous or anything like that. He kept it under control, figured out the problem and handled it.

I thought one part of the agreement between my parents must have been about the woodshop, because my father dismantled his tools and moved them to the garage and the green and brown bottles disappeared. He paneled the room in a blonde wood, laid a dark red-and-black-mottled carpet down and installed a suspended ceiling with fluorescent lights to augment the scant light from the two ground level windows; it became Brian's bedroom.

Chapter Eight

I thought of those familiar days riding to the pool
for fun and games, my mom at the wheel. We would
pass the public library and Mom would cluck and
sigh at the "sorry hippies" stoned out on the grass. I
would seek to spy these sorry people yet never saw.
Hell, they all looked like boys and girls to me. Yet I
crossed the street when I came to the public library.

—Brian Hurley, senior English class journal, 1976

In the renovation of the basement, my father installed a huge
tank in the wall between the basement water-heater room
and the play area. Brian transferred his fish from upstairs and
bought a large and growing Oscar fish to command the fifty
gallons of water.

One Christmas, when I was in middle school, Brian gave
me an African frog for Christmas. I lifted the water-filled bag
with the small brown-green creature and wondered what Brian had been thinking. "He looks dead."

Brian flicked the bag with his fingernail. The creature
kicked out and then down. "Let's get him in the tank downstairs. He'll be more comfortable."

Ah. The frog was really for him. Still, I followed him
downstairs. As he'd taught me, I put the bag in the tank water
to float for a few minutes. I looked up at Brian, his face ka-
leidoscoped with the slippery light from the tank. He gazed

down into the water as if he could see when the temperature equalized. Finally, he said, "OK. I think it's time."

I dashed out to look from the rec-room side. I could just see Brian's fingers dipping into the water to untie the bag. The frog kicked out as the bag was drawn from around him, and when the water stilled, he'd disappeared behind the fake neon green coral. He was hard to spot after that, but I liked knowing he was there, somewhere. When I had friends over, I'd make them look with me, and it was my best friend, Valerie, who first said, "The water's really cloudy."

I took a step back, a bit embarrassed. She was right. And there were tiny wisps of green algae undulating from the spire of one of the brightly colored ceramic pagodas that sat at the bottom of the tank.

When I asked Brian about it, he was impatient. "It's not a big deal. Every tank gets algae; I'll clean it." And he did. Until he didn't. This time, it was my father who brought it up while we were eating dinner. "The tank needs some attention, Bri," he said. "When's the last time you cleaned it?"

"I'll clean it tomorrow." Brian's tone was low and annoyed.

My mom stepped in. "We know you have a lot going on, with football practice and then going to the gym, maybe it's too much."

Brian glanced at my father and shook his head. "It's not too much. I'll do it tomorrow."

"Sounds good." My father let it drop.

We all knew that Brian was playing football mostly for him. Our high school was much smaller than the one where my dad was the athletic director, and we didn't play his teams. The football games were on the same days, and often my father would miss seeing his son on the field. Still, he listened closely to the verbal replay my brother would give him, with my mother adding in details or criticisms of the coach. Though she had no love for the game, she went to them all.

Brian didn't clean the fish tank the next day. Or the next. That was because my mother had to pick him up early from football practice and help him in the house. He had a charley horse from being hit head-on in the thigh by a helmeted player. I'd never heard of an injury like this, and it didn't sound very serious. But it must have been because Brian couldn't bear weight on that leg, the muscle cramping was so severe. He spent the evening in and out of a hot bath. Floyd came to the house with a portable whirlpool, which looked to me like an outboard engine and sounded like one too. After it was set up and Brian was back in the tub, my father walked Floyd to the door and shook his hand. "Thanks, Champ. I think that will make the difference."

Floyd nodded. "No problem. Keep it as long as you need it." He didn't say, "Brian shouldn't be playing football anyway." But, within days, Brian finally quit the football team to focus solely on boxing. As far as I know, my father didn't disagree. But the fish tank got even cloudier, the algae thicker, the filter gummier.

Alfie

[2004]

It's the smile I first noticed when I was … eleven? Probably. Walking with Brian and Alfie and two or three other fighters. Not Floyd. Not my parents. We were on a sidewalk in a city. There was someone we passed. He made a remark, snide in tone. I sensed the collective pause, a slight drag on the forward energy. Over my head, those young men had a little conference with quick intakes of breath and significant turns of the head, with brief but meaningful looks at each other. Some of the tension wafted down and prickled on my neck. I looked up at Alfie. The plump of his cheeks rode high on the bones, even when he was not smiling, which was rare. His jacket made small scratchy-squeaky noises as he moved his left hand onto my shoulder and said in that gentle voice of his, "It's nothin'. Don't worry." And in a moment, our group was released from the tension, like we were all one big, rough hand that had snagged the soft silk of a scarf and then slid away.

At the match that night, Alfie sent that left out again. It connected with a jaw, and he won his match by technical knockout.

Given that memory, I don't know why it took me so long to call Alfie after Longo found his number. I was nervous, despite how everyone I talked with about Alfie said this: He is the nicest guy in the world. I knew Alfie had a lot to tell me about the gym, about Floyd, about Brian. I also knew that he left the gym to turn pro in the city, going by the ring name Cool Breeze, and then came back upstate and struggled with addiction. I didn't know any of the whys, only that he got clean. Finally, an evening came when my husband, David, had taken the kids somewhere and there was enough quiet. I had no idea if Alfie had a family or if he lived alone or if he might be home on a cold night in early December. After two rings, he picked up. Still the nicest guy in the world.

Now, it's late afternoon, at the Best Western, off I-84 in Newburgh, New York. I open the door to see Alfie, long dreads pulled up under a black, green and gold knit tam. The sharpness of his features has softened with his fifty-odd years, his goatee a mix of gray and white with stubble along his jaw-bones. He's wearing a khaki-green pea coat, a scarf and that smile that starts in his eyes.

The chair I offer Alfie is really too small for the length of his frame, but it's the best I've got. He lays his coat on the bed and sits down, palms flat on his thighs, long fingers moving a bit as we chat about his girlfriend and her little boy. Maybe he's nervous too. He turns his head a bit as if to hear me better, nods with the rhythm of my voice as if to affirm it, encourage it, and I feel it settling, smoothing out in response as I position the tape recorder and ask my first questions.

"Everyone was so close at the gym," Alfie says. "We were like brothers. That's what I liked. I miss the club for that. When I think of my closest family, it was when I was at the gym. It was just the respect. Everybody gave each other respect. Nobody was really like jealous over anybody. We had a lot of middleweights, and they wanted to see you win. I wanted to see everyone win."

We share our memories of the different gym characters, Alfie chuckling, sometimes shaking his head as if with the sheer wonder of being encouraged to ramble into these long-ago places.

"Brian was a natural. Brian was really intelligent. Real friendly nice guy. When Brian fought, anyone fought, we all worried. We all got together and said, oh my." Alfie puts a hand up to his mouth as he says this.

I repeat it, "Oh my!" He nods and laughs with me.

After a while, I bring up Floyd, wondering what light Alfie has to shed on this man who sits in my peripheral vision and moves every time I look directly at him.

He tells me that Floyd let him live in the gym apartment for three years, that he was invited to eat supper with the family often, that one time, Floyd gave him five hundred dollars at Christmas because he knew he was broke, that he was like a big brother to him. That once before a fight, Alfie's hands were shaking, and he said to Floyd, "I need you to tie my shoes. I'm not sure I should fight this guy." And Floyd had answered, "That's good, that's good, I wouldn't let you fight if you didn't feel like that." Alfie nods as he tells me, "And so, he tied my shoes for me."

Alfie at a match bout.
COURTESY OF THE ALFRED
BEVIER COLLECTION.

Chapter Nine

[1975]

In the gym, Floyd's personality and talents shine most. It is here that Patterson relaxes, laughs and talks freely. Sparring with his pupils, he chuckles after being hit, "That was a good punch," he says. "A damn good punch. I just watched the ring post dance from here to there."

— Brian Hurley, "Character Portrait: My Impressions and Learnings of Floyd Patterson," 1983

The gym was loud with the thumping of heavy bags, the rat-a-tat-tat of the speed bags and the slap of jump ropes. Though the workout area was on the third floor, the sound shook all the way down through the second-floor loft to the bottom level where Floyd worked with Brian in the ring. Longo stood with his arms crossed over his chest and watched. Brian kept his head turned, listened out of his one good ear, the one not scarred by childhood ear infections, and paid attention to every instruction Floyd gave. Sweat dripped from under his knitted ski cap. He wore it to tame his curling hair, wore it to school, wore it while hitting the heavy bag or speed bag. The gym was cold now, but he wore it no matter the heat.

Longo called to Floyd: "We got some waiting to spar. Alfie with Brian?"

"Yeah, that's a good idea," Brian said. He threw a few more

shadow punches. He was sixteen now, his body well developed and strong.

Floyd nodded. "Yeah, that's fine." He turned to wave Alfie into the ring. "You ready? Let's go then."

"Sure, Floyd, I'm ready." Alfie flashed a smile as he slid through the ropes and turned to accept a mouth guard from Longo. His laid-back demeanor meshed well with Brian's sense of humor. They had enormous respect for each other in the ring, which made their friendship comfortable outside of it. Now, with headgear on and cups worn over sweatpants, Alfie and Brian started to spar after Floyd rang the bell. Despite the chill in the room, they warmed quickly, the sharp smell of new sweat blending with the musty smell of leather. The ring filled with the popping sounds of blocked blows, the occasional thuds as a glove connected to the body, the loud exhalations of the fighters as they threw their punches.

Everyone at the gym knew about Brian's "move." After a few jabs to his opponent's head, he would bend over to the right and throw a stiff, heavy shot to the midsection. Usually, the other fighter moved to deflect and lowered his right hand. Brian would bend over as if he was going for another body jab but, instead, shift his weight and come around with the full-power left hook to the head. But as a southpaw, Alfie mixed things up. Brian had to judge his timing differently, watch for different cues, remember Alfie's jab and that strong, straight left cross as he moved in. Alfie's low-key demeanor, angular frame and surprisingly quick and powerful reach had more than once prompted the comparison to a praying mantis.

While Longo kept up a steady stream of encouragement and commentary on style and technique, Floyd watched Brian and Alfie without saying a word. He had a toothpick in his mouth, which rolled slowly from side to side when he was content with what he saw, faster when he wasn't. When the third round was over, he talked to each of the fighters after they climbed out of the ring.

As Floyd moved away, Alfie said to Brian, "That was good, really good man. You gonna run with us later?"

Brian hesitated. "I got a paper due tomorrow. Think I'm gonna have to skip it."

Alfie used his teeth to pull the laces on his gloves and then said, "Not to be your mother or anything but you didn't run yesterday either."

Brian nodded, now with laces in his mouth too. When he spat them out, he said with good humor, "I'm honored you desire my presence. Tomorrow, I'll run double miles, how's that?"

Alfie shrugged. "Hey, they're your legs, man."

Chapter Ten

It all takes time and practice that prove to be the refiners fire, and the skills attained are the salt of these athletes. To have these to fall back on when hurt in the ring, to know what you are capable of in any given situation, to fight intelligently and almost instinctively is paramount.

—Brian Hurley, untitled essay on boxing techniques and training, 1983

At the sound of the gym door slamming, Longo looked up to the balcony where two boys in heavy winter jackets peered down. "Yo, Salt and Pepper, you gonna change and join us down here?"

The Bobbsey twins, they were called by some. The Gold Dust twins, by Floyd. Salt and Pepper, by Longo. They were both thirteen, both in eighth grade. They'd arrived at the gym for the first time some months before. Andy was slender, with reddish-brown hair that fell into his blue eyes, skin pale and freckled. Sammy was taller by about four inches, which made him look thinner than Andy, with smooth, brown skin and a wide baby face, short-cropped black afro, eyes blacker still.

"You're late," Longo called up to them. "Go and get changed."

"OK, OK, we just got here," Sammy said. He had a unique voice, high in his throat, reedy almost, a quality that would

never change, even when his voice got a bit deeper in deference to puberty.

The two boys had met in school when Andy's family moved
to New Paltz. Sammy listened to Andy's stories about getting
boxing gloves for Christmas one year, about how his older
brother would set out logs to mark a ring in the backyard and
then act as boxing promoter by inviting boys over to spar with
his little brother. Everyone in New Paltz knew about Floyd
and his gym, but it was Andy who persuaded Sammy to check
it out. And so, the day after the middle school basketball try-
outs and making the team, he and Sammy walked up that
long drive to the gym together, figuring they could always play
ball if Floyd said they were too young to box. They weren't
turned away. Neither one returned to the basketball court.

In the gym, the boys were as competitive as they were
inseparable outside of it—or, at least, Andy was. If Sammy
threw twenty jabs in training, Andy threw thirty. If Sammy
spent twenty minutes on the heavy bag, Andy put in forty.
When Brian gave Andy handgrips to strengthen his forearms,
he encouraged Sammy to use them, and then worked with
them twice as long. And the running. Andy always did his
running.

Now, Longo helped them get wrapped and gloved and
cupped and ready and Floyd motioned the boys into the middle of the ring.

Andy stepped forward and took the center of the ring.
Sammy circled to his left. He flicked out a long, light jab with
a reach that Andy didn't have. But he was a step or two further
back than he should have been, and the blow didn't land.

A moment later, Sammy found some space and threw another jab. This one connected, not cleanly. Andy kept his eyes
open and plowed right back in. Sammy lost concentration; it
was almost imperceptible, a slight relaxation in the shoulders,
a swift slide with his eyes to see who was at ringside, then

closing them as Andy took the moment to step in and snap Sammy's head back with a jab.

Floyd put up a hand. "Hold up." He climbed in the ring and grabbed both of Sammy's arms to talk with him, his voice low. "I saw it again. You gotta keep your eyes open. When a punch is coming your way, when you are throwing a punch, if you're in the corner, you gotta keep your eyes open. I'm not going to let you get in a ring in a real bout if you can't do that."

Sammy nodded impatiently, his mouth full of his guard. He was sweating, breathing hard.

"All right then," Floyd said. "Why don't you go upstairs and work out. Andy, I want to work with you on a couple of things."

Longo shook his head as Sammy disappeared up the stairs. "That kid has a lot of talent."

"He's glove shy. He's got the worst case I've ever seen. Either he'll get over it or he won't. Doesn't really matter how much talent he has if he doesn't." Floyd said.

Longo laughed. "He'll get over it. Just give him time."

It was months before Andy got his chance to spar with Brian. Floyd motioned Andy over as he came down to the ring area.

"I'm gonna put you in with Brian today," he said. "Just a round, maybe two. You're getting too good to spar with the other guys your size." He glanced around. "Where's Sammy?"

Andy shrugged. "I don't know. He wasn't at school."

The truth was, he hadn't seen him since Saturday when the two of them went to a keg party hosted by Sammy's older brother in the field behind their house. Sammy stayed close to the tap all night. For every beer he drank, Andy took a sip out of his white plastic cup, finally going to the bathroom and dumping it down the sink.

At the end of the night, Sammy was so drunk his brother picked him up and slung him across his shoulders like a laundry bag, carried him into the house, through the blue-lit living room where their parents were watching TV and into the room they shared. Andy followed, and when he saw the pile of Sammy on the floor next to the bed, he decided to call his parents and get a ride home.

Of course, he couldn't tell Floyd this, so he said it again. "Wasn't at school and didn't call after, so I don't know what's up."

Floyd nodded. "All right, you and Brian, you're up."

Andy was nervous. Sparring with the middleweights, sparring with Brian. Longo rang the bell. After a few moments, Andy relaxed. He could see that Brian was going to be gentle and slow with him. Andy ignored Longo, who chattered at him over the ropes, and just concentrated on what Brian could show him. He noticed that Brian let him get in pretty close, and he wanted any punch he threw to be worth the opportunity. He didn't want to look like some little kid flailing around the ring.

It was an uppercut that connected with Brian's nose, and suddenly there was blood dripping down on to his upper lip. Andy took a step back, shocked that he connected so cleanly, sure that the nice slow pace was about to change. But Brian just nodded at him, took a moment to shake his head and wipe at his nose with the back of his forearm. And they continued, same pace, same patience from Brian.

After, Brian spat out his mouth guard and said, "That was a good uppercut. If I had known you had that already, I wouldn't have let you in so close."

Andy shrugged. "I was kind of surprised myself. I thought that was it for me. I thought you would really step up the pace on me."

"What?" Brian looked puzzled and then realized what Andy meant. "Nah, I wouldn't have done that."

Andy shook his head. "I would have."

Andy Schott,
age 13, left, and
Floyd Patterson.
COURTESY OF THE
ANDREW SCHOTT
COLLECTION

Andy

[2004]

After I talk with Alfie in Newburgh, I drive north on the New York State Thruway to Albany, where I'll meet Andy Schott for lunch. The Andy who boxed in Floyd's gym with Brian, the Andy who was salt to Sammy's pepper, the Andy who I dated in high school, whose friendship kept me connected to my brother through so many years. I'm just getting out of my car when I see him pull in. I wait, my fleece coat pulled tight against the winter raw, though I'm shivering as much from nervousness as from the cold. I haven't seen him in thirteen years, and we haven't communicated in at least ten, until I found him via the internet and sent an email to the campus address where he now teaches psychology. I turn to lock my car, and when I turn back all I can see is his smile.

Inside the restaurant, Andy shrugs out of his black leather jacket. He's dressed for work as a prof: button-down striped shirt and dress pants. That brown-leaning-toward-red hair is close cropped. He fought as a middleweight, tall and thin. He's still slim but with the authority of a light heavyweight. After a few moments of half-hearted consideration about what to eat, I ask him if he still keeps a notebook to track all of his workouts and runs.

He laughs. "I do. I'm still that neurotic guy. Not as bad, maybe."

He tells me about teaching and about working with some amateur and pro fighters and shows me pictures of his two children. They are a couple of years older than mine, also a girl and a boy. His wife is someone I have known since I was in elementary school, but my husband is a total stranger to Andy. We share the facts of our lives like kindling for a conversation, which soon enough produces an easy, honest blaze. It's fed with a connection that is more than history and pops with a mutual humor that means we laugh more than we eat. I tell him about the book I want to write about my relationship with Brian. I tell him that I can't do it without him. It's a bit dramatic, sure. But he nods because it's true.

Chapter Eleven

[1975]

> It is unwritten law never to speak to the other
> fighters in the locker room; the atmosphere is tense,
> created to allow concentration. It seems concen-
> tration clears the nervous system for those vital
> electronic impulses that could spell the difference
> between a victory and defeat. So you concentrate
> on an object. A bench. Its splinters. Its dimples and
> creases. The moisture, the sweat, the years and the
> athletes it has soaked up during its existence. You
> come to know that bench like no other object and it
> is the fight.
>
> —Brian Hurley, "The Other Side of the Ropes,"
> *The Huguenot Herald*, New Paltz, New York,
> June 23, 1976

The Golden Gloves. Just the name excited me, and that was before I knew that the winners received bejeweled boxing gloves.
"A glittering array of honors and awards await the contenders,"
read the call for entries in the *New York Daily News*, "Each
champion will receive diamond-studded Golden Gloves. The
runners-up receive ruby-studded silver gloves. Those losing in
the semifinals will receive a single silver glove."

I could just see those glittering gloves, like something from
a fairytale, on the shelves already laden with Brian's trophies.

Some came from tournaments; others honored the Fighter of the Night at interclub matches. Most of them featured small figures in perfect boxing stance, faux silver or gold. Some sported a fighter with one arm extended to the side, the other glove above the belly button, and we teased Brian that those were for excellence in ballroom dancing. But diamond and ruby gloves weren't something to tease about—they'd be sacred.

Even the location for the Golden Gloves felt thrilling—the Felt Forum, in Madison Square Garden. It was the mecca of boxing, where Floyd Patterson first made his name and Joe Frazier met Muhammad Ali in the "fight of the century" in March 1971.

One of the main sports networks decided to follow Brian as the protégé of former World Heavyweight Champ Floyd Patterson. Not only was Brian going to fight in the Felt Forum of Madison Square Garden, he would also be on television.

On the big day, I watched with my mother and Nora. My father was in New York with Brian. There, on our television, was my brother, hitting the heavy bag at the gym; Brian running along Springtown Road, hood on to protect against the winter chill; Brian sparring with Floyd. Floyd himself on camera being interviewed not about his own impressive accomplishments but about the accomplishments he saw in Brian's future.

Then there was a live interview with Brian in the locker room as he waited for his first fight in the Golden Gloves. His comments were spare and delivered without a smile. "Floyd's the best trainer on the East Coast. I think I'm ready for this fight. Ready for the whole tournament."

"Do you see yourself winning the weight class?"

"You gotta see yourself winning," Brian said. By this time the camera was in so close I could see his eyelashes. He was obviously uncomfortable, glanced down as he spoke.

"Well good luck to you." The reporter was gentle.

"Yeah, thanks."

Then the camera pulled out, and the reporter looked at us in our living room. "Young Brian Hurley, protégé of Floyd Patterson, former World Heavyweight Champ, here to start the long road to the Olympics by winning the Golden Gloves."

The next day at school I asked everyone I knew if they saw Brian on television and knew that he'd won his fight. No one had. At lunch time, my disappointment kept me sipping on chocolate milk through a straw while I listened to friends chatter about television shows or teachers or who was "going out." As I stood up to take my empty brown bag to the trash, a girl got up and followed me.

"I think that's cool," she said. "About your brother."

Joan was a year older than I was. She was tall and thin with brown hair that hung straight down on either side of her face, eyes that looked too large behind her glasses, and tiny little pimples that hid in the creases on either side of her nose. I didn't know her, really. Still, she was my only taker. And so, I recruited her into the fan club.

By the time Brian was headed to the quarterfinals, Joan was all in. She made him a poster with oil-based crayons, drawing a pair of golden gloves in the center. At the top, she wrote *Middleweight Champion* and at the bottom, *Brian Hurley*. As I put it on Brian's bed, I wondered why I hadn't thought of doing something like this myself.

Brian's next fight was on my birthday, and none of my family was going down to watch. I raced out the front door to the porch to catch Brian just as he was climbing into Floyd's Lincoln. "Good luck!"

He lifted his gym bag and smiled, then ducked his head to get into the back of the car. He hadn't said happy birthday, but

I didn't mind. Later, as I was listening to my family sing off-key over the cake and blowing my wish to Brian in New York, I kept glancing at the phone, so squat and silent on the kitchen counter. When would he call to let us know what happened?

I finally went to bed around 10:30 after dashing to the phone every time it rang only to dismiss birthday well-wishers. I was in that hazy place just before sleep when the phone rang again.

My father picked it up. "Yeah, Floyd, how did it go tonight?"

I slipped out of bed to stand in the doorway to the dark kitchen. "He did. Well. How's he doing?" And then, "No, no, we'll just see him when he gets home. Thanks for calling." He hung up and stood for a moment. I took a step forward and flipped on the light.

"Dad," I said, just as my mother came to the door at the other end.

My father glanced at me and then my mother. "He lost. Floyd said it was a bad decision, that Brian won the fight. He said that everyone booed the decision."

I couldn't quite get what my father was saying. "Lost?"

"Floyd said they would be home in a couple of hours."

"How's Brian?" My mother came to me, put a hand on my back and rubbed in light, steady circles.

"Floyd says he's tired." My father looked at me. "There will be other fights."

But by this time, I was crying so hard I couldn't answer him. My mother finally patted my shoulder. "Go back to bed, honey," she said. "There's nothing you can do about it. Just go to bed."

I cried when Brian came in, though I didn't get up to see him. I cried when I heard the murmur of my parent's voices. I cried when I heard Brian going down the stairs to his bedroom. The next morning, I felt sick and worn out as I got ready for school. I thought that by the time that I got to school

I would be able to put it aside and let myself be distracted. But the first person I saw was Joan.

And, of course, I cried. "He lost."

"Lost?" Joan was appropriately incredulous. "How?"

"He lost a decision that should have been his," I said and felt an odd comfort in the injustice. "The crowd booed the decision." As if I had been there.

And so it went through the day. My friends inquired about my swollen eyes, and I told them the whole unfair story. Unfair because he should have won, according to Floyd. Unfair because I never considered that he would lose. Unfair because I wasn't prepared. He was in the newspapers, he was on TV, for God's sake.

In the free time we could go outside after lunch, I saw Sammy and Andy. I barely knew them then. Brian had recently brought home the news that Andy had broken his hand during a sparring session. He'd said this off handedly, just a part of the news from the gym. A week or so later he was more admiring. "He's still in there every day," he said. "Floyd says it'll make him stronger on the other side."

I hadn't noticed Andy's cast until that day. They came toward me, looking for information, I could tell. I shook my head as they got near. "He lost!"

"Lost?" Andy said. "How?"

"Decision," I answered and took satisfaction in the shaking of their heads, their disbelief.

"No way," Sammy said.

"Floyd said it was a bad decision," I said. "He said Brian was robbed."

Andy and Sammy nodded knowingly, as if bad decisions were old hat in their young boxing careers.

That night, I examined Brian's face as he sat across from me at dinner. There was a swelling, a small "mouse" of raised tissue on his right cheekbone that was just starting to purple.

Other than that, he looked fine. As I chewed on a pork chop, I imagined the scene, exaggerated with my loyalty: Brian standing in the middle of the ring after the fight, flushed, sweaty, but basically untouched. His opponent with a gash torn over his eye, a bruise on his rib where Brian cracked it, raising his arm over his head in bogus victory and then spitting out teeth, letting them drop to the canvas as the boos mounted in the Felt Forum. If only.

After the meal, my mother brought out dessert. She offered Brian a piece of the chocolate birthday cake. He shook his head no and then glanced at me. "Hey," he said. "Happy Birthday. I meant to tell you that yesterday."

The next day, I didn't bring in the newspaper clippings to school, the ones that quoted Floyd about the bad decision, then quickly moved on to report on other winners and losers.

Joan never asked me about Brian again.

Harold

[2004]

> I thought at the time and still believe that of all the
> people I knew in high school, Brian had the finest,
> most clever mind, the best sense of humor, the most
> impressive physique and the best understanding of
> human nature.
>
> — Harold Issen, letter to Bill and Sonia Hurley,
> September 1990

I greet Harold on the sidewalk outside of his home near Or-
lando. I haven't seen him since 1980. He looks much the same:
small, wiry wrestler's frame; dark wavy hair; cut very short
now; high cheekbones. His house is a low-slung, one-story
ranch in the true Florida style. Inside, I meet his wife and two
children and chat for a few moments before Harold gestures
toward the front den, where we'll talk about Brian.

He says, "I'd like to do a reading and light a candle before
we start."

I'm not sure exactly what he means and hesitate to answer
him. He picks up a lighter from a small table just outside the
den and lights a candle. It's an altar of sorts, with pictures of

Brian and Harold and other high school friends propped up against various objects. "Did you do this just for me?"

Harold smiles. "Well, for me too. I was looking through stuff for you and found pictures and decided to put these up while you are here." He picks up the book that lies in front of this collection, *Young Men and Fire* by Norman Maclean, and opens it to a marked page. He reads aloud in a voice that is slow with a reverence that I sense is not only for his history with Brian, but for his love of good writing. There is a rightness to these moments that feels familiar. This reading, making this small altar is exactly what Harold would do. It's not sentimental or instructive. It's a stopping, a commitment to full attention. This is why, out of all the people who knew Brian well during those high school years, he is the one I most wanted to find.

The first thing that Harold shows me when we begin our conversation is a poem that Brian wrote in high school:

Humble
So in order to see
He lowered himself
And found that he was free

He tells me that the poem made a huge impression on him, on Fred, on Jamie, a girl who was a regular part of their high school crew, that Brian was the first of the three to really start considering Zen. Harold picks up a marbled composition notebook from a stack of other papers on the floor. "You should have this. It's from an English class when we were seniors."

"How did you get this?" I've never seen it before.

Harold grins and shrugs. "I saw him throw it away. I

couldn't believe it. I loved his writing. So, I just picked it up out of the trash can."

I hold the notebook on my lap as we talk, aware of its slight weight on the top of my thighs. I have so little of Brian's writing, just two notes, written on scrap paper, and the article he wrote for the local paper when he was a senior in high school, which he titled "The Other Side of the Ropes." I resist the urge to open it, to flip through the pages immediately. On the front, Brian wrote his name in blue ink. Below it in bubble letters is an instruction obviously intended for a teacher: *To be read when in a good mood.*

And under that, as if an afterthought, he had added in small script, *please?*

Chapter Twelve

[1975]

> They pull the mouthpiece out and pour water
> down your parched throat. It is a bother, but you
> go through it to appease your corner men... Your
> mind clicks, thinking. Supplementing itself with the
> instructions it receives... There are so many things to
> compare and align. It is you that decides what the
> next round will be and your senses beseech you to
> abide their instructions.
>
> – Brian Hurley, "The Other Side of the Ropes,"
> *The Huguenot Herald*, New Paltz, New York,
> June 23, 1976

"Meatballs, garlic bread... my mom makes the best spaghetti." The voice was low, as if sharing a wonderful secret.

Another equally wistful voice says, "There's this dish my grandmother makes. It's like a stew almost, vegetables and potatoes, lamb. You eat it with this great bread you can't get here in the states."

I watched the passing lights on the thruway and smiled as I listened to Harold and Fred talking in the rear-facing back seat of my family's enormous station wagon. They were riding with us to watch Brian fight in Albany. It was wrestling season and time to talk about food, not eat it. I'd gone to cheer for them and Brian for two junior varsity seasons at the high school. They were all good, though Harold was the most serious about the sport, and Brian left the team before they moved up to varsity, when he'd decided to devote all his energies to boxing. This would be the first time that Harold and Fred would see Brian fight.

Brian drew a good opponent that night, and the two were on even footing until late in the second round when Brian maneuvered the other fighter against the ropes. He delivered blow after blow that his opponent couldn't answer, finally just curling in like a threatened millipede, his head down, gloves over his face. The ref surely should have stopped the fight or given a standing eight count, but he let the punches fly, perhaps as in awe of the number as we were.

I wanted Brian to stop, but I wanted him to win. But I wanted him to stop. What if he really hurt the other fighter? Really hurt him? Killed him, even? I felt suddenly embarrassed as if I had been surprised by a pop quiz. Of course, these were possibilities. Always were and I had never considered them. Had Brian? I wanted to see his face, but his back was toward me.

The bell rang and the two fighters went to their corners. The other kid didn't come out for the third round. As Brian came down the steps from the ring holding his trophy, I grabbed at his robe from where I was sitting. My father was next to me, and Brian leaned over us slightly, one gloved fist resting on the back of my seat. He breathed with raspy intakes and reluctant gusts and sweat dripped onto my hair and knee. I looked up into his face and felt relief. This was the Brian I knew, freckles and all.

"That was something," my father said. "The ref should have stopped it. You hurt him pretty early on."

"Yeah," Brian said. "I kept thinking the ref was going to step in. I'm glad the guy didn't come back out. I didn't have a punch left in me."

I glanced at Fred and Harold. They were slowly standing up to talk with Brian as if they didn't know what to say and wanted to postpone the inevitable.

"Hey," Brian grinned at them. "Thanks for coming."

"Good fight," Fred said and glanced at Harold.

"Yeah," Harold said. "It was. A good fight." But his tone was uncertain.

Two hours later, we were with the caravan of cars that followed Floyd's Lincoln into the diner parking lot in New Paltz. I loved these post-fight gatherings, the chatter of the fighters and, if we were lucky, a story from Floyd about his pro-career. The hostess, recognizing Floyd from other evenings, scrambled to assemble a long table for the five or six fighters, their respective families and fans.

Brian looked pale and exhausted as he took a seat. The waitress moved about the group, like a hummingbird amongst bee balm, flirting and scribbling. When she reached Brian, he glanced up and said, "Yeah, yeah, just a Bud for right now."

Andy was sitting next to Brian. He'd fought that night, too, winning his bout easily. I saw him lean hard against Brian's shoulder and nod toward Floyd. Sammy, who didn't get a fight that night, sat on the other side of Andy and covered a smile with his hand. Floyd didn't seem to pay attention, but then he glanced at Brian. As the waitress moved away to the other side of the table, Brian sighed, then raised his arm and clicked his fingers. She looked back. "Just a Coke," he said. "Make it a Coke."

Floyd didn't say anything, he probably hadn't heard. Or maybe he had.

"Boxing isn't just filled with Neanderthals that want to beat each other's brains out," Brian said. "I just like that I can take this body, shape it, you know. That it's just me out there. Think about the Olympics. They were based on purity, that idea that the human body should be worshipped, be divine."

Harold shook his head and said over his shoulder to their friend Jamie, "So he says as he lights up for the third time in the last hour."

The three of them were riding around on a Saturday night as they usually did, with Harold driving, Brian joking, and Jamie as the arbiter or provocateur of good-natured, often hilarious, debates. Harold braked hard as he came down a hill to a stop sign. The back seat slid toward the front, and Jamie giggled as her shoulder-length straight dark hair swung forward like a curtain over her face. She smashed against the front seat, right between Harold and Brian. As Harold accelerated, she pushed herself back.

Brian took a long drag, leaned over and blew the smoke in Harold's face.

"Jesus Christ." Harold turned into the parking lot near the main intersection downtown and stopped the car. "We're gonna have a wreck if you do that again. So, OK, purity thing. You're really thinking Olympics with this?"

Brian shrugged. "No telling. But boxing and the Olympics, they kind of go together. That idea, that you represent your country in this pure form … and it's just you. There is no team. I mean, yeah, there is a team, but it's not like you are playing a game. It's just you." Brian's face flushed with earnestness, though he kept his tone noncommittal.

"You and whoever you are beating on," Harold said.

"No, he means no excuses," Jamie said. "No one but yourself to blame if anything goes wrong."

"Exactly." Brian turned to grin at her. "By Jove, you've got it."

She grinned back. "OK. Now that's settled. I'm starving. Let's get something to eat."

Brian peered through the windshield at a group of young men in front of one the seamier local dives, illuminated by a fluorescent orange sign. "Yeah, I'm not that hungry. I think I'm going to join those fine gents over there."

Harold followed his gaze. "Who are they?"

Brian shrugged and opened the car door. "Some guys I know."

Harold, Ulster County Athletic League Wrestling Champion, 112 lbs. 1976.

COURTESY OF THE HAROLD ISSEN COLLECTION

Jamie

[2004]

A boxer with style, an athlete with brains. His sardonic wit never missed the irony of life's absurdities. He laughed easily and often, and never threw punches. Where others might put a person at the center of a joke, Brian didn't. Humor was situational—not personal.

– Jamie Rhein, email to Janet Hurley,
August 17, 2004

Brian never had a steady girlfriend in high school. I knew he had his crushes and brief dalliances, mostly with girls who escaped notice by other guys because they were too smart or unconcerned with popularity. Brian used boxing as an excuse to ward off sisterly inquiries he found uncomfortable. "I'm training," he would say. "You know what Floyd says." Then he would wink.

We all knew what Floyd said. When an overzealous relative had pinched Brian's cheek and asked if he were breaking any girl's heart, Nora had jumped right in. "No, he isn't. Floyd says women weaken legs."

I write to Jamie after visiting with Harold. I vaguely remember her interest in Brian. She isn't hard to summon to mind. When they were teens, both she and her brother, an artist and friend who was my age, had dark hair, very white skin, with large smiles and freckles that lent a jauntiness to their expressions. Now, a professional writer of articles and essays, Jamie takes the time and care to send me such well-crafted and deeply felt prose that all I can do is ask her permission to share a part of it.

"*When Brian Hurley entered a room, I knew he was there. He was my friend, but also the type of boy who sent my heart racing … Ski jump nose, sharp jaw, perpetually fair skin, even in the middle of summer, and the slightly pink hue of his knuckles immediately come to mind when I say his name.*

[He] moved with an elegance that was unusual for an adolescent. Whether sliding into a chair at the beginning of class, walking across a gym floor during a wrestling meet or perusing the streets of New Paltz, his body looked like it fit. Even from far away in a dimly lit hall, his walk marked him. With his head tilted forward, shoulders slightly hunched, and feet moving with a gentle bounce, Brian's time spent in a boxing ring gave him his signature stance.

He was a toned-down version of a high school hunk. This wasn't the role he chose to play, even though he had the attributes. His role was a loftier sort. Brian was a champion—not a saint, but a boy a girl could trust.

A couple of times, I spent time with Brian alone. With Harold's friendship between us, there wasn't much time or inclination to head down the path of a full-blown involvement, but a bit of dabbling was too alluring to pass up. Afterwards, the friendship stayed with no hurt and no regrets. Besides that, our lips were sealed. Brian did not kiss and tell and neither did I."

I'm glad she did. Tell. I'm grateful for Jamie's writing, not just for its content, but because she has saved me from speculating on paper about my brother's teenage love life. I just can't imagine him making out with a girl in the back seat of a car or having sex on someone's basement couch, though, of course, anything was possible. Jamie chose the best words to describe it: he seemed lofty, above such things.

Brian, winter 1976.
COURTESY OF THE
HAROLD ISSEN
COLLECTION

Chapter Thirteen

It seems that he became frustrated and tangled within his thoughts. The fibers of him crossed and raveled into irretrievable abstractness. And no one noticed.

– Brian Hurley, senior English class journal, 1976

I was envious of Brian's room, so much like a club house, tucked away and out of the flow and inspection of family life. My room was right off the kitchen—and on top of Brian's room—and included the closet where we kept the vacuum cleaner. I liked lying in bed, listening to *The Dark Side of the Moon* by Pink Floyd coming up through the floor, or Stevie Wonder, or one of Brian's other favorites.

When he wasn't at school or at the gym or out with friends, Brian spent hours in his room on his own, leaving occasionally to take long baths in our one bathroom, ignoring the pounding on the door by his sisters. He would finally come out, steam surrounding him, and push past us, with a towel around his waist, and drops of water still clinging to the curly hair on his head and chest. The bathroom always felt like a cave to me when I'd rush in, water still in the tub, mirror fogged, everything a bit damp to the touch.

One Saturday morning, when Brian must have been seventeen and I was thirteen, we sat at the dining room table together. He read the paper while eating bacon and eggs that he fixed for himself. I remember his blue terry cloth bathrobe and ubiquitous ski cap as being stylish and cool. Brian hadn't said a word since I sat down, but I still enjoyed the implied companionship while I ate an English muffin. It was rare that we spent time together at all these days.

My father came up from the basement, through the TV room and into the dining room. He stopped by the table, almost as if he didn't want to and might change his mind. He hesitated a second and then said to Brian, "What are you growing in that trunk down there?"

I wasn't in on Brian's efforts, but I guessed immediately what it might be. I knew all about pot. With my friends Cathy and Robin, I had purchased a joint for a buck from a twelve-year-old dealer and then returned it. We were too afraid to smoke it. What was Brian doing? Floyd would kill him if he knew. Not to mention my parents. I couldn't stand the thought, so I jumped right in. "It's a science experiment."

Brian, whose face was flushed, looked at me with a raised eyebrow. "Yeah," he said slowly. "Artificial light...or natural light. Which is better? Another kid has the natural light plants." Brian calmly put another bite of omelet in his mouth.

My father nodded. Surely, he knew this wasn't true. "I just went in there to change out the dehumidifier," he said. "Seemed wet near the trunk so I opened it."

Brian nodded. "Yeah, I'm sorry. I have to figure a better way to water. I'll deal with it right after breakfast."

"Use the shop vac to get up the water out of the carpet," my father said. "Otherwise, it will mildew. And...I think using that trunk is a bad idea."

He went into the kitchen then, and Brian widened his eyes at me. I could feel the blush warming my face and had to glance away. Now, I wonder, why did my father let this lie ride?

Sometime in the weeks that followed my father's discovery, I lay in bed and listened to Brian thunk thunk thunk down the stairs. I felt Led Zeppelin vibrate through the mattress and pillow to my cheek. I couldn't sleep but not because of the music. I was angry with my parents. I'd just listened to them badger Brian about concerns that I considered to be blown out of proportion. Lately, they'd been having the same argument with him. They'd set his curfew at 11:30 p.m. and he'd come home late, again. The exclamation from Brian was always, "Everyone can stay out until after midnight!" The answer, disguised as a question, was always, "What can you do after eleven-thirty that you can't do before?"

Like every other night, Brian didn't respond to this hopelessly naïve parental inquiry, or to any of their other questions about what they thought they smelled on his clothes or on his breath. Tonight, my mother had started in on which friends he needed to avoid, only to be interrupted by my father, who said he just couldn't understand why Brian would put his boxing on the line with these shenanigans, not after he'd worked so damn hard.

I'd wanted to get up and go into the dining room to confront them. What about Brian just getting quoted in *People Magazine* as Floyd's "star pupil"? I imagined saying. Brian was still the golden boy at the gym. That's what matters, I thought. That matters most.

I heard Brian say, "I'm not! I won't! OK!"

A few weeks later, I surprised Brian in the bathroom on the night of the prom. He was usually a stickler for locking the door, particularly during his annoyingly long baths. I walked right in to find him in his cream-colored tux, black bowtie limp around his neck. He leaned across the pink Formica counter to examine his eye in the mirror. The delicate skin was a purplish-blue, like a smear of eye shadow without any glitter. He recently won a fight by a technical knockout in the second round but obviously only after taking a good blow.

"I can hide that," I said impulsively.

He looked at me in the mirror. "Really?"

I nodded and dashed to my room to return with a makeup stick. "Turn around."

Dutifully, he faced me, but didn't look at me, as if I were a drill sergeant calling him down. I stroked the makeup stick across the soft skin under his eye and then smoothed it with my pinky finger. I had to stand on tiptoe, chest to chest with him, a proximity that was rare. Everyone in our family was wary of Brian's need of inordinate personal space. It was the closest physically that I had been to him since we were both children. I finished and immediately stepped back to a safe distance.

He twisted to examine my work in the mirror. "That's good. Will it come off?"

"Maybe," I said. "Don't rub your eyes. I'll bring it in my purse to put some more on if you need it."

"Nah," he said. "This is good."

I was disappointed. "OK."

Brian and I were both going to the same prom. He as a senior asked by a junior girl, Molly, and I was an eighth grader asked by a junior boy, Matt. What Brian thought about that, I couldn't tell. My parents didn't approve of me dating a high school boy. They rightly assumed that forbidding the relationship would just send it underground. Brian never commented on Matt, though I am sure he was surprised to find a boy so near his age now sitting on the couch every evening with his younger sister.

I was glad that he would be at the prom too. I was nervous, intimidated by the idea of being with all those older girls. I wanted my dress to be sophisticated even if I wasn't. The dress

I chose was coral red, sleeveless, with a plunging neckline that ended in a stitched diamond on my solar plexus. I bought four-inch-high white platform shoes to wear with it. Mike's mother took great pains to help him pick out a tux with a shirt that would match. She even had his boutonnière tipped with the same coral red. It was as if she thought we would make up for our out-of-sync ages with color coordination.

On that day of the prom, I was dressed hours before Matt would pick me up. Brian hastily dressed in the forty minutes before his date would arrive. My mother took pictures of us out on the patio behind our house. It was a beautiful day, the air warm and full of early spring scent. There isn't a picture of Brian and me together. But in his, there isn't a trace of that black eye.

Once at the prom, held in a turn-of-the-century hotel complete with dinner and a lazy band that played so many slow dances they looked bored themselves, I lost track of Brian. Matt and I sat at a table with his friends, where I cut my roast beef into tiny squares so that I wouldn't attract attention with a mouth opened too wide. The girls around me were very polite, engaged me to pass the salt, offered me rolls, but their stories were like news reports from a foreign country, so I just smiled when everyone laughed and took comfort in the occasional squeeze Matt gave my knee under the table. As soon as we finished the white cake with off-white icing, he whispered, "Want to walk out in the gardens?" I nodded and stood immediately.

As we headed for the door that led out to a lake, romantic dark paths and gazebos, I saw Brian sitting at a table filled with plates of half-eaten food, scrunched up napkins, sweating water glasses. On the other side, a girl sat on her date's lap with a dreamy just-kissed look. Brian leaned back in his chair. His bow tie was off, his tux shirt opened at the throat. The bruise near his eye had slipped out from under the makeup.

He watched the dance floor where Molly was with someone in a pale blue tux. I knew Brian didn't care who she danced with, was probably glad he didn't have to. But he looked tired, not really comfortable. He lifted his chin up to greet me when Matt and I stopped next to him. I was delighted and relieved to find him.

"What's up?" he said.

"Not much," I said. "Did you like the dinner?"

He shrugged.

"How's your eye?" I asked.

He shrugged again, turned his gaze not on the dance floor but somewhere slightly lower. I felt a bit embarrassed, wanted some invitation to sit down, wanted him to include me, wanted to be seen with him, laughing and at ease. Wanted my relationship with Matt to be anointed and approved in front of everyone.

"Well, we're going to walk out in the garden," I said.

"See ya later," Brian answered absently, glanced back up, and shook Matt's hand like a father.

Brian and his ubiquitous ski cap at our dining room table, circa 1974–1975.

Sanctity

[2004]

"The sanctity of your body..." Longo considers the can in his hand. "I drink beer. I drink beer all the time. And I drank beer back then. I didn't drink when I was in college athletics; I didn't smoke. I still don't drink or smoke, other than beer."

"So, do you think Floyd knew that Brian was smoking or drinking while he was in training?"

"Well..." Longo relaxes back into his seat a bit. "Floyd Patterson hated alcohol and drugs. Hated them. Patterson never did alcohol or drugs, never. Never ever." Longo stops for a second to take a swig of beer and check my face to see if I got that last never ever. I nod to show that I got the point.

Longo crumples up the empty beer can, disposes of it in that mysterious place I can't see, leans back and gets another from the refrigerator. As he pops the top on this one, he says, "I think Floyd was pretty oblivious to any partying that Brian was doing. If Floyd woulda known, I woulda known. I was around him as much as Floyd was or more. And I would be sensitive because I know about that stuff."

Indeed. I think of Brian's stories about Longo always having a six-pack in the car on the way home from fights—and he was willing to share. But I'm nodding as Longo talks, just want to see where this goes.

"Floyd was o-bliv-i-ous," Longo chuckles. "If you asked him what a joint was, he would think it was a goddamn thing between two two-by-fours. I don't think he knew about the drugs or knew about smoking. But then Brian wouldn't do the running, slacked off that. For Floyd, not running was worse than shooting dope."

Chapter Fourteen

Opinion

I don't need this knowledge
to get to no college
I'm afraid I must say
I can find a better way
than finding the rhyme for orange.

—Brian Hurley, senior English class journal, 1976

"OK, OK." Brian grinned. "Let me see the book again."

Harold pulled out the Royal Canadian Air Force Fitness Program, something he'd proposed they follow this summer before their senior year. A couple of summers before, he, Brian and Fred trained at the college track with the goal of running six miles in thirty-six minutes. They started with an eight-minute mile and worked down. Through repetition and dedication, they were convinced they could achieve most any goal. Of course, they didn't spend that whole summer running. They taught themselves to juggle in the same way, had loud and focused ping-pong matches in our basement, and grunted through individual push-up, chinning, and sit-up routines.

That summer, 1975, it would be just Harold and Brian. Fred had plans to travel with his family overseas. Harold had already lined up a job in the kitchen of one of the mountain resorts to subsidize his true love: flying. Brian worked in the kitchen of a Chinese restaurant and was training at Floyd's. Still, they had time every morning to do the Canadian Air Force thing.

Brian flipped through the pages, examining the sketches of muscular men doing jumping jacks or sit-ups, all with square rectangular faces, shoulders straight and broad, chests and stomachs tapering perfectly to hips that were just hinges to connect with huge muscular thighs. "Cool. Very cool."

"So, I think we're in pretty good shape," Harold said. "Let's start at level three."

Brian flipped a few pages further. "Nah, let's just go for it. Level six."

"I can't run a mile in five minutes."

"Sure we can."

I don't remember this period when Brian and Harold were hell-bent on Canadian-inspired fitness. From Harold, I know that Brian was just a tad overconfident, which, I imagine, became clear after just a few days into their training. They were outside of Harold's house, gasping, bent double, with hands on their knees as they shook their heads to make sweat-drip patterns on the pale cement sidewalk.

"I...told...you." Brian probably pushed the teasing out with great wheezes. "No way we should start at level six."

Harold rolled his eyes and played along. "You were sooooo right, Hurley." He walked up to the front porch of his house and picked up the book. "I am now looking at chart three."

"Yeah, yeah, what's next?"

"Sit-ups."

"Cool."

After they finished, Brian reached into his gym shorts and pulled out a plastic bag with a joint and lighter in it.

Harold shook his head. "I got a flying lesson this afternoon."

Brian shrugged. "So?"

Harold made a face and shook his head. "No way. Catch me later with that."

"When are you going to take me up?"

"I gotta learn to fly the damn thing first, but I hope it's soon," Harold said.

Brian nodded, holding in a drag as long as he could. After he exhaled, he asked, "Hey, you know what 'calisthenics' means in Greek?"

Harold smiled. "No, I don't think I do."

"Strength and beauty."

"No shit."

Harold, Brian, Phil Eulie, Fouad Boulos, winter 1976.

COURTESY OF THE HAROLD ISSEN COLLECTION

The Party Party

[1976, 2004]

> I don't feel that school is necessary from the aca-
> demic point of view. Sometimes I think that after all
> this intermingling in this great melting pot of ours is
> said and done that everyone will think and behave
> the same. And you will feel that you are talking to
> a mirror all the time... You live in a perpetual echo
> chamber.
>
> −Brian Hurley, senior English class journal, 1976

Harold loans me the 1975–1976 high school yearbook because I can't find Brian's. There's a picture that I keep coming
back to, of Brian, Fred and Harold. When I ask Harold about
it, he tells me that they ran for senior class officers as the Party Party, campaigning on the platform of More Party! They
made a single campaign appearance: eating Chinese takeout
in the cafeteria during lunchtime while wearing silly hats.
They endorsed a good-natured friend, Mike, for secretary, and
they were all elected, no surprise to anyone.

Three out of the four boys would soon be featured in the
local papers for receiving commendation letters from the National Merit Scholarship program. Out of 1.2 million students taking the PSAT/NMSQT in 1975, 35,000 received
commendation letters for outstanding performance, including Brian. When my parents congratulated him at dinner, he'd

shrugged. "You know I didn't study for the PSAT," he'd said. This wasn't a surprise to me. It seemed like he didn't study much for anything anymore. Not like he used to. More than once, I'd heard my parents talking with him about his report card or the lack of time he was putting in on homework. He always agreed with their worries, always promised to turn things around. And now he was commended for an outstanding performance.

"Well," my mother replied carefully. "This just shows how smart you are. And it's great for college applications."

"If I go," Brian said. "If it fits in with training."

Now, I look at the picture of these senior class officers, all smiling, as they sit on the landing of a stairway, legs through the railings. Fred, Harold and their friend sit straight up. Brian holds the middle railing at the crooks of his elbows and leans back, his legs kicked up, grin full shine.

When I first look at it, I know there's something amiss. I take a second look and then a third and see that Brian has one socked foot, one sneakered foot. The missing sneaker lies along the length of his left forearm. I'm reminded of those find-the-hidden-object picture pages in children's magazines.

It's a feeling I always had with Brian—that just when I thought I saw him clearly, got the picture, something else would come into view. And now, while writing about him, talking with people who knew him, and knowing that his story will stretch into my own children's lives, it's stronger than ever. I want to circle the shoe with a red pen. *Aha, there it is.* Just a moment of satisfaction before I search again.

Chapter Fifteen

Once there was a person who strove to become
himself, his potential. He carved and chiseled for
years and yet a rough him remained. I guess you
could say he was striving for him-ness.

—Brian Hurley, senior English class journal, 1976

Brian entered his second Golden Gloves competition in 1976
without the television crew but with plenty of newspaper cov-
erage. It was the golden anniversary of the Golden Gloves, and
Floyd registered his largest and most experienced squad.

"This year," he told a reporter, "we're aiming to make the
finals."

Brian was no longer in the sub-novice class. He was now in
the open class, come what may, at 160 pounds. The returning
two-time champ of that weight class was Tom Chestnut, a
man at twenty-three, trained by the Police Athletic League.
Another boy eyeing that same crown was Tom McNeece, a
big-boned redhead from Long Island who had dropped down
a couple of weight classes and was making a reputation for
himself as a middleweight. After winning his first fight, Brian
drew McNeece for the next.

As we sat through the earlier bouts, my father worried aloud
about McNeece, but I didn't pay much attention. I was simply
in awe of the cavernous venue and the number of people. It

was like being in the cross section of an ant hill. Thousands of tiny people scurried along in half tunnels formed by the different levels of seating, the stairs and the rows of seats. On the floor of the arena, reporters and trainers and fans swarmed as if the queen were under attack in the ring.

My father's leg did its usual jiggling when we finally saw Brian, Floyd and Longo come down to the ring. McNeece and his father appeared moments later in their corner, son looking like a younger version of his square-shaped dad. The boxers moved to the middle of the ring, each with white skin that was bright under the lights. They were equal in height and had to be within the limits of the weight class, but somehow, McNeece seemed thicker, and more powerful.

Within moments, the bell rang. Brian knocked McNeece to the canvas early and I relaxed until McNeece got up, took his eight count impatiently, and then seemed to have twice the energy.

Tom McNeece was clearly as good a fighter as Brian, with the same tenacity. He was a powerful puncher. Every punch Brian threw, McNeece returned it, and they were equally damaging. During the second round, I closed my eyes more than I opened them, so I wasn't sure who was throwing or taking more blows. I thought back to that night when Brian was so relentless on his opponent and felt somewhat reassured. I knew that whatever McNeece threw out, Brian could answer it. Though the reverse was obviously true too. By the third round, the people around me were standing, and so was my father. When I stood up, I could see that almost everyone in the arena was on their feet. My father yelled and then yelled again, but there was so much noise, so many yowls and whistles, even screams, that I could barely hear him at my side. My own throat was so tight that my screaming came out as if through a kazoo. I looked down for a moment at my mother. She sat, elbows on her knees, head in her hands, rocking slightly forward and back. She didn't make a sound. Every once in a while, she lifted her head up, and made herself look.

The third round was my mother's nightmare, worse maybe than a knockout. Brian was winning but it was taking everything he had, and he had to take everything that McNeece had to give on top of that. But he was winning. I knew he was winning. When the bell rang on the third round, the crowd gave a collective whoop, the applause lasted minutes. And then minutes more as the judges totaled their cards. I could hear some yelling, draw! Draw! Draw! But there was no draw in an amateur fight. Someone had to be the winner, someone the loser. Behind those yells, I heard another refrain begin, *Hur-ley, Hur-ley, Hur-ley.* A slow clap syncopated the name, and then a stamping started.

The announcer came to the center of the ring and motioned for the fighters to meet him there. The crowd continued: *Hur-ley, Hur-ley, Hur-ley.* Brian and Tom's faces were both bloodied and swollen; both of them had split eyebrows, McNeece had a cut under his eye, Brian a split lip. *Hur-ley, Hur-ley, Hur-ley.* The announcer motioned for the spectators to quiet down. Twice he started to speak into the mic and twice he stopped, glaring up into the stands. *Hur-ley, Hur-ley, Hur-ley.* Finally, the chant quieted down to an uneasy murmur.

"The winner by a split decision, from Long Island, Tom McNeece." The announcer raised McNeece's arm into the air to boos and clapping, jeers and cheers. The chant and the stamping resumed: *Hur-ley, Hur-ley, Hur-ley.* Brian walked back to his corner where Floyd was ready with his robe. Longo wiped my brother's face, draped the towel around his shoulders and parted the ropes for him. McNeece stood in the middle, and I almost felt sorry for him. Almost. There were a few cheers that came from behind me, and I turned to find the traitors even as I stamped and chanted myself. For some moments I honestly believed that maybe the judges would realize their mistake. That they would climb into the ring and say, no, no you got it wrong, and snatch the paper from the announcer. I looked at my mother, who had remained in her seat the whole time. She had her coat on, her purse slung over her shoulder, though there were other fighters to watch from Floyd's gym. She knew the decision was final. And she wanted to leave. But first, my father wanted to see Brian.

Longo was standing next to where Brian lay on his back on a bench, taped hands over his eyes when my father came into the locker room. "I never seen a fighter so exhausted," Longo said. "Brian won that fight."

My father never looked at Longo—just at Brian. He must have seen the sweat still rolling off his son's stomach, arms quivering just a bit with all that lactic acid called up in the relentlessness of the fight. Maybe he saw Brian's chin move a bit as if Brian were talking to himself. Other fighters in the locker room were giving the bench a wide, respectful berth. Finally, my father stepped around Longo and went to stand next to Brian.

"Bri…"

Brian shook his head, arms still covering his face.

After a few moments, my father sighed, put a hand on Brian's forearm for just a second and then turned to leave. Longo still stood a few feet away, now with Floyd. Both had their hands clasped behind them.

"I have never seen two fighters throw so many punches," Longo said. "Look at Brian. I'll say it again. He's as exhausted as I have ever seen anybody. I guarandamntee you that McNeece is around the corner there lying flat on his back too."

Floyd sighed. "It was close, I think Brian took it. But my fighters never get the close decisions down here."

My father nodded. Everyone knew the Golden Gloves were New York City and Police Athletic League-centric, begrudging of teams that came down from upstate. He held out his hand.

The New York Daily News would proclaim Brian's bout one of "the most exciting in many years," reporting that Tom McNeece "edged out a hairline decision as the fans howled for a draw." *The Kingston Daily Freeman* would say that there was "a stormy scene in Madison Square Garden" and carried the headline "Hurley Is Eliminated in Controversial Bout."

Longo was quoted, "It took a heavyweight to beat Brian. He scored a solid knockdown, counterpunched beautifully with left hooks, but McNeece threw a lot of leather that must have impressed those judges."

"It was a bad decision," Floyd told the reporter. "A bad decision."

Chapter Sixteen

Real life heroes are open to various people's
interpretations.

–Brian Hurley, senior English class journal, 1976

As senior class officers, Harold, Brian, Fred and Mike were
responsible for making sure there was enough money in the
treasury for their class trip. Brian came to a meeting with a
photo—him and Floyd in a ring at a charity exhibition held a
few years before. The Huguenot Boxing Club could do something similar as a fundraiser for the senior class, he said. Despite Floyd's retirement, Brian explained, he was still a celebrity, not so long out of the boxing world that he wouldn't draw
a crowd. And instead of an exhibition, they could do a real
show, sanctioned by the Amateur Athletic Union. Bringing in
clubs from other places—and their fans. Brian's fellow class
officers thought it was a brilliant idea.

Brian talked with Floyd and came home to report that he
was totally on board and would work on getting the help of a
promoter. My father volunteered to find someone who might
donate the use of a ring. I volunteered to hang posters and sell
tickets. The club had never fought in New Paltz. It was my
chance to show my friends what I was always talking about.

A local printer donated the posters for the exhibition.
Black ink on salmon-colored card stock, 11 x 14. Brian

brought them home, wrapped with brown paper, and tore the package open with an impatience fit for a much-longed-for birthday present. Fred's artwork was front and center. The boxers looked almost like martial arts fighters, highly stylized, with bodies that seemed too lithe for the gloves that were exaggerated at the end of their arms. But the most important information about why to come was there in big bold letters: Two-Time Former Heavyweight Champion Floyd Patterson. And underneath, in smaller print: To benefit the New Paltz High School Senior Class. And in yet smaller type: Appearing with the Huguenot Boxing Club. Brian's name was first on the list of fighters.

Eager classmates helped Brian staple the posters onto telephone poles and taped them up in the windows of supportive businesses. My father took some to Kingston and gave them to a few of his athletes to post around the school and town. He took a bundle of tickets as well. I found it hard to imagine that anyone could or would dare to refuse him.

I took a poster to school and asked permission to post it on the bulletin board near the office. The assistant principal looked puzzled as she scanned it. I pointed to my brother's name.

"Sure," she smiled. "Just don't cover up any of the other notices."

I had a harder time selling tickets to other eighth graders, though my best friend Valerie said she would buy one, which didn't really count.

Years later, Harold told me that he'd never seen Brian so energized. That Brian was hoping to fight someone who was good—but not a southpaw. If this was to be his one fight in New Paltz, he wanted to win. Brian trained hard, Harold said, to impress. Who? His friends. Girls. My father. Ticket sales were strong, equipment rented, publicity out. Harold figured it wouldn't be a huge moneymaker, but they'd have enough to give something back to the Huguenot Boxing Club and still go on the class trip. Everything was falling into place.

When Brian walked into the gym on that afternoon, he was a little late, for the first time in weeks. He had been training with a focus he hadn't had since before his first Golden Gloves. He called hello to the other fighters who were already there and then went to the ring, where Floyd watched two boys spar. "Floyd, I want to give you the update on the show seeing as it's next week. Ticket sales are going pretty well, and the way we figured it, we'll have some money to just give to the gym." He held out a piece of paper.

Floyd's voice was louder than anyone had ever heard it. "GIVE the gym? GIVE THE GYM? WHO are YOU to say WHAT MONEY THE GYM GETS?"

Brian took a step back from him.

"I DECIDE. I don't care what is on that paper. Here is how it works." Floyd named his percentage for the club. "Period. End of discussion."

Brian was stunned for a moment. "Floyd, that's not what we agreed on."

"If you are going to argue with me then it's off."

"But Floyd," Brian said, "the class will lose money. It's supposed to be a benefit."

"Then it's off if it's not good enough. Or you can do it. But not with me."

"Jesus Christ, we sold tickets," Brian said. "Everyone is talking about it. We have it all ARRANGED."

Floyd motioned to the sparring partners. "Let's go. I don't have all day."

Brian looked around the room at the fighters frozen in their various positions. "We can do it ourselves," he said. "Are you in?"

When he didn't get a response, he started a slow circuit to make his appeal. Most of the guys just shook their heads. Brian even climbed the stairs to talk with some of the guys who'd heard the argument all the way up on the third floor and came down to watch from the balcony as if it were another sparring session. More shaking heads. Finally, Brian came back down to the first floor and stopped in front of Andy. He was waiting to spar, hands taped. Brian stepped close to him. He could still look down at him despite the new inches and pounds on Andy's frame. "What about you?"

Andy lifted his eyes up to Brian's face. It was set, unsmiling. He glanced over at Floyd. He hesitated as if Brian should just know what he would say and then move on without him having to say it. But Brian waited.

"I … can't fight without Floyd," Andy said. "You know that. None of us can fight without Floyd."

Brian came home that evening looking worse than he did after one of his tougher fights. He sat down at the dining room table and put his head in his hands. I could see him from where I sat in the living room and was just about to ask him what was wrong when my mother came in from the kitchen and put a hand on his shoulder.

"Bill?" she called to my father. I heard the television go off, and my father came in a moment later.

"Bri, what's the matter?" The question sounded like a reluctant invitation, as if my father was exhausted from the number of talks he and Mom had with Brian over the recent years. About late nights. About school. About spending too much time alone in his room or watching late-night TV. About the worries he didn't seem to share. I'd overheard parts of so many of them.

"Floyd's not doing the show."

My parents sat down and pulled their chairs in close to Brian. From where I sat, I could barely hear their collective murmuring. My father's voice and Brian's rose and fell with the same cadence, their heads close together. My mother's voice became shrill, and she leaned back in her seat to let it out.

"This is just rotten. Just rotten. How could he do this? You boys worked so hard on this; everything is set up. Why is he doing this?"

More murmuring from Brian.

"He is a sick guy," my mother said. "He is crazy. You don't do this sort of thing to a boy! I'll call him right now."

Brian and my father both lifted their heads and looked horrified by the thought.

"No," Brian protested. "No, Mom, really. You gotta let it go." He stood up then and said, "I'm going down to my room."

My parents watched him go, and then my mother said, "Bill, this is ridiculous."

My father nodded and rubbed a hand over his ever-increasing bald spot. "I know, but there is nothing we can do to change it. All we can do is support Brian through it."

"I know that!" my mother snapped, and then her voice became softer with tears. She got up and fetched a tissue from the kitchen counter, blew her nose as she came back to sit down. "But Brian was so happy. I had so much hope for him about this. I thought it might help him through the end of the year. Hasn't Floyd noticed how hard it's been for him lately?"

My father continued to rub his hands over his head as if he could just wipe the situation out of his consciousness. "I don't know."

When I went to bed, I listened to see if Brian was still awake below me. There was no music, no sounds at all. How could Floyd do this to him? What would happen now? I thought about all the posters that were up around town, that would have to be pulled down, thrown away.

The day of the canceled show, Floyd came up to the third floor where Andy and some of the other fighters were pushing their clothes into their gym bags. They were idly exchanging small talk about workouts and who did what in the sparring session. Brian hadn't been to the gym since the day of the argument, but they didn't mention him.

"Listen," Floyd said. "I know you guys are all feeling bad about Brian. I just want you to know, I did most of the work. I called the promoter, made some other calls. Without that, there woulda been nothing. What did Brian do? I thought Brian and I had figured it out, and then he comes in with this stuff about what he's gonna give the gym. If I hadn't made those calls there wouldn't have been anything to give anyone."

The fighters didn't look at each other. Finally, one said, "Yeah, Floyd, well, thanks for telling us all that."

Floyd nodded. "Yeah, well, all right then. See you guys tomorrow."

After they heard the door slam downstairs, Andy looked at the other boys. "I don't know what to think. I didn't know Floyd did all that." He hesitated and then shook his head. "I—I think it will blow over; it can't be that big of a deal. Brian'll be back. This is his place." He nodded slightly, as if confirming it with himself. "Yeah, he'll be back. It won't be a big deal in a few months."

Brian did go back. He won a fight in May, at an outdoor show in Warwick, NY, by stopping a New York City fighter in the second round. The follow-up article referred to him as Floyd's protégé. I remember going to the fight with my whole family, looking up through the ropes, Brian so white in the glare of the lights he seemed like an apparition.

Another article from *The Kingston Daily Freeman*, promoting a show in Kingston at the end of the month, carried the headline "Amateur Fight Show to Feature Brian Hurley," referring to him as "Patterson's outstanding 160-pound protégé" and "son of Kingston High School Athletic Director." I don't remember that fight at all, and there is no newspaper clipping to consult. Fights fall through all the time, someone gets injured or sick, hasn't trained enough, or trainers aren't happy with the match.

Histories

[2004, 2021]

"What did Floyd expect of Brian?" Longo bends his head to one side so that he can look me straight in the eye. "When you think Floyd, think money. Floyd, until recently, didn't drive down his driveway without making a dollar."

I wince, because I know this is simply not true and because I am familiar with this point of view, having heard it from my mother through all these years. From what I knew, and according to Andy, Floyd never charged for the use of his gym or for the training he offered to amateur fighters. There were many tournaments and match bouts that he traveled to with the club where he wasn't paid for his appearance—and then he took everyone out to eat. But even if it was true, don't elite athletes, in their prime and retired, rely on endorsements and appearance fees?

Maybe Longo notices this change in my expression because he rushes on. "I don't think he had dollar signs in his brain with those kids at that point, but he knew he had to keep his hand in boxing to bring in the income. He saw Brian's natural ability, and then he saw Brian sneaking out of the gym after sparring… and then when he dealt with him business-wise, on that project, I think Floyd thought there was a little bit of competition going on and I think that was where Floyd didn't want to be involved."

The seeming bitterness of his first statement is diluted a bit with this effort to be reflective, to speak on the argument, not about his own difficulties in his relationship with Floyd. My sympathy for his disappointments is tempered, though, by my inability to talk with Floyd about his side of the story.

After I didn't hear back from him or his wife, I learned that he has been struggling with prostate cancer.

When I ask Alfie to tell me about Brian's argument with Floyd, he, too, looks me straight in the eye. But his response is slower in coming. With a finger laid to the side of his nose, he nods slightly as he muses. "Floyd was hard when he had to be. Floyd was hard. He had funny ways…but I had funny ways too."

Alfie shifts a bit and thinks some more. His voice is low and a bit sad. "He could be paranoid. Sometimes I would hear Floyd talk, say that someone was trying to get him, he always thought someone was trying to get him. I believe that a lot of that came from his pro career. They used to mess with his money a lot. I think a lot of that paranoia came from that. I heard he was taken for a lot of money early in his career. I don't remember the argument [with Brian] but I must have been there." He pauses, trying to remember. Finally, he shakes his head. "But that's cold, that is cold. 'Cause it was for the kids, I always thought that show was about the kids."

"What do you think the show meant to Brian?"

"That was a good thing for him. It was kind of like Brian's project, and you wouldn't think that Floyd would be the one to do that to him."

When Andy tells me about the argument between Floyd and Brian, his memories are unsullied by adult perspective and opinion. I can hear the bewilderment of that young boy who sees his idol behave in a way that seems so unreasonable, so unexpected. And I can hear the regret for having to refuse Brian. My parents only ever spoke of the argument in terms of its impact on Brian. I see now, it's part of Andy's history too.

Now in 2021 , I am still caught in this question of what might have moved Floyd to react the way he did to my brother on that day. He died in 2006, from prostrate cancer and afflict-ed with Alzheimer's. Andy doesn't seem surprised when I ask him to connect me to Floyd's adopted son. I tell him I am hoping that Tracy can give me perspective on the argument as a fighter who Floyd trained and managed, as a world cham-pion who ultimately broke with Floyd over what Tracy said, publicly, was a need for a new direction.

Tracy responds to my text and agrees to meet, adding, "I re-member your brother as being well-liked and a talented fighter."

A few weeks later, as I drive to meet Tracy at the Floyd Patterson Boxing Club in Highland, New York, I am still pondering, not about what I want to know, but how to ask the questions so that the inquiries themselves aren't dismissed or harmful.

The truth is, I have my own suppositions about what might have motivated Floyd. They're probably closest to Alfie's, about people who took advantage during Floyd's career, specifically white managers working with this young Black man. Perhaps my brother's declaration of what the class would give to the club touched on a rawness of history and disrespect, and he just didn't feel like the effort was worth his time. Or maybe it's just simple: Floyd was having a bad day.

Tracy and I sit across from each other at a long plastic table set up with a view, through glass windows, into a space where several young men train on heavy and double-end punching bags. Tracy and his partner, Tony Bongiorni, opened the gym in 2015. Tracy comes to the gym a couple evenings a week after his day job as a corrections officer.

Tracy was adopted by Floyd at fifteen, when his family de-cided to move back to Alabama and Tracy wanted to stay in New Paltz to continue training. Eventually, he won two world titles, the WBC (World Boxing Federation) Super Bantam-weight title and the IBF (International Boxing Federation) Super Featherweight title during the '90s. He's still very fit, and I see the fourteen-year-old I knew in high school still in his face, even at fifty-six. He's pleasant and guarded, which I expected. Pleasant because Andy connected him to me and I am Brian's sister, guarded because we don't know each other. Not really. I share a memory of him in the New Paltz High weight room, how I'd teased him that Floyd better not find out that Tracy was lifting, wanting his fighters to be more agile, not muscle bound. Young Tracy had just looked at me, unconcerned. Now, he laughs a little and says, "Well, I was into other sports too."

I ask him about memories of Brian, and he says, "I was a sponge when I got to the gym, I was just eleven. I watched everyone to see what I could learn. Brian was the total package. He had the moves and the heart. And everyone liked him. My dad told me he was the best fighter in the gym."

I don't linger on this too long because I hear this as a package of sorts: of memory and generosity, along with a bit of professional courtesy, which doesn't mean it's not true.

When I tell Tracy the story of the argument, without any of my own take on it, he looks surprised. "That doesn't sound like my dad. I don't remember this. I wasn't there, at the gym, when this happened. I never heard about this. I can tell you, my dad would never hurt anyone. Not intentionally." He pauses for a moment. "I don't know. I can't speak for my dad. I don't want to disrespect him."

I rush to agree with him. "Really, I just wonder, from your own interactions with him, would you have a perspective on what he might have been feeling?"

He shakes his head. "The only thing I can think is that someone got in his ear. You know, might have said something. But other than that, I can't say."

I offer my own additional reasonings as possibilities. Maybe Floyd felt disrespected after building a career without the benefit of any privileges other than his own physical ability and persistence—and having his trust betrayed over money. Maybe he felt frustrated with Brian, in particular, for not sticking to his training and partying when Floyd was training him for free.

Tracy listens to my maybes and says it again. "I think there must have been someone talking in his ear, that gave him ideas."

This time, I get it. Tracy is speaking from experience. A little later, we talk about that new direction he had to take, away from Floyd, in 1994. It boiled down to his need as a world title holder, a man with a wife and five children, who needed to share in the decision-making about his career and finances. Splits between top athletes and their trainers or managers are common. Even, or maybe especially so, when family is involved. Arguably, any of these relationships might feel like family, even without blood or legal connection, and the break-ups are deeply personal and devastating.

Tracy doesn't get into this with me, though he does share the pain of not being recognized at times by his dad, toward the end of his life.

As I gather up my pad and phone to leave, Tracy reiterates that Floyd never had a bad word to say about my brother, that he always said that Brian was one of the best fighters to come through the gym. I get his email address and, after we move outside, I shake his hand, effusive with thanks. But he offers to walk me down to my car and, on the way, we chat about his mom, who still lives in Alabama. I tell him I think she was brave to recognize what her son wanted and let Floyd adopt him. Tracy shakes his head and says, "I was fifteen at the time. I was staying."

I laugh. "I'm a mom. I can tell you. She was brave."

I am done with this wondering about Floyd, or maybe I have just folded it up and tucked it away as yet another of the baffling artifacts from Brian's life.

There's so much history that came before his argument with Floyd, so many endings that I barely noticed or didn't notice until they all added up, so subtle and, for all I knew, as natural as puberty.

My parents, of course, noticed more than I did, long before I did. I know that now. At the time, what got my attention were the noises. From my bed, I could hear their cajoling as they sat with Brian. Sometimes, long after the house grew quiet with expectation of sleep, I would get up to go to the bathroom and pause by their door to listen to low, weary voices. Other nights the house was filled with shouts and crying. Once, there was the sound of broken glass as one of Brian's drunk or tripping friends fell through the glass panel next to our front door. Another night it was the sound of splintering wood coming up at me through my pillow as Brian punched his fists through the paneling in his bedroom.

I know for sure all of this didn't begin with the falling out with Floyd. But after the argument, Brian stepped back into himself, like stepping into a room that was only big enough for one with the door closed.

Chapter Seventeen

[1976]

> One night, during a typical evening of cruising and partying, a close friend turned to me and spoke... not with his reeking breath and cherry eyes. He asked me if I realized that I was the person my mother warned me about as a child. And I knew it wasn't an original thought, but under the circumstances, very appropriate.
>
> —Brian Hurley, journal, spring 1977

Just after Brian left high school, I entered it. It was a small school, and I knew many of the upper-class students already, so I didn't feel nervous about the transition. But in my second-period Earth science class, Mr. Cameron called the class roll and paused on my name.

"Brian's sister, I presume?"

Brian had already forewarned me about wacky Gene, a brilliant, award-winning teacher who teased unmercifully and, sometimes, cruelly. I nodded.

"Do you box too?"

The class laughed.

I laughed with them. "Noooo..."

"Are you as smart as he is?"

I looked around the room, felt suddenly unfamiliar with anyone who was staring at me, though I had known most since kindergarten. Slowly I said, "Of course."

Mr. Cameron nodded. "OK then, let's just keep the smoking to a minimum." Except that he didn't say smoking, just put
his fingers to his mouth as if he were holding a joint, pursing
his lips and screwing his face around, eyes crossed so that he
looked like a lunatic. It was over in an instant, but the class
laughed long and loud. As he continued with the roll, he got
more laughter with his teasing, more reddened faces. He never
said, "Just kidding, guys." I couldn't tell if that was because he
didn't have any sense of decency or because everything he said
was basically true. I guessed it was a bit of both.

I liked my English teacher, Ms. Ecton. Earnest and endear-
ingly frumpy despite her youthful face, she required all students to keep a journal. She read through them at the end
of each week. She promised not to read sections that were
entitled *Please don't read*, but she would still count those pages toward the total for the final grade. Quantity not quality
was the prevailing standard. Elsewhere, she made comments
about what was written. Most of my journal dealt with boys
and my friends and she remarked, in tiny, beautiful cursive,
Most relationships are like that, or *Can't you just say all of these
things to him?*

I was under a strict gag rule from my mother after she
overheard me talking on the phone with a friend about Brian's
latest troubles. She demanded that I hang up. "We don't tell
other people our family business."

I trusted Ms. Ecton enough to write out the thoughts I had
about my brother, my frustration and growing anger. *Why can't
he just get his act together?* She never commented on these pas-
sages. Not until the story about Brian and my grandfather.

Just after his eighty-ninth birthday, my grandfather, Per-
cy, moved into an apartment a few blocks from our house.
It was a compromise between my mother's concerns about

him living alone an hour away and his insistence that he was perfectly capable. He moved in wearing his baseball cap and blowing bubbles with the gum he chewed constantly. He seemed content, and his neighbors were kind to him, though he blasted his favorite show, *Donny and Marie*, throughout the complex. Except for the day he had his first stroke. My mother found him and called my father for help. Brian went too. And, over my grandfather's protests, carried him, like a bride on her wedding day, down the stairs to our car.

Brian didn't have a job just then, so he helped my mother with my grandfather, whose stroke was pronounced a mild one by his doctor though he couldn't return to the apartment. He sat in the living room and watched TV most of the day, fiddling with his hearing aid and making loud cracking sounds with his gum that he couldn't hear himself.

I was on the phone with a friend one afternoon, stretching the cord from the kitchen into the dining room when I saw Grandpa begin a struggle to stand in the living room. Brian was at his side in an instant. "What do you need, Grandpa?" he asked, leaning over him like a parent with a toddler.

Grandpa muttered something, and my brother repeated it. "Bathroom, sure, just take your time."

He held my grandfather firmly under his elbow as he stood. Grandpa took a deep breath and moved one foot forward as if feeling for the edge of an abyss. They turned toward me as I sat on the kitchen stool, listening to my friend chat away, not helping at all, though I had a clear view of their slow progress. When Grandpa's drawstring pajama pants slid down his legs and created a puddle of plaid at his feet, he didn't seem to notice, he was so intent on the next step. I felt sick, frozen on my stool, horrified and embarrassed. My grandfather's legs were now just contraptions of bone and muscle, each clearly marked for their job. He wasn't wearing underwear, and his genitals swung gently to the side as he shifted.

"Wait Grandpa," Brian said. He bent over and pulled the pants up, and then he leaned Grandpa's body against his own, like a book at the end of the shelf, to tie the drawstring. Brian's cheeks were flushed, and his eyes were glittery. "C'mon, Grandpa," he said. Their journey resumed and so did my phone conversation.

In the days that followed, my mother and father debated the option of a nursing home for my grandfather, something that my brother bitterly opposed. He thought it was wrong, to put a family member under the care of strangers. He said he could care for him. But my grandfather didn't want his family to see him so weak, so childlike in his needs. He urged the move.

I wrote in my journal:

My parents and brother took my grandfather to the rest home today...I guess he had another stroke when he got there, and they had to rush him to the hospital. My brother was pretty shaken up, but as usual that didn't interfere with his going out and getting drunk.

The entry on the next day:

My mother thought it was all right if I went to the wrestling match, so I did. Brian came about 8:30. He just walked up to me on the bleachers and said that my grandfather died.

And that's where Ms. Ecton wrote, *Oh Janet, I am so sorry.*

Chapter Eighteen

I don't know if the shadows are getting darker or if
the light is just getting brighter. The days, weeks,
and months are undistinguishable at present but
then again it has been a very long and hard winter.
I hope that I am optimistic as I am not sure of much
of anything lately.

– Brian Hurley, letter to Harold Issen, Spring 1977

Most of Brian's friends left New Paltz after high school graduation. Harold to the Army, Fred to college upstate, pre-med.
Brian lived at home and reluctantly took a few classes at the
college before switching to community college, which he as-
sessed as high school regurgitated and stopped going. Harold
came home on leave before he shipped out to Korea. He and
another friend, Bob, rode with Brian in my father's Volkswagen to a New Year's party hosted by a former classmate. It was
a garbage-can party where everyone brought a pint or fifth of
something and poured it into the can. By the time they left
they were drunk and stoned and not even the slap of the cold
air could sober them.

Harold climbed into the back seat of the Volkswagen and
Bob took shot gun. The night was clear and cold with snow
banked along the mountain roads, pavement clear though
pot-holed and bumpy from the annual freezing and buckling.

"Hey," Bob yelled, minutes after Brian started the car. "Slow down." But the beer and pot conspired to stretch the O's and exaggerate the W's. Sloooowdooown.

Brian laughed, kept up the speed. He used a hand to wipe away the condensation that built on the windshield from the combined breath of the three young men, bent his head a little to look out. It was right then that they reached the fork, left to town, right heading back up the mountain. He hesitated. It was in that moment, Harold told me later, that he knew they wouldn't make it either way, when the street sign looked as if it were running straight at the car and then jumped out of the way as the car plowed on, bucked up over a high ridge of snow, bumped forward, and came to rest, tail end still out on the road.

The three were quiet for a moment, just the creaking of the car as it settled a little. Brian opened his door, and it scraped into snow and leaves as he squeezed out. Harold and Bob sat still, listened to him walk around the car, though it was hard to hear over their own heavy breathing. Harold moved his arms and legs. He hadn't been wearing a seat belt, but felt OK. Bob wasn't wearing a seat belt either, and was holding his nose as if he had bumped it on the dash. He reached up and turned on the interior light, turned the rearview mirror so that he could look at it. From where he sat, Harold thought Bob looked OK, too, except for that small trickle of blood out of the left nostril. But Bob's voice rose. "I said slow down, I said it. I said SLOOOW down."

"Goddammit!" Brian yelled, and they heard the thud as he kicked one of the tires. He stuck his head in the door, looked for a moment at Bob, shook his head, and then looked at Harold.

"Well," Harold said, "that was one way to slow down." He was shaking as he pushed on the driver's seat to get out. He squeezed through the door and past Brian to stand in the snow at the edge of the road, the cold rushing to claim his face, to grab at his bare hands.

The Volkswagen was totaled. For the next couple of weeks, Brian was home every night. After Nora and I went to bed, I could hear the conversation: my parent's voices insistent and his sometimes strong, but mostly toneless. Once, I got up for a drink of water from the kitchen and saw him in the dining room with my mother. He had his head in his hands as my mother rubbed his shoulder. Neither said anything.

The next day, as I came in from school, Brian passed me, heading out the front door with his gym bag. I let him go by me without saying anything, though once inside I tracked my mother down. After leaving her position as director of the Poughkeepsie Schools Drug Prevention Program, she'd decided to stay home full-time while Brian was still in high school. Though she never said as much to me, I figured that it was to be close by in case of "Brian emergencies ."

"Where is Brian going?"

"To Floyd's."

"Floyd's?"

She glanced up at me as she stuffed the washing machine with sheets. "He wants to get his life back on track. I'm not crazy about this either. I don't care if I ever see Floyd again, but it's what Brian wants to do, get back into training."

"How's he gonna get there?"

"I told him he could use the station wagon." Her voice took on a wary tightness.

"Oh," I said. "So, he can wreck that too?"

"Stop it," she snapped. "He's trying."

I thought he wasn't trying hard enough, though I wasn't exactly sure what trying hard enough would be.

Brian came home from the gym that day to report that Floyd wasn't there, that he was on a trip with the family. I couldn't tell if he knew that before he went up or not. He was

mildly enthused, reported that Longo was the same old character, that Andy Schott was getting really good, that Alfie was
still there. For a moment, as I listened to him, I believed him,
maybe. Maybe he could make a comeback; maybe something
would stick, as if he were a walking wall of Velcro and things
like focus and dedication and common sense had peeled off
and just needed to be reattached.

A few days later, Brian called my parents from a pay phone.
He'd slid the car off the road into a telephone pole on the way
back from the gym. It was rainy and slick, he went too fast
around a curve, he said. So, for the second time in a month,
my father called a tow truck and went to wait with Brian until
the station wagon was hoisted like a mangled metal whale and
carted away. Brian didn't go back to the gym. Instead, he went
back to his basement bedroom. When he wasn't at the bars.

I wrote in my journal for Ms. Ecton:

*He was such a good kid, talented, on the ball. I wish I could
have stopped him from drinking and smoking pot. He ruined his boxing career and high school and going to college.
He's nothing but a bum. I can't get through to him, that we
do care. He says we don't understand. I used to and maybe
I still do. I can understand how he just can't get it together
and drinking helps. But why does he fight us?*

Later that spring, my mother came home and told Brian
that she'd found a job for him, driving a cab for the only outfit
in town. I was stunned when I heard this. Brian was going to
get a job *driving?* He didn't seem particularly excited, but he
started almost immediately and loved it.

He was often requested by seniors for rides to the grocery
store or doctor's offices. He dropped them off with a promise
to return and was always right on time, loading the groceries
into the trunk and then unloading them again at the other

end, carrying them into small kitchens, helping to unpack as long as he didn't get called for another fare. But I'm sure it wasn't the carrying of groceries that so endeared him to these older people, it was his attention, his listening, his real interest in their stories.

He came home from a day of driving with stories to tell, jokes he learned from passengers. It reminded me of the days when he came home from Floyd's with stories that made me laugh and sometimes thrilled me. I began to look forward to the stories about regular riders. Harry with the ear hair that sprouted like sheaves of wheat. Ms. Dunkirk, who bought the exact same items every week from the grocery store, had a regular rotating schedule of what she ate and was appalled by Brian's suggestion that she should have dessert sometimes. Brian played chess with Sam if he had time between fares and changed the light bulb on Mrs. Hall's front stoop. After a few months of driving, his boss let Brian use the cab for personal use. It was a Volkswagen, a fitting taxi for a small town.

One night after listening to a story, I said, "You should write all these things down."

Brian laughed. "Nah. It's their lives. I don't have time anyway."

What else did he have to do? I wondered. He didn't go back to the community college, wasn't training. Besides driving a cab, he was just hanging out. With friends who, like him, were waiting for something to stick.

Chapter Nineteen

[1977]

I just happened to glance into my parent's room as I went past and was surprised to see my dad sitting at his desk, writing something into a journal-like book. "What are you doing, Dad?" I asked, not shy at all about interrupting him.

He glanced up and seemed stuck on the question. After a moment, he said, "I'm what you call ten and tenning. It's something Mom and I learned at that weekend."

Ah. The weekend. The Marriage Encounter Weekend, which had happened a couple of weeks before. I didn't know a lot about it but some of my friend's parents had also gone, though at a different time. As I understood it, it was a program of the Catholic church, and that might have been the only reason my dad said yes to going, having grown up in a devout Irish Catholic family, nuns at school and everything. I was sure it was my mother who was the instigator for their attendance, even though she'd been raised Protestant and neither of them went to church anymore. When they told us about their decision to attend this retreat, my mom said it was for couples who wanted to deepen their marriage. It wasn't couple's therapy. This was all said very carefully, cheerfully almost. Like they didn't want us to worry.

Nora and I stayed over with friends while they were gone, and Brian was given a firm admonition about not having anyone over to the house. Julie was at college. Now, my parents were home and, truly, they did seem a bit easier with each other, a little more tender.

When I asked my mom about the ten and tenning thing, she laughed. "Well, it's not really a verb. Dad and I have a list of questions and we each write for ten minutes to answer the same question. Then we share our answers and talk about them."

This sounded really boring. "What kind of questions?"

"Well," my mom said, "questions about how we feel about things."

"What things?"

My mother paused for a minute and then shook her head with a chuckle. "So many things. Too many to tell you. But it's about being in the habit to communicate, to talk with each other."

"OK," I said. It was really boring.

A few weeks later, I lied to my parents and told them I was walking up to see my friend Valerie, would spend the evening at her house. Instead, I walked to the parking lot in front of the deli, where the high school kids hung out, watched traffic and spun their intricate web of high school drama. I did meet Valerie, but then we in turn met up with three boys, all older, and walked over to the college campus. One of the boys had a six-pack that he carried in a brown paper bag, as if no one would guess what was in there. No parent or cop stopped us, and the evening felt light and fun. It wasn't much beer to split, but we made the most of it, giggled ourselves around the lake on campus until it finally occurred to me that I should go home. My parents were watching TV when I came in. "Where have you been?" my mother asked from where she sat on the couch.

"I was with Valerie," I said, keeping my distance, chewing cinnamon gum.

She shook her head. "I called Valerie's mother. She said you never went there, that Valerie was supposed to be here."

I was stumped. My mother never called to check on me.

"Have you been drinking?"

"Just one beer," I said.

"Janet, you lied to me." My mother didn't bother to raise her voice over the sound of the television. Her words were clear. "When you leave here, I need to trust that you are going where you say you are going."

My father stood up. "Your mother and I have been talking about this and—"

"You're grounded," my mother finished. "No seeing Valerie, no going out at night on the weekends."

"For two weeks," my father said. "Starting tonight."

I was stunned. I had never been grounded before. "Fine," I yelled, and put all the injustice I could muster into my voice. "It was hardly anything. It was one time. I am not Brian. I do everything I can to be perfect. I get good grades and try to do good things. I am not Brian!"

It was my parent's turn to be stunned. After a moment, my mother said quietly, "No one said that you are like Brian. Don't talk about him like that. Now go to bed."

More than being grounded, what I really hated was that I might be the subject of my parents' ten and tenning. But soon enough, my grounding was forgotten by everyone, even me. And I never saw my dad or mom writing in a journal again.

Chapter Twenty

My generation in high school was probably more apathetic as an after effect of the sixty's revolution. Many felt overly stressed and emotionally battered. For a decade they had lived under the nuclear threat. They were numbed by the assassinations of three national leaders. On television, we watched the fall of Phnom Penh and our president slink from office.

– Brian Hurley, "My Generation: Society's Effect on the Generation and the Generation's Effect on Society," 1983

Larry was a friend of Brian's from high school, a bright boy with a quick wit. He'd been one of the regulars in Tommy's basement boxing matches so long ago, taking his chances in the ring. During high school, he was always around, on the periphery, not Brian's close friend, but still in the orbit around him. He'd even gone to New York to watch Brian fight in the Golden Gloves. Now Brian and Larry had more things in common: they both watched their senior class friends leave town after graduation, head to college, like Fred, or to the army, like Harold, or out west. They both lived at home. His parents, like mine, probably talked in whispers about their son late at night, after they were in bed. That summer, he and

Brian often played basketball in our backyard as the evening waned toward the drinking hours. Larry spent more time laughing than playing. I never knew if his trademark bandana, which he tied around his forehead to keep hair and sweat from slinging into his eyes, was saturated from the exercise of the game or the effort he put into acerbic one-liners that he laughed at himself.

Brian and Larry came into the house for water after one of those backyard pick-up games, carrying their conversation on around me in the kitchen as I got a snack. After he gulped several glasses of water, Larry was suddenly serious. "I think I am going to go back out west," he said. He'd traveled out west after high school and his conversations often centered on Colorado and what he would do if he lived there.

"Really?" Brian took a long draught of water. "I thought you are going to college. Here."

"Yeah, maybe. But I think, if I save some money, I could get outta here," Larry said.

Brian nodded. "I hear you. Maybe I'll go too."

Larry's face was suddenly eager. "Yeah? That would be cool. You'd love it out there, man."

"C'mon," Brian said. "Let's head downtown."

Would he really go out west? I doubted it. Julie was now a student at the University of Arizona at Flagstaff, home for part of the summer. She transferred after her sophomore year at our local state college when she met a man who loved Arizona, the guitar and Eagles songs. The relationship didn't last that long, but she said she loved being out west. Beyond asking her about Carlos Castaneda and peyote, Brian didn't seem to pay much attention to her stories. They didn't hang out together, had different friends.

But that night they would end up in the same bar, Zach's, at the same time. Even shared a table with some other high school alums: Lynn, a friend of Julie's since elementary school, and Steve, a slight boy with heavy eyebrows and a mustache, more of an acquaintance of Brian's than a friend. Larry must have seen them through the plate-glass windows as he walked by. He came in, pulled up a chair and jokingly went to take a sip out of Brian's beer. Brian pushed the glass toward him. "I'm done man. I gotta drive the early shift in the morning."

Later, Julie would remember he'd only had a mug and a half of beer in the hour or so that they'd all been talking, and she'd assumed it was because he'd felt self-conscious in front of her, a known one-glass-of-wine-a-month drinker. She was glad to hear that, instead, he'd been thinking about his job.

"Cool," Larry said and topped off the glass from the pitcher that was still on the table. The conversation meandered for a while until Larry pushed back his chair. "Gotta hit the head." He made his way through the crowd to the back of the bar.

Brian stood up as well. "I gotta get going." He looked at Steve. "Need a ride home?" Steve lived right in town, but he nodded, took a last swig of beer, and followed Brian out the door.

A few moments later, Larry came back to the table. "Where's Brian?"

"He left to go home," Julie said.

"Damn," Larry said. "I was going to ask him for a ride home. My car still isn't up and running."

Julie waved him toward the door. "They're probably still out there; he parked down at the bank, I think. If you run, you can catch him."

Larry saluted. "Then I'm off. Catch ya later."

"Hey," Julie called, and he stopped at the door. "If you miss him, I have to take Lynn home a little later, I'll drop you off."

Larry waved and was gone.

Chapter Twenty-One

Eventually, "now" did not exist for him. Only then and whenever.

— Brian Hurley, senior English class journal, 1976

It was the sound of Julie wailing that interrupted the night-time buzzing and peeping outside my open bedroom windows. "Mom, Dad. Mom, Dad."

By the time I reached the front door, my mother and father were already there, my mother wearing a light summer night-gown, my father tying on his blue cotton robe. Julie stumbled into the house while clutching her stomach. I thought at first that she was sick.

Lynn was right behind her and tried to straighten her up. "Julie, stand up and tell them. Stand up and tell them."

My mother's voice sounded as if it were being squeezed out of her. "What is it? Are you hurt?"

Julie shook her head, gasping, and then said, "We drove up on it."

"What?" My father sounded tense, almost irritable. "Drove up on what?"

"Brian had an accident. With the taxi. I was taking Lynn home and we came around the curve and there were all these cop cars and ambulances. They loaded them all into ambulances and took them to Vassar Hospital."

"Oh my God," my mother said, opening the front hall door and searching for her coat, as if she would put it on right over her pajamas and head to the hospital.

"Wait, wait," my father protested. "Who was with him? Was he hurt, were they hurt?"

"They wouldn't let me near the fucking ambulance," my sister wailed, bending over again. "I tried, I told them that I was Brian's sister, but they wouldn't tell me anything."

"Julie," my father said sharply, "who was in the car?"

Julie's teeth chattered. Lynn took a deep breath. "We think Steve Russo and Larry Young. We had just seen all of them at Zach's."

My mother had her coat in her hands. "Let's go, Bill."

"I want to go with you." Julie was already moving to the door.

My mother hesitated and then said to Lynn, "Can you stay here with Janet and Nora while we go? I can't believe Nora has slept through all of this." Coat in hand, she hurried back up the hallway to her bedroom to get dressed.

Lynn looked at me as if noticing me for the first time. She smiled in a way that was an agreement, though it seemed apologetic, as if she knew I was old enough to stay at home by myself. But I wasn't sure if I was old enough to stand the wait by myself.

Before my father followed my mother, he asked quietly, "What about the cab?"

Lynn shook her head. "The whole left side was just flattened."

At close to 4:00 a.m., my sister called. "Larry's dead," she said without saying hello. "Steve's leg is broken all to pieces. He's got some other injuries. Brian's pretty banged up. The steering wheel shoved into his stomach and then up, messed up his diaphragm and his lungs."

"Larry's dead," I repeated. I sensed Lynn stir and turned to see her put her head on her arms.

"Watch out for that car!"

Who said that? Brian never remembered. This is the point at which all the details were lost for Brian and Steve and conjectured by so many others in the following months. After listening to the theories swirling about me, discovering that, contrary to the newspaper report, a telephone pole hadn't been smashed into and adding what I knew of that road, that curve, that very time of summer night, my own version settled like sediment—not firm, but undisturbed.

Because Steve was already riding shotgun, I imagine that Larry must have squirmed about for a few minutes in the back seat of the Volkswagen when he first got in, then crooked his long legs up, lay his head against the rim of the window, his elbow providing support. I don't know why Brian decided to take him home first—perhaps Larry asked him to.

Larry lived a couple miles out of town. Within minutes, just a couple of miles, they reached the S curve on Route 32, the one the town supervisor later said was dangerous and should be straightened out. Halfway through, there was a left-hand turn that led to the high school. Ahead, the curve uncurled into the country highway, with Larry's house about a half mile beyond.

"Watch out for that car!"

I decided that Brian must have jerked the steering wheel to the left to avoid a car pulling out from the high school road and then crossed over into the other lane. He probably saw the telephone pole just off the edge of the road and jerked the wheel back, but the two left-side tires dipped off the asphalt and the speed turned the car over onto its left side with such force that it bounced back up and rolled back across the road to come to a stop. The engine stalled at this point, and with no one conscious in the car, I've always imagined that the early summer night noises took over—cicadas and crickets, maybe a bullfrog sermonizing from one of the nearby farm ponds.

Chapter Twenty-Two

Brian was released from the hospital the afternoon after the accident, walking slowly and breathing with great difficulty. He was in the living room when Larry's parents and four sisters arrived to see him and stood up as one of the girls moved quickly to hug him before he could take a step. One by one, they embraced Brian, each lingering longer as he cried.

My parents urged me, Julie and Nora out of the room, and then they stood respectfully in the kitchen. As I turned to go, I saw Mr. Young sit in front of Brian, and their knees touched. Mr. Young reached out a hand and placed it on the back of Brian's neck, leaned in close so that their foreheads were touching too. Later Brian told us what he said. That Mr. Young was asleep when the accident happened at around 1:30 a.m. He never went into a deep sleep until all of his children were in the house, but he was drowsing. Finally, he heard the front door open, footsteps came up the stairs. He roused himself enough to say, "Good night, Larry. I hope you didn't forget to lock the door." The steps paused outside his door and then continued on. Satisfied, Mr. Young let himself fall into that deeper sleep, of which he would only get an hour more before he got the call from the police.

When he told this to Brian, I think it was with the expectation that Brian would get some comfort from the suggestion that Larry's spirit found its way home. Mr. Young obviously did, at least then. And he and Mrs. Young reassured my parents that they didn't hold Brian responsible, that they'd already talked with the DA about dropping charges. And those charges were, eventually, but not because of the Youngs' request.

I went outside with a pen and a pad and sat in the grass in the shade at the side of the house, just out of sight behind the large cedar. My hand hesitated and then came down to touch pen to paper, then lifted again as a bird would, unsure about alighting on a branch. Finally, I pressed down, and found myself committed to a poem: "For My Brother."

I lay back and watched the sky until I heard the slam of car doors, heard the Youngs driving up the hill, let the sound fade completely before going back inside. I ripped the page off my pad and folded it in half, intended to walk into the living room and give it to Brian right then. I saw him sitting in the brown swivel chair, turned so that he could look out the window. My parents sat nearby on the couch, faces weary. I felt silly, suddenly. How could my little poem be in the room with such immense sorrow? I went into my room, where I tucked the folded paper between two books on the shelf over my bed.

The day of the funeral was a clear and warm one. The service was held at the Catholic church, a large modern structure I had rarely visited with friends or family. The Young family sat in the front pew, the younger girls squirming, turning around to look at all the people slowly filling the seats behind. As we came down the main aisle, the smallest one shrugged against her mother, and she turned to see Brian on the arm of my father, walking slowly, taking long but shallow breaths, arm in a sling. She and Mr. Young stood up and came into the aisle to hug him, urged my family to sit behind them, and so we all filed into the pew, though my mother moved to the very end so that we wouldn't be right behind them, as if she wanted to protect Brian from the grief. Brian sat and studied his hands, not looking up. Like the Young girls, I had to look, had to know who was there. I saw Steve come down the aisle on crutches, followed by his sister and parents. He came all the way to the front, and again, the Youngs stood to receive him. He looked over Mrs. Young's shoulder at Brian, who didn't lift his head to meet his gaze.

The service was short by Catholic standards, with statements by weeping girls in miniskirts and a song that a friend of Larry and Brian's sang while strumming a guitar.

We didn't go to the graveside.

If we thought Brian spent too much time in his room before, now he virtually exiled himself to the basement. Friends came to visit during the day, tromping down the stairs, several at a time, several times a day, until they came alone, maybe every couple of days and then maybe made a phone call before they headed out to the bars. Fred took a bus down from Boston where he was attending a summer Christian convocation. He came several times during the weekend. When he left for the last time, Brian followed him to the front door, said goodbye with obvious forced cheer and then came back to sit in the dining room. He tried to laugh, but it ended up a painful squeezing of his tender lungs.

"He's really into Christianity now," he said. "He talked about it a lot. He thinks this was my penance for my sins." He leaned his forehead into his palms and slowly shook his head back and forth as my mother rubbed his shoulders.

A few weeks after the accident, Andy and a couple of other fighters were heading to a match with Floyd. Floyd surprised them by turning left onto our street. He cleared his throat and said, "This'll only take a moment. Just picking up Brian."

Everyone, of course, knew what had happened, that Larry was dead and that Brian was hurt. But they didn't know that Floyd had called and invited Brian to come along to watch these fights. Into the silence that greeted his remark, Floyd said, "The least we can do is show up and take him to a fight. He'll like that."

Andy thought, Maybe now. Maybe now Brian'll get serious, come back up, get back on track.

When they pulled into the driveway, Floyd left the car running. He went up the walkway, disappeared inside the house for a few moments and then returned with Brian following behind. Brian's whole body looked crumpled, his face whiter than usual, with some faded bruising following his jawline. His arm was still in a sling. The fighters quickly shuffled their places so that Brian could have the front seat. Brian slid in, breathing heavily, grimacing and grunting as he adjusted the trunk of his body to give his lungs more room, his arm some more comfortable space. He glanced over his shoulder, not quite able to turn his head as far as he needed to and said, "Good evening gentlemen. Ready to fight, are we?"

At the fights, Brian stayed close to the corner, watching the club members fight from a chair next to Floyd's. Andy glanced down at him as he climbed into the ring and Brian gave him a thumbs up with his good hand, the blue fabric of the sling on his other arm bright in the lights, his smile even brighter. Andy was glad he was there and thought again, maybe he'll come back, maybe this is it. But then he forgot all about Brian and moved forward to get his instructions from the ref.

On the way back from the fights, the car was full of chatter. All three of the fighters had won, Andy by a technical knockout. Brian was happy to provide his ringside assessment, to which Floyd nodded and disagreed with only once or twice in a good-natured way.

When they pulled into the drive, Brian waved off Floyd. "Nah, don't get out. I can do it." And he did, taking a moment to regain his breath and energy before pulling himself out with his good arm.

"'Night, you princes," he said, then turned and made a slow ascent up the stairs and to the front porch. The light came on as if someone had been watching for him.

"Maybe he'll come back," Andy said.

Chapter Twenty-Three

I'm afraid we weren't very enlightened. We weren't
cool; we weren't hip. We were pretty old-fashioned;
we were trying to be men. So, by the accident of
birth order and adolescent male sensibilities, I think
that you got the short end of the stick, and that's
just the way it was. Perhaps you should cut Brian
some slack on that issue.

– Harold Issen, email to Janet Hurley, 2004

When the accident happened, I was dating a boy, a senior to
my freshman. Wayne was a star athlete, a handsome boy, with
a slender athletic build, olive skin, light brown hair that waved
down the nape of his neck and fell into his hazel green eyes.
He was popular at school, famous for a temper and a quick
fist that gave him a bad-boy glamour but charming when it
came to me and my parents. I was fifteen and loved how his
attention to me never wavered. It had an intensity about it
that was thrilling. Brian didn't disapprove or ignore; he just
didn't notice. Or so it seemed, because after Larry died, Brian
spent most of his days in his room, only coming out of the
basement to watch late-night television.

Once school was out at the end of June, I usually joined
him. Joining is not the right word. I sat behind him, he in the
easy chair almost squarely in front of the television, me on

the couch. If he laughed at something, I did too. Sometimes, I would make a remark and he would cock his head, turning it slightly to acknowledge me, but never turned around, rarely replied, just took deep drags on his cigarette. He'd started smoking in later high school, which he'd slack on when he was training for a fight. Both my parents were smokers and maybe they'd let this slide because it wasn't worth the argument, given all the other challenges. Now, he smoked more than ever. I grew bold, sneaking a smoke myself, figuring my parents would think it was Brian. Bold enough to sneak my boyfriend into the house and down the stairs to the rec room. I didn't think Brian would notice and, if he did, that he wouldn't care.

But one night, Brian thudded down the stairs and swung open the door so fast I didn't even register the sound until he was just suddenly there. He stood still and silent, taking in the scene. He didn't take his hand off the doorknob. With the only lighted lamp closer to where he stood, I saw his face plainly; every muscle was visible on his jawline, top teeth set into his lower lip so hard it whitened.

"Get dressed," he finally said in a low voice, turned and went back up the stairs.

By the time Wayne was out the back door, Brian was again in front of the television.

"Bri…"

He turned to look at me. "Where's Wayne?"

"He left."

Brian moved faster than he had since the accident and headed to the front door. It took a moment for me to recognize his intention, and then I ran after him, hissing in a loud whisper so that my parents wouldn't wake up, "Brian, stop. Wait, Brian, please, please."

As we got close to the door, I grabbed on to his arm, and he tried to shake me off. When this didn't work, he stopped, turned just a bit and. with his arm across my chest slammed me into the wall so that I had to let go. By the time I caught my breath, the storm door was screeching to a close and I was terrified. Brian was in poor shape, and I thought he'd be no match for Wayne's fists. I was about to follow him when my mother appeared, pulling on her housecoat. I told her that Brian and I had argued, that we'd work it out. She must have known that the truth was being packaged, but given the time of night and her general exhaustion, best left unopened. To my relief, Brian came back in just as she went back to bed, and I followed him into the dining room where he sat down to have a smoke. He didn't look up when I slid into the chair next to him. "Couldn't find him," he said.

I put my hand on his arm. He didn't shake me off this time, but there was no response to my touch. "Brian, do you love me?"

He made a small purse of irritation with his lips.

"Do you love me?"

"You don't know guys. He is just using you."

"No, no, it's not like that."

"Yeah right," Brian muttered.

"Brian, if you love me, please don't tell Mom and Dad, please. They'll kill me; they won't let me see him. Please don't tell." I leaned forward, my hand still on his forearm, and tried to catch his eye.

Brian stood up. "I won't!" He was impatient, as if this was a trivial concern. "I don't want to see him again," he said and went back to the TV, back to the cigarettes, leaving me to ponder how I would manage that. It never occurred to me that he meant he didn't want *me* to see Wayne again.

In the morning, things seemed better. I felt giddy with my narrow escape. A couple days later, Brian told my parents the whole story.

"We don't need this," my mother said during the inevitable dining room conference.

"Brian's mental health is in question here, and if he is going to hate the sight of Wayne, we have a problem. I think it will take some time for him to get over this. How could you do something like this after all that we have been through?"

My father was quiet the whole time, just nodding when my mother pronounced my three-week grounding. And then he got to the point that seemed to be bothering him the most. "Jan," he said in a low voice, "can you tell us that you are still a virgin?"

I hated those questions, hated Brian, still so angry a week later when we all got into the car to drive to Duck, North Carolina in the Outer Banks. My mother had reserved the cottage back in the wintertime, and she thought it would do all of us good to be away. It was a break in the tradition of going to the Jersey shore every summer for a week, sometimes more, usually to the same cottage a few blocks back from the beach. The Jersey shore had gotten really crowded in recent years. My mother had heard the Outer Banks were unspoiled and uncrowded. A refuge. During the fourteen-hour drive, Brian slept or looked out the window, saying little. I followed suit. My father had packed all the fishing gear in hopes that Brian would get back to that long-ago love. My younger sister had her own reel and badgered Brian all the way down. "Will you show me how to cast beyond the breakers?" she asked over and over until I thought I would scream. The cottage, octagonal and contemporary, sat a couple blocks back from the beach. It was small, just two bedrooms, with a pullout cot for Brian in the living room.

The first full day we had there was beautiful and hot. We lugged all our chairs and towels and toys and tackle to the beach. After we set up our encampment, my mother handed the sunscreen around to her Irish-Swedish-British melanin-deficient family. Brian lay down immediately and closed his eyes, pretending not to see the bottle.

"Brian, put some on," my mother said.

"I will," he answered lazily. "The sun's not that high. I'll do it in a few minutes."

But he fell asleep. With swimming and walking the beach and helping Nora to bait her hook, none of us noticed that the sunscreen never made it on to Brian's white, white skin.

That night, my mother rubbed Noxzema on Brian's burned body. The burn stayed flushed and furious. My mother made sounds of exasperation and worry. "I can't believe I didn't make you put that sunscreen on." She tenderly rubbed some of the cream along the neon rim of Brian's ear. I was disgusted. He knew he should have put on sunscreen. He'd been living in that skin all his life. He was a grown man, for God's sake!

By the time Brian was ready for bed, the first blister appeared. By morning, they covered his body, some of them as big and viscous as jelly fish. They drooped from his shoulders and above his collar bone, the parchment skin barely holding their heavy loads. There was no way to be comfortable, no position gave relief, so he was just in pain, fevered, nauseous, forced by my mother to drink glass after glass of water. My parents talked about taking him to the mainland to the hospital, but Brian refused. "I'll be all right," he said.

Life After Death

[2010]

> I got your letter and found you were very perceptive
> of the sitch. I have resigned myself to the reality of it
> and I am busy picking up the pieces. To sum up the
> accident itself, what I have to say is that it may have
> been my fault (this I may never know for sure be-
> cause I have no recollection of the accident; neither
> does Steve). But I didn't do anything wrong. But this
> kind of reminds me of Mr. Nixon's famous responsi-
> bility/blame quote.
>
> – Brian Hurley, letter to Harold Issen, summer 1977

> In any organization, the man at the top must bear
> the responsibility. That responsibility, therefore, be-
> longs here, in this office. I accept it. And I pledge to
> you tonight, from this office, that I will do everything
> in my power to ensure that the guilty are brought to
> justice and that such abuses are purged from our
> political processes in the years to come, long after I
> have left this office.
>
> – President Richard Nixon, The President's
> Address to the Nation, April 30, 1973

I'm driving to pick my son up from soccer practice and listening to *This American Life*, one of my favorite radio shows.
This week, the theme is Life After Death. The first segment

is interesting, though I find myself tuning out, thinking about work, maybe, or a grocery list. The second essay is by Darin Strauss, who, as a high school senior, hit a classmate with his car after she veered in front of him on her bike. She died. The police determined that Strauss wasn't at fault, and he was never charged. Strauss describes the accident, the immediate aftermath, visiting with the girl's parents, detail by vivid detail that my own experience amplifies. I can't listen to this and drive at the same time, so I pull over in a restaurant parking lot just as Strauss says that a year after the accident, the girl's family sued him for five million dollars. The suit took five years to settle, out of court, with a small payment of "go-away money" by his insurance company—because the parents had no case. But whether or not there was a case, Strauss felt the responsibility of the girl's death and it changed his life. He's written a whole book about it.

It would turn out that the two officers on the scene of Brian's accident had different versions of what they thought happened in the accident and what they witnessed when they arrived at the scene, as my parents relayed it. They were brothers in their early thirties and knew all the boys in the car—courtesy of a small town. They had dealt with Brian before—for bar fights, public intoxication, maybe his car accidents. I'm sure Brian was never easy to deal with at those times—just too smart and sarcastic to keep his mouth shut, but then, none of the charges against him ever kept him in jail—not by then, anyway. Perhaps the cops weren't unjustified in assuming they knew what happened. But, according to my parents, blood wasn't drawn from Brian until the next morning, four or five hours later, a breathalyzer was never used, so his blood alcohol content at the time of the accident was never determined. No one knew who had made the 911 call. And no one ever came forward as the driver of the phantom car that might or might not have caused Brian to lose control of the Volkswagen.

Four months after the accident, the Youngs talked with a lawyer and filed suit against New Paltz Taxi and my brother for civil damages, $1,824 for funeral expenses and $50,000 for "anticipated pecuniary loss." At the time, the filing of the suit naming Brian stunned all of us, especially after they'd first told my parents that they didn't want him charged.

There is nothing in official court records but the initial filings, which means it never went in front of a judge. Perhaps there was a settlement. At the time, I understood that with the criminal case dismissed against Brian, the civil suit was dropped. Mrs. Young taught at the high school, so I saw her and the Young girls. But we never spoke after the lawsuit, and neither did our families. Of course, it doesn't really matter, what a criminal or civil court might or might not have determined. Larry was dead and Brian found himself guilty, every day.

At the end of the *This American Life* episode, there is mention of research on traffic fatalities by a Dr. Ed Hickling. He has found that drivers involved with fatal motor vehicle accidents who aren't found at fault are more likely to develop post-traumatic stress disorder. When I look up this research, I'm surprised by the title: *Overcoming the Trauma of Your Motor Vehicle Accident: A Cognitive-Behavioral Treatment Program*, published by Oxford University Press in 2006, twenty-nine years too late.

///////////////////////
Part 2
///////////////////////

Other fighters from your club come and go and you
try to act happy or sad depending on the outcome
of their fight. But it is a mere formality like saying
hello to a stranger is passing politeness. The time of
the fight draws near as others speak of how it was
and how it should have been. They have lived for
the night. Pass or fail, they have lived.

–Brian Hurley, "The Other Side of the Ropes,"
The Huguenot Herald, New Paltz,
New York, June 23, 1976

Chapter Twenty-Four

[1978]

Boxing requires more than toughness and natural ability. It requires a love of the process, a love of the journey, a desire to work and dream and work some more.

– Andy Schott, email to Janet Hurley, 2004

I walked into math class at the start of my junior year in high school with a pragmatic eye on my grade point average. Andy walked into that same class at the start of his senior year with the dream of winning an Olympic middleweight boxing title. We saw each other and nodded in mutual recognition tinged with a little surprise, as if we both could say, oh yeah, I forgot about you.

That first day of class, he took a seat behind and a little to the right of me, stretching long blue-jeaned legs into the aisle. He was six feet tall now, some fifty pounds away from that skinny kid who walked into Floyd's gym when he was just thirteen. I vaguely knew Andy was still training at Floyd's, but I'd put boxing behind me, ignored any memory just as I tried to ignore Brian and his roller-coaster life. I didn't know that Andy was now the golden boy at the gym.

I couldn't remember having talked with him since I was in seventh grade. That memory was clear, still had a sting:

watching Andy and Sammy come toward me across the athletic fields, both expecting to hear that Brian, the fighter they admired so much, won in the Golden Gloves. I knew that Sammy had stopped boxing and started hanging out in the smoking lounge and downtown on the streets after school. He was stabbed one night, outside of a bar, and wore a colostomy bag under his T-shirt for a while. I saw him at a party one time, lifting his shirt to show off the bag with one hand, a beer in the other.

In the first week or so of math class, I paid little attention to Andy or anyone else, just focused on doing the work in my least favorite subject.

"C'mon," I heard a low voice coming from behind me one morning. "You have to wait to open the book. You can't have it open and ready. You'll make the rest of us look bad."

I glanced behind me to find Andy smiling. His hair, a brown that wanted to be a red, was long enough to pass the collar of his sweatshirt, falling partially over one of his blue eyes.

It was true. I had my book open to the page we were assigned the day before. I moved a piece of paper over it. "I didn't finish all the problems," I lied.

"Yeah, OK," he said. He flipped open his notebook and showed me a page with the homework assignment dutifully noted at the top, the rest blank. "This is not finishing the problems." And he tapped the page with his pencil, like a pointer to a blackboard.

"Now, that could be a problem."

He flipped through the math book and sighed. "If you would stop bugging me, I might be able to get something done before class."

I turned back in my seat and stared down at the desk, recognizing the arrival of blood and heat in my face and not wanting him to see it.

"Hey, how's Brian doing," Andy asked one day as he slid into his seat.

I stiffened. "He's good."

"Yeah? What's he doing?"

I hesitated. The short version was that my mother had convinced Julie to take Brian out west when she returned to Arizona, to get him out of New Paltz, give him a new start. The problem was that she'd never convinced Brian that this was a good idea and he'd been angry about it, even though he was a fan of Carlos Castaneda and, it seems, did find someone willing to share peyote buttons while he was there. After he blew through all the money my parents gave him and squandered the good will of my sister and her boyfriend, my parents funded his bus ticket back home. After just six weeks away. But even the short version was too long for me to share. "He's living at home again. For a while."

"Do you think he'll come back to the gym?"

I shook my head. "No. That's over. Far as I can tell."

"That's too bad," Andy said, and his tone caught me by surprise. He really did think it was too bad. He brightened then. "I remember you came to the fights one time."

"I came to a lot of fights."

"Yeah, well, I think Brian fought Christiana that night. It was pretty tough, very exciting. I had a great fight, too, one of my best in the earlier years. Do you remember it?"

"No. I don't."

"Oh," he said and looked disappointed. "I thought I might have talked with you afterward."

"Maybe. I don't remember. But I don't really remember Brian's fight either. I mean, I remember him fighting but I don't remember the specifics." I turned around as class started, wishing that I'd paid more attention back then, to fighters other than Brian.

Some weeks after discovering Andy in math class, I brought him up during dinner. Just to say his name, just to try it out, see if it felt as good to talk about him as it did to think about him.

"Guess who's in my math class?" Brian and my father turned expectant faces. "Andy, Andy Schott."

Brian raised an eyebrow. "Oh yeah? Cool."

I was disappointed. Was that all? Didn't he have any questions? Any memories to share with me? "Hey, did you know Floyd took them to Ireland this past summer to fight?"

Brian looked at me for a long moment. "Yeah," he said. "I heard about that."

My father cleared his throat, jumped right in. "He looked really good against that Italian kid down in Warwick," my father said. "But I've always thought Andy wasn't talented so much as a hard worker."

"Everyone said you were the most talented fighter to go through Floyd's, Brian," my mother said. "Andy works hard, no doubt, but you were the one with the talent."

I was still dating Wayne who, in the two years since Brian found us together in the rec room had somehow worked his way back into my parent's tolerance. His intensity had long felt controlling and jealous, then violent whenever I tried to break away. I didn't confide in my parents, tried to keep our perpetual arguments hidden, though one time, my father said, with a shake of his head, "Wayne can just pick a fight with you out of thin air."

Years later, at a reunion with my two closest girlfriends from high school, they told me they'd thought about going to my parents to ask them to intervene but were afraid. Of my boyfriend, of causing my parents more pain when they had Brian to think about. They'd just hoped, they said, that I would find the strength to end it.

And I did. We were on the front porch, my parents inside, maybe watching *Barney Miller* or *Taxi*. I remember stepping back from Wayne, with his clenched jaw and fists and the so familiar threatening question: why do you have to make me so crazy? How good it felt to close the front door on him . Of course, there were repercussions, but by then, I'd met Andy and remembered who I was.

By the end of that fall semester, I had laughed more with Andy than I had since I was a kid listening to Bill Cosby records with Brian or even, not so long ago, listening to Brian's post-dinner stories about the odd characters he met at the gym or at fights or at work. Andy and I wrote notes to each other on an almost daily basis. His were always signed Andy "The Cat ." This was his ring name, given to him by someone at the gym, who apparently thought Andy's moves were feline in nature. I loved the idea of a ring name. Brian had never had one.

When Andy asked me to spend New Year's Eve 1979 at his house, I felt like I was finally in the right place. A safe place. If my mother was surprised about our plan, she didn't say, but then, she was mostly preoccupied with trying to figure out what she should do next to help Brian get his life on track. Despite a steady snowfall, she drove me up the mountain to Andy's house. When I told her that the Schotts had invited me to spend the night if the roads got much worse, she surprised me by agreeing that this was a sensible plan. Maybe she was just glad that Wayne was out of my life.

Andy's parents were home that night until about 10:30. Then they poked their heads into the den where we were sitting on the couch with the family dog, a large, dark-furred Akita mix named Kayo laying in front of us. We were not quite one at each end, but with a noticeable, suddenly shy distance between us. We had been talking for hours, Andy showing me his training notebooks where he kept track of miles run and rounds sparred. He put the notebook between us, rather than sliding over to be next to me.

Mr. Schott wore a scarf wrapped tightly around his neck, a ski cap protecting his bald spot. "We're headed to the Thompsons'. We're just gonna walk down the hill. If you want, there is some wine in the fridge, some beer."

Andy nodded. "Yeah, thanks, but no thanks, Dad. Have a great time."

Mr. Schott nodded, and I could see that he was amused. "Have a good time yourselves."

After they left, I said, "You don't drink."

"Nah," Andy said. "I'm training. It's not worth it. What about you?"

"I've had my share," I said and then hastened to say, "But I don't anymore."

He nodded. "That's good, don't you think? I mean, after Brian and everything."

"Yeah," I said. "I think that's good." I picked up the training notebook and scooted next to him, slid my hand into his, while I flipped through the pages. "I can't believe you keep track of all of this."

He laughed. "I know, a little compulsive, but it helps me stay on target, keeps me focused." He took the notebook off my lap and dropped it on the floor.

Andy says that I called his parents cool that first time I spent the night.

A writer and a painter for whom, I sensed, convention was a spiritual trap, they were a well-educated, middle-class white couple who moved their family to this small upstate town of New Paltz hoping to live their ideals. Or so it seemed to me. They were probably surprised to discover that they had a son choosing a path that was noisy with the crunching of noses and the cracking of ribs. While his father painted early in the morning, Andy was running his miles, no matter the snow. His mother, finishing her typing in the late afternoon, could be sure that her son was waiting to spar. Equally perplexing for them, being parents in the mid-seventies, must have been that their son refused to party, partake, imbibe, even have just a little taste. Of course, it was a blessing, but it was a little, well, odd for a teenager. Hard to set curfew when your son went to bed before you did.

So, when I appeared, and something completely expected happened in Andy's bunked bedroom with the huge windows that faced the woods, maybe his parents were reassured by something they understood about teenagers. They must have presumed Andy's good sense, if not mine, would prevent a pregnancy. And they were right. We even shared the cost of the birth control. They might have also presumed that I told my parents that I shared Andy's bedroom when I spent the night. And they were wrong. My parents followed a more traditional standard of what was appropriate between teenagers. But this spending the night with the consent of Andy's parents felt honest, respectful, healthy and safe to me at a time when I needed, or any teen needs, to feel that most. I wouldn't have dared to share this with my parents if they had asked me about the sleeping arrangements at Andy's. And they never did.

Not long after that first New Year's Eve, I walked into the cafeteria for lunch and was hailed by one of my friends.

"Look at this," he said and grinned. He waved the school newspaper, *The Deja Vu*, at me. I sat next to him, and he pointed to the odds and ends column which queried: Is it true that Janet Hurley is dating Andy Schott because he is the only one who could take out Wayne Wilson?

I was stunned. Wayne's intensity had jiggled my very cells, kept a light buzz in my ears at all times. Andy's energy was a constant low-frequency, soothing. Always playful and fun. That was what made me feel safe, not his fists. The thought of him taking out anyone seemed ludicrous.

"That's crazy," I said and laughed.

My friend raised an eyebrow and agreed. "They must be talking about that other Andy Schott, you know, the one that is ranked as one of the best amateur middleweights in the country."

Andy Schott, right, amateur fight circa 1978.
COURTESY OF THE ANDREW SCHOTT COLLECTION

Sammy

[2004]

It was Alfie who gave me Sammy's number and forewarned me, "I think he's still using." I'm willing to take my chances. I call him from my cell phone while sitting in the parking lot of Stewarts, a convenience store in New Paltz.

"Yeah?"

I'm stunned that I recognized the voice immediately, that reedy high pitch unusual in a teenager, now odd in a grown man. "Sammy? This is Janet Hurley. Alfie gave me your number, said I should give you a call."

"Oh, yeah, yeah, he said you were coming up. How are ya?"

"I'm OK. I guess Alfie told you that I'm working on this book about Brian. I was wondering if I would be able to talk with you."

There isn't the pause I expected. "Yeah, yeah. When?"

"What about later this afternoon or tonight?"

"Yeah, well the thing is, I'm working right now. I do some painting and construction stuff. And I got some stuff tonight. What about tomorrow night?"

I hesitate. I'm going up to Albany for some research at the state library. I wouldn't be back in New Paltz for a couple of days. "Well, how about Thursday night?"

"Thursday? Yeah, yeah, well, that's better. That'll give me some time to think, you know, just pull up some memories."

"OK, I'll call you the night before to confirm."

"Sure."

I spend the next day scrolling microfiche at the state library for hours, looking for articles about Brian and the Huguenot Boxing Club. Sammy's name came up once, just a quick mention in a rundown of a match bout. I didn't expect more than that. His tenure at the gym was only about eighteen months.

That night I call him. He answers on the second ring, and I jump right in. "Sammy, this is Janet Hurley. I just want to confirm we're getting together tomorrow night."

"What, hold on a minute." He fumbles the phone. "Who is this?"

"This is Janet Hurley."

"Yeah, yeah right. I'm sorry. I didn't hear you very well."

"That's OK. I'm just calling to confirm. About talking tomorrow night."

"Yeah, yeah, that should work. I thought you said tonight."

"No, tomorrow."

"Just as well. I just got back in, and I got this court thing that has me a little worried. But it should be settled tomorrow."

"But you can get together after?"

"Yeah, yeah," he tells me the name of the apartments. "They're like a couple blocks from your parent's house." He gives me the number and worries that I need directions.

I can see them clearly in my mind. "No, it's a small complex. I'll find you. And Sammy, you know, I just want to talk about your memories. Just what you want to tell me."

I think, now he'll take that big pause. That pause that will precede his changing his mind.

But he doesn't. "Yeah, I've been thinking a lot about that this week. You know, Brian was really a mentor to me when I was at the gym. He taught me a lot."

It's a raw January night, rainy and foggy. When the door swings open, Sammy leans his tall body against the frame and holds on to the knob. He looks like the boy I knew so long ago, but it's as if he was put into a dehydrator, as if his bodily fluid was minimized for more efficient storage. His hair is still short, a mustache wraps around his mouth to a sparse, stubby lichen of beard that creeps down under his chin toward his neck. Sammy wears a T-shirt and jeans cinched tight on his hips with a belt as if the pants once fit. He looks down at me. I can see that he is puzzled.

"Hi, Sammy. I'm Janet."

"Oh, yeah. Yeah." Sammy dips forward and down a bit, smiling. "Man, you look different. No, no, it's just your hair. Otherwise, you look the same."

"So do you," I lie uneasily. I wait for a cue to come inside. "I thought we had a plan for talking tonight."

"Yeah." Sammy runs a hand over his close-cropped Afro. "Yeah, tonight's not a good night."

"No?"

"Actually, I got off from this DUI today. Thank God!" He pauses, and I realize that I am supposed to share in the sentiment. I just nod. "Yeah, well, me and some friends, we're celebrating, you know. I am just too inebriated to talk with you."

Inebriated strikes me as an attempt to be polite and to deflect attention at the same time. I sigh. "OK, well…"

"Tomorrow?" Sammy smiles at me, almost tenderly.

"No, I have to start back to North Carolina tonight," I say. "Can I call you sometime?"

"Sure, sure, call my landline." He leans forward slightly to see that I write it correctly. I smell beer and the sweetness of pot, but the energy around him comes from something I can only guess at. "Hey," he says. "I like your hair. All curly like that."

"Yeah. It's a lot longer than when I was in high school."

"You perm it or something?"

I take a moment. "No," I say finally. "I just have curly hair. Remember Brian's hair? It was so curly he kept that hat on it."

He nods and seems tickled to think about that. "Yeah, must be the Irish in ya."

"Must be. Well, good luck, Sammy."

"Yeah, drive safe!"

I get back in my car and cry. What did I expect to find behind door H-12? I'd wanted to hear his stories about Brian, sure, but, more, I'd wanted to find Sammy doing well, maybe not prosperous, but well enough.

I head down the thruway to Newburgh and stop at Alfie's apartment to give him back some photos he let me take to photocopy. I tell him what happened with Sammy, and he nods. He seems unsurprised but sad. He introduces me to his partner, Tonja, whose smile is warm and lovely, and a curious little boy, Jason, and then to his dogs and cat. It's a rainy night, so he doesn't take me out back to show me his pigeons. He walks with me to the car and hovers close to be sure nobody bothers me, though I'm parked under a streetlight, just across from his door. As I drive away, I see him in my rearview mirror, still standing in the street, still watching. He raises a hand.

Chapter Twenty-Five

Disdainfully, Floyd tells us that women have brought
about the downfall of many a promising fighter...
There is silence as the younger fighters blush and
Floyd grins and walks out with a mischievous gleam
in his eyes.

— Brian Hurley, "Character Portrait: My Impressions
and Learnings of Floyd Patterson," 1983

Though I'd talked about Andy for months, Brian seemed surprised to see him at our house. Brian sat at the dining room
table with his girlfriend Titi, playing Trivial Pursuit as Andy
and I came in the front door. It was a late Saturday afternoon, without much to do in town. Brian must have heard us
talking and laughing as we stamped snow off our feet on the
front porch. He stood up when we came into the dining room.
I was used to either casual indifference or pointed dismissal
when it came to my boyfriends. But he stuck out his hand.
"Andy, hey, how are ya?"

Andy smiled. "Cold. How are you?" He took Brian's hand,
covering it with his other, and then pulled it back awkwardly.

Brian nodded. "Good, good." He hesitated. "This is my girlfriend, Ti. Have you met?"

I thought, Now where would they have met? A bar?

But Andy was gracious. "No, no. Haven't met. What's the name? Sorry, I didn't catch it."

Ti reached to flick off the ash on her cigarette with one hand while holding out the other to shake Andy's hand. She was a waif in the tradition of Twiggy, so thin that a tube top and hot pants seemed modest on her. With long, fine blonde hair, blue-eyed, she was pretty in an anemic way. "Titi. I know, it's weird. It was my little sister. My real name is Elma, and she couldn't say it and tried to say sister and it turned out Titi and now I am stuck with it. Better than Elma anyway." She smiled up at Andy. "More than you wanted to know."

"Nah, no, it's an unusual name, people must ask you. Very efficient of you." Andy glanced at me, his voice trailing off.

Brian picked up his glass. "I was just heading in to get a glass of water. We're finishing this game. You're welcome to join us."

"No," I said. "We're not going to be here that long; we're just gonna hang out a little."

"Oh," Brian nodded without looking at me. "Yeah, well, how's the training going?"

Andy nodded. "Good, good. It's... yeah, it's good."

Brian stepped past him, laid a hand briefly on his shoulder and said, "All right. Well, have fun."

Andy and I moved into the family room, which was just off the dining room. As we sat down Andy said in a low voice, "It's good to see him. He looks... OK. When you told me how depressed he's been I kinda expected something else."

"It's one of his good days."

Brian had let my mother convince him to try classes again at the community college. To save money, he lived at home and worked one of a long line of forgettable and sometimes regrettable jobs. It might have been the garbage truck or furniture-moving company or the lab-mouse sexing facility. He also went to see a psychiatrist, which was a secretive and irregular activity that I learned about only through eavesdropping when my mother and father were talking about it in the kitchen.

I shared this with Andy as we were driving to a mall in Poughkeepsie.

"Wow." He was appropriately shocked. Neither of us knew anyone in any sort of counseling or therapy.

I suddenly felt anxious about betraying the family code. "Don't say anything to him, or anyone."

Andy shook his head. "No, no, of course not. I'm glad you told me though."

Brian spent all his free time with Titi, or Ti, his first real girlfriend that we knew of. She was one of a crowd that hung out regularly at the bars downtown, and Brian met her through a friend. Older than my brother, she had a little girl from a previous relationship who didn't live with her. She worked as an assistant in a nursing home and lived there in a basement apartment. As if to make up for her small use of physical space in the world, Ti had a voice that was declarative, a laugh that dominated any social scene. Hers was a large, smooth forehead behind which, I was sure, whirred a machine of smoothly clicking parts, not the gray-blue softness the rest of us had. I think now that she was seeing her future as a day trader even as she sat on a bar stool with Brian and drank until she passed out. But that would be much later, after the years of living and not living with Brian, years of consensual push and pull.

At this earlier point in their relationship, Brian and Ti were sober, a pact made with each other that they would stop partying, be clean, accountable, and bored together. To deal with the boredom, my mother had bought them the Trivial Pursuit game. They played for hours in our dining room, sometimes with us, sometimes with friends they invited.

Ti was the first person I knew who was admitted into Brian's physical personal space. My family was so accustomed to his distance that we all operated as if there was a force field around him. She obviously knew how to deactivate it. He often lost track of his turn, too intent on tucking her hair behind her ear so that it didn't fall in her face, or busy with the preparation of a snack for her in the kitchen. They both smoked, and the haze around the game board felt intimate, private, as if I stepped into the bedroom with them. I never really felt comfortable with Brian and Ti, probably no one did. They exchanged too many knowing looks with each other, laughed often at some private joke that seemed to always be lurking. I never felt quite smart enough around them.

I was glad that Brian welcomed Andy so pleasantly to the house, but at first, I really didn't want to share my boyfriend with him. And besides, I told myself, Andy wouldn't want to be breathing in all that smoke. But there was more to my reluctance. It was obvious that Brian noticed Andy, had changed his usual modus operandi of ignoring boys I brought home. Because of the boxing. Not just any boxer, but that skinny kid who had looked up to him in his glory days at the gym, a fighter who was now touted in the papers, who had the confidence of Floyd.

But it turned out that Brian and Andy had more in common than boxing. They shared a similar sense of humor, manifested in quick, witty observations. They both liked to tease, though Andy was always playful and Brian could veer into uncomfortable edges. For a while, I relaxed around Brian and Andy, just enjoying their tag-team humor. There were times when they would riff off the other until I had to just say, "OK, stop, enough. We have to go," and tug at Andy until he reluctantly stood up.

There were moments when we were all together and Brian looked at me and I actually felt seen, so different from the first time I brought Andy home. My relationship with my brother was still distant, but it was as if Andy were a bridge that could, for a time, span that gulf.

Brian and Ti getting ready to play Trivial Pursuit, 1980.

I met Floyd again in my new role as Andy's girlfriend at a club match upstate. It wasn't a role that Andy was anxious for Floyd to know about, given his views on girls and training, but this just made me want to go to the fight more. My anger toward Floyd about Brian and the cancelled boxing exhibition had dissipated over the past two years, scaled down next to all that had happened since. I just wanted Floyd to know that I would be around, cheering for my boyfriend, as any girlfriend would do, especially one that had a history with boxing and who liked going to fights.

After the fights, held in a recreation center, I waited with Lou, my ride for the evening as I didn't have a car and my parents were wary of letting me drive out of town in theirs. He was new at the gym, a very green heavyweight in his late teens. I didn't know him well, but then, I didn't know many of the fighters well. Alfie was gone from the gym, had turned pro with a trainer from New York City because Floyd was now the head of the New York State Athletic Commission and couldn't represent him in his professional career. I missed Alfie's easy way and broad smile. Longo wasn't fighting anymore, though he helped out some at the gym. He now had two small children and worked full time at his own shoe repair shop.

Lou and I were in a large room with a ping-pong table. Some of the mothers and girlfriends of the local fighters had put together a table of cold cuts and bread and condiments. None of the fighters from the Huguenot Boxing Club had yet appeared from the locker rooms. Most of them had won, Andy by an easy decision.

The door opened and Janet, Floyd's wife, came in with their girls, Janine and Jennifer. They were about nine and ten. I remembered when they were tiny and sitting near ringside at some of the first fights I went to with my parents. They wore their hair in much the same way as they did then—one had tight soft curls, the other girl wore hers longer. They were both pretty and, to me, looked like Floyd, particularly around the eyes. Janet was a slender white woman with a sharp face, fair skin, dark hair streaked with red and blue-green eyes lined with black. She wore black high-heel boots with jeans, a leather jacket and a blue turtleneck that set off her eyes. Red lipstick gleamed under the fluorescent lights, accentuating her slight overbite.

"Do *not* eat that food yet," she called to her girls as they made a beeline for the table.

She glanced at me and Lou. "Hey, no one's come up yet?"

Lou shook his head. "Not yet."

She looked at me more closely and held out a hand. "Janet Patterson."

I stepped forward and took her hand; it felt small and soft, not intimidating at all. I introduced myself and was grateful that her face lit up when I mentioned Brian.

Lou piped up. "Janet's Andy's girlfriend. She came up with me."

Janet smiled broadly, eyes bright. "Really! Andy's girlfriend. I didn't know he had a girlfriend."

I was eager to confirm it. "We've been going out a couple of months."

"A couple of months! I am going to have to give Floyd heck for not telling me!"

The door opened just then, and several of the fighters came in, gym bags in hand, including Andy. Janet immediately switched gears and greeted each fighter, dispensing a comment on each of the fights before patting their shoulders and pointing the way to food.

Andy smiled at me. Janet laughed. "OK, Andy. Keeping secrets from me will never do!" She noticed Floyd as he came in and called him over. He still had his head turned, talking with someone over his shoulder as he joined us. "Floyd." Janet slapped her small hand on his big shoulder. "Pay attention. This is Janet. Janet Hurley. Brian's sister."

Floyd turned. His face was so familiar to me, not just from studying him in person during the years, but from all the pictures I'd perused in *The Ring Magazine* or the boxing history compendiums that were now growing mold in Brian's room. He never seemed to age. He looked hard at me and then nodded slowly. "Yeah, yeah, I remember."

I wasn't sure what to say, just stuck out a hand to shake his. "It's good to see you again."

Janet leaned in close to his ear. "She's Andy's girlfriend now."

Floyd glanced at Andy, conveniently involved in a teasing conversation with Janine, helping himself to cookies off her plate.

Floyd looked back at me. "I didn't know that. About Andy. So, you're Brian's sister. You look just like him. Same eyes, same nose… same… sad face."

Janet gave him a playful push. "Oh, shoot, Floyd. She doesn't look sad." She winked at me as they moved away. "We Janets have to stick together."

"How was that?" Andy asked a few minutes later. "Sorry I missed it. I was talking with the girls."

"No problem," I said. "Don't worry about leaving me to fend for myself." I kept my tone light. I didn't tell him what Floyd had said, how his comment had startled blood into my cheeks, created this smile I now wore to refute any implication that I was like Brian. At the same time, I found it hard to talk, as if the words that I should have said in Brian's defense were still queued up in my throat and blocking the way for any other.

It wasn't until we were lying on Andy's bottom bunk later that night that I was able to cough them out. Andy shook his head as he listened. "He can be weird sometimes. Just ignore him. And you're not like Brian."

But I was wary of Floyd. I felt his disapproval at all times, so I made sure that I still knew my way around the fight scene. I understood the ten-point-must scoring system where officials must award the winner of a round ten points if he hasn't fouled or been knocked down and the loser nine or fewer points. If the round is even, each boxer is awarded ten points. I understood the basics of the different moves, the strategies at play. I knew the local amateur rankings and the international professional rankings from flyweight on up. I could drop this into conversations with the fighters while we were waiting for everyone to come out of the locker room. If Floyd noticed my boxing acumen, he never said, though I hoped he did. Whenever he saw me with Andy, he gave the smallest of nods, his face impassive. I always smiled at him and said hello and thought, I won't let you scare me off.

Floyd still had very clear ideas about women, sex and boxing. When he was fighting, he would tell his fighters, he just didn't. Not for six weeks before a fight. He swore off, put it out of his mind, he abstained. Which was understood to include no flirting, no foreplay, nothing.

He might have punctuated his comments with one of his ubiquitous lollipops. Or maybe he ran a huge hand nervously over that close-cropped hair. He was still in great shape, still a powerfully built man, but he was shy about the topic of sex and delivered his message as delicately as possible.

"But Floyd," Longo told me he protested one time, "how can it drain your energy? For me, it's three or four minutes tops."

Floyd didn't want to hear more details. "It's about getting the sex. Staying out all night looking for it."

"I'm married!" Longo couldn't let it go. "I don't go out all night lookin' for it."

Floyd glanced around at the couple of fighters who were listening to the discussion. "You just don't want to be losing anything right before a fight. That's what weakens you."

Longo snorted. "Yeah, yeah."

I don't think Floyd ever worried about Andy until I arrived on the scene, and even then, I think he was more concerned about other fighters. With his star well on the rise as a middleweight, Andy already abstained from alcohol and drugs, adhered to a rigorous training schedule year-round. He was focused, determined. He had those calendars and notebooks full of data on every workout. And, while listening to Floyd talk about sex, like all the other fighters, he nodded his head every time. But Andy and I were both seventeen, and despite all of Floyd's warnings, we were not to be denied.

I felt smug that I prevailed over Floyd's admonitions, sure that my love and young passion made such concerns about sex trivial—maybe even lent energy and power to Andy's pugilistic endeavors. *Floyd didn't, but we did.* And then one afternoon, as I waited for Andy to come back from the kitchen with a snack, I absent-mindedly picked up his calendar where his upcoming fights were marked. I noticed little dots of ink on certain days. I flipped back through the calendar and saw the dots stretching back into the months before.

When Andy walked into his room, I said, "What are these dots for?"

He was silent for a moment, and I knew immediately. "Are you keeping track of when we have sex?"

"I just wanted to see," he said. "I just wanted to find out if it matters."

From an article by Wayne Allen Hall, "Hard Knocks," in the *Hudson Valley Magazine*, January 1978. Brian is to the immediate right of the heavy bag. PHOTO BY WAYNE ALLEN HALL

Chapter Twenty-Six

Before any of the tools of the boxing trade can be
learned, one has to be in shape and then one must
be able to discipline himself and sacrifice much.

– Brian Hurley, untitled essay on boxing technique
and training, 1983

I could see the Golden Gloves logo at the top of the forms
Brian had in front of him. He sat at the dining room table, fill-
ing in the spaces on his application with his neat block print.
I couldn't believe it. "What are you doing?"

Brian looked up. "It's the Gloves. I went up to Floyd's today,
and he said he would be in my corner if I stopped smoking."

"What weight class?" I asked.

"Middleweight," he said.

Andy's weight class.

That night I helped my mother with cleaning the kitchen.
"Why is Brian going in the Gloves?"

My mother glanced at me. "Why not? I just hope that he
and Floyd can get along and that this works out. I think it's
good, gives him a focus."

I was having none of it. "Yeah, right. That's not likely. Why
does he have to be in Andy's weight class?"

My mother seemed surprised. "Why wouldn't he be?"

"He could go up to light heavy."

My mother shook her head. "He hasn't had a fight in two years. He can't go up to light heavy. It'll be a miracle if he gets in shape at all."

"Fine," I said. "But if he and Andy meet up, I'm rooting for Andy."

"That is awful." My mother's puzzlement turned to anger. "Brian is your brother."

"I don't care," I said. "He had his chance. Andy's doing everything he can to make it in boxing. Brian never did that."

"That is my son you are talking about." My mother snapped rubber gloves on and plunged her hands into the hot sink water. "I know he messed up his chances. But he needs something right now, and if this is it then, by God, we all better get behind him."

When I talked with Andy about it, he seemed unconcerned. "I'm glad he's back in the gym," he said. "He's got that same old Brian style. It's good to see. I just hope he really stops smoking, takes it seriously this time."

"But what if you and he meet up?" I asked.

Andy looked surprised. "We won't. It'll never happen."

I wasn't so sure. Brian could still have a punch that could level a better trained boxer whose attention had slipped; he could move forward in the tournament. I didn't question that he would lose, it was just a matter of when and if he would be hurt. And if he did win and met up with Andy, he would force my allegiance and discover that it wasn't with him.

There wasn't much time before the preliminary bouts in the Gloves, roughly a month, hardly enough time to get the nicotine out of his system. But Brian went cold turkey. His first run, just around our neighborhood, left him gasping and lightheaded. He went out again the next day and came home to report that he threw up on a neighbor's lawn.

My mother shook her head. "You're trying too much too soon."

"No," Brian wheezed. He bent over, hands on his knees to catch his breath. "I don't have time to hold back."

Listening to this, I was tempted to roll my eyes and say, what is the point? But I was quietly unsupportive and figured he'd give up by the end of the week. He didn't. After the second week, I knew that Brian was really going to fight in the Golden Gloves. I gave up wishing that he would quit training and instead just gave myself over to dreading his first fight.

"I sparred with Brian today," Andy said one evening. We were at his house, sitting on the couch in his family room. Andy played with his dog Kayo's ears.

"How did that happen?" I asked.

"Floyd just put us in together," Andy answered, thumping Kayo on the side. The dog slid his tail back and forth on the rug.

I took one of Kayo's ears between my thumb and forefinger and rubbed it like a magic purse. "What does Floyd think about Brian being back?"

Andy shrugged. "You know Floyd. He doesn't say much about stuff like that. Right now, it's like Brian is just one of the fighters. And that's good, really. I mean, Brian's got to do the training himself, and Floyd will be there when he spars and then in his corner. Floyd isn't going to give anyone extra special attention."

"No," I said. "No, I don't mean he should. I thought he might give him less attention."

"Nah. We all would be happy with more. But anyway, Brian did OK sparring today."

"Yeah?" I couldn't help it. I could feel a little rise of something in me, and it felt familiar.

Andy pushed Kayo off and bent over to rub the dog's stomach. His voice took on a muffled quality. "Yeah, it was OK. I went slow with him, you know. Held back. It was his first time in the ring since before the accident, right?"

I sighed. "I think." The familiar feeling—maybe pride, maybe hope—slipped away.

The first Golden Glove bouts for both Brian and Andy were on the same night. My family had a station wagon at the time that would seat, oh, fifty people, it seemed. With a back seat that offered the rear view, we had plenty of room for my parents, my sister Nora, Ti, me, and the Schotts. Brian and Andy, of course, rode down much earlier, in Floyd's Lincoln.

We found our seats in the Felt Forum and settled in as the fights got underway. It felt like hours before Brian came to the ring with Floyd, though it was relatively early in the program. I felt my mother stiffen next to me. Floyd looked like he always did, strong, in shape, wearing a Huguenot Boxing Club T-shirt. Brian climbed in the ring, his pale skin looking bright and vulnerable. He turned and threw some punches into the air, shrugged his shoulders, bounced from the ball of one foot to the other. His opponent climbed into the other corner: Noel Tucker, a Black teen with broad shoulders. The announcer stepped to the center of the ring and made his usual comments to the crowd, ending with introductions. "And in this corner, weighing 165 pounds, from the Huguenot Boxing Club in New Paltz, Brian Hurley."

And that was it. I knew in my heart that it would be the last time I would ever hear those words. That knowledge slid down into my stomach to join the turmoil there, that writhing ball of anticipation that wouldn't let me eat anything earlier.

The bell rang while Ti and I yelled, "C'mon Brian!" and "This is your night, Brian!" or, from Nora, "Get that guy, Brian!" I don't know if he heard us, we weren't too far away, but not on the main floor. The constant buzz of conversation in the huge arena made me feel as if I were in a vacuum. It was hard to breathe.

The two boxers moved in, sizing each other up. Tucker was a southpaw. Brian never liked a southpaw, the way that he had to reverse his strategies to match the way they fought. The gym had more of its share through the years, and he had lots of experience with them, but that was a long time ago. The crowd stirred as Brian brought the fight into Tucker, but Tucker covered well. By the end of the first round, despite Brian having a lot of forward energy, he couldn't get in a solid blow while Tucker had several counterpunches that found the mark. The round ended in what I thought could be a draw, though it probably edged to Tucker.

"Brian lost that one," my father said, and I almost disagreed, was surprised at how fast I wanted to jump to Brian's defense. I noticed that my father's leg was jiggling, and I felt as if I would cry. The second round was almost a repeat of the first, though Tucker stayed constant and I could see Brian working to pull in breath. When he returned to his seat, his chest heaved, he sat forward on the stool for a moment to let the sweat drip down and to ease his lungs before Floyd wiped his face and leaned in to talk into his ear. I could see Brian nodding.

My father's voice was regretful. "Lost that one, too, not by much."

My mother was in her usual position, curled in a bit at the stomach, elbows on her knees, hands close to her eyes for instant covering. She watched Floyd tend to Brian. "C'mon, Brian!" she yelled unexpectedly, and I jumped.

Mr. and Mrs. Schott exchanged glances I could read plainly, empathetic in the way that only parents of a boxer could be.

From the moment Brian stepped away from his corner in the third round, I knew that he wouldn't even have this round to claim and take home as consolation. He held his own, but he was moving slowly. The round was unremarkable, nothing exciting from either fighter, but Tucker still was in charge, and everyone knew it. The last bell rang, followed by a smattering of applause and some whistles. I looked over at Ti, who had curled her small body into her seat next to Nora. Tears slid down her face. As the ref lifted Tucker's hand in victory, Nora said, "I can't believe Brian didn't win!" with such incredulity that it made the rest of us smile.

My father cleared his throat, tapped his leg with his program and glanced at my mother. "I'll go down and see him," he said. "I think I've got a couple of bouts before Andy fights." He stood up and squeezed past Andy's parents.

"I'm really sorry," Mr. Schott said.

My father put a hand on his shoulder. "Thanks."

My mother wiped at her nose with a tissue, leaned over to offer one to Ti. They both blew their noses noisily. She waved one at me, and I shook my head. Despite the pressure of tears all through the fight, I no longer wanted to cry. It was over, and I was relieved. No matter how good this win might have been for Brian, the next fight might have been with Andy. And if not, and he won that too, then the next fight. Surely. Because Andy would win all his fights up to that point. And he would win that one too.

According to the program, Andy's opponent was Charles Hecker, and I knew nothing about him. All through the day my anxiety and anticipation had swirled around Brian's impending fight. I'd let my confidence in Andy's record lull me along. And while that writhing ball in my stomach was calmer, it seemed now to have unfurled into a straight hard edge that made me want to push time and get Andy's fight behind me.

Within moments of the first bell, it was obvious that the pairing was one-sided in Andy's favor. He looked strong and confident, not even breathing hard each time he went back to the corner. His opponent boxed well enough to stay on his feet, but the fight seemed half as long as Brian's with the end never in question.

Nora and I yelled for Andy during the fight, with Mr. Schott chiming in occasionally. Ti was out near the concessions somewhere, probably having a smoke, something she gave up when Brian did, just to be supportive. My mother watched Andy's fight with little interest, lost in her own thoughts. Andy left the ring with almost as much energy as when he entered, lifted a gloved hand over his head and then was gone in the crowd.

My father hadn't returned. I thought maybe he was in the locker room with Brian, and then saw them both standing in the crowd, not far from the ring. I realized they'd watched the whole fight.

We all gathered outside the forum, my family, the Schotts, Brian, Ti and Andy. I hugged Andy, smelling soap and shampoo. Neither of us said anything about his fight, not with Brian a few feet away. We stepped away from the others. Andy squeezed my hand and said, "Look, I'll catch Floyd. That'll be a cramped ride on the way home if I go too." He glanced at Brian and then away. I could see it would be better if Andy went with Floyd.

"Let's go then," my father said. "It's too cold to hang around here."

Andy raised his gym bag as a farewell wave and then trotted off to find Floyd and his Lincoln.

The rest of us walked to the side street where we left the car. Brian walked arm in arm with Ti, hunched into his coat. He carried his gym bag with a bare hand despite the frigid air.

The station wagon was gone. My father and Mr. Schott had debated the wording on the signs. It was obvious they'd gotten it wrong, and the car had been towed. The eight of us stood in front of the empty space in silence, as if hoping to conjure it.

My father moved forward and out into the street, with his hand raised. A taxi slowed, and it became clear that my father intended to get in it. Mr. Schott crowded behind him, with my mother following, protesting. A few moments later, she came back to us, shaking her head. "They told the cab driver to take them to where they put the towed cars."

"Well, there goes the night," I said. "That cabbie isn't stupid. What are we supposed to do?"

"Wait," my mother said.

And so, we stood, lifting our feet up and then putting them down, like gulls on the edge of a pier. Brian and Ti cuddled together for warmth, a few feet away from us. We probably would have stayed there if a cop in a small golf-cart-type of vehicle hadn't noticed us and pulled up to warn us of the dangers being on the street at that time of night in that neighborhood and sent us to a nearby all-night restaurant. "Just tell them that the guys from the Ninth (or maybe it was the Seventh?) sent you in. They'll take care of ya."

The folks in the diner were unimpressed that the guys from the precinct sent us. They took advantage of a slow post-midnight shift to get a little cleaning done. With ammonia. The vapors were so strong they caught in our throats, made our eyes water. But it was warm, and the hot chocolate and tea and coffee seemed like tonics. We waited for hours, taking turns to go out into the cold and peer down the block. Nora fell asleep against my mother's arm. Brian drank coffee, and after a moment's hesitation, reached into Ti's purse and grabbed a cigarette. His hand shook a bit as he lit it. I knew then that he wouldn't go on, that the training was over.

"Was it hard?" I asked him. "Getting back in the ring?"

Brian took a long moment to reply. "Nah," he said. "I coulda fought better, that guy wasn't that good. Not enough training, I guess." He watched Mrs. Schott come back into the diner. "My turn to go," he said, stubbed out his cigarette, shook another from Ti's pack and walked out the door.

Before the fight, I had been so angry with him for losing his way, for wanting a piece of something that he gave up and, in my mind, no longer deserved. Now, as I watched him through the plate glass as he cupped his hands around the lighter and then leaned his head back to blow the smoke in to wobbly rings, I felt only grief and regret and what if.

Finally, Brian stuck his head back in the door. "I think that's them."

My father and Mr. Schott were already out of the car by the time we reached them. My father beckoned us to hurry, gestured toward the door he held open to the back. Once we were all in and my father pulled out into the street, my mother said in a wary voice, "OK, what happened?"

Between the low and spare mutters of my father and the bemused commentary from Mr. Schott, we learned that the cabbie had taken them all over the city before dropping them off at the right lot for towed vehicles. That the radio had been jacked but, according to the guy in the exit booth, they were lucky it wasn't worse. In addition to the cab ride, it had cost a hundred dollars to get the car back.

"Oh, my God!" My mother shook her head.

Mr. Schott leaned forward and wagged a check between my mother and father. "Here. Let us pay for half."

My mother said, "Oh no, no, no. That's not right. It was our car; we were driving."

Mr. Schott kept his hand in place. "Really, I insist. It was a joint decision to park there, I thought so as much as Bill. I insist." He put the check in my father's upraised hand.

"Bill!" But then my mother fell silent. It was as if the fights had happened ages before, forgotten in the calamity of being marooned in the Ninth (or Seventh) Precinct. But of course, that wasn't true.

Andy lost in the quarterfinals of the Gloves and then re-doubled his efforts to earn a spot in the Nationals. As he was getting ready for that tournament, a full-page article appeared in the *Middletown Sunday Record* by Mark Schwartz, "Schott Does His Boxing in the Ring," where Floyd described Andy as lacking in ability when he first came to the gym but said that he'd found his way with dogged determination.

Brian brought up the article at the dinner table, and I was surprised. He agreed with Floyd, bringing up examples of Andy's training regimen, remembering when he still came to the gym with a broken hand and cast. I told them about Andy's scrupulous tracking of runs and workouts.

My mother said what she always did, in one form or another. "Out of everyone at the gym, you were the one with talent, Brian. Don't forget that." And, as he always did, my father agreed with her. Brian shrugged. There was a quote by Floyd we were all avoiding. "Between his willingness to sacrifice and the way he's developed his skills, his quickness, his defense, his timing—Andy's worked his way into the best boxer I've ever had."

Talent

[2004]

I get an email from Andy not long after I visited with Longo in Florida. He tells me that Longo called him, with lots of opinions and strong feelings about the fighters who came through Floyd's gym. Longo focused in on Sammy who, he said, had more talent than Andy, with great hand speed. When Andy pointed out that Sammy never won a round out of the thousand they sparred, had no heart when he fought in a real bout, had the worst case of glove shy that Andy—or anyone at the gym—had ever seen, Longo conceded it all, "Yeah, that's true."

I can almost hear Andy's calm, reasonable voice when he told Longo that he had to evaluate the entire fighter. That talent comes in many forms. Looking good throwing punches is the most obvious talent, but not necessarily the most important. That the ability to take a punch, the will to fight when tired and hurt and the determination to overcome setbacks might be more important than looking good on the heavy bag.

The talent vs. hard work discussion. It is the conundrum, the central issue of any sport, any endeavor, but for some reason, boxers debate it endlessly. I think back to my father and brother and their discussions. It was exactly the same every time I heard it, as if they had a template.

Andy and Longo have a different template, of course, cut out with scissors sharpened on their long relationship, their respective boxing careers, the differences in their present lives.

Andy's perspective is analytical, based on the review of the data. He still trains fighters, has new debates to attend to. Longo has all the old ones.

During his conversation with me, Longo's perspective was a mix of the time of day, the number of beers he had downed, a soft spot for what he thought a sister would want to hear, a loyalty to what needed to be said: Brian was a warrior who went in for the kill if his opponent was hurt. He had good hand speed and combinations, a decent chin and defense. But he didn't like any of the training that wasn't in the ring.

And after another hour, several more beers, Longo said, "Brian was the most talented boxer to come through that gym, punches-wise, concentration-wise, hand-eye coordination-wise, listening-wise, adapting to Floyd's suggestions-wise." He brings up Andy, though I haven't asked for a comparison. "You know how Brian used to think and think and think? Andrew used to think and think and think. They were both philosophers. But it seemed to me that Brian could make those punches come out without thinking TOO much."

Then Longo added, "Andrew had no talent, but Andrew was the hardest workin' motherfucker I ever saw in my life. And you can quote me on that."

I am not afraid to quote him. Through the years, Andy and I have had the talent vs. hard work discussion many times. I email Andy with the relevant parts of my conversation with Longo and he replies, "I wonder how much talent I had, outside of the hard work."

He brings up his ability to take a punch, that out of 128 amateur fights he was knocked down once, for a second. He was never knocked out. This is a talent, in his perspective. And when he first went to the gym, he was immediately noticed. Within a week, Floyd saw something in Andy and told him he could do something special. "But," Andy writes, "maybe it was determination more than talent even initially."

I am struck by the responsibility to be accurate prevailing over a wondering he knows can never be proven. Maybe that's why he documented the hard work all those years in note-books: all of his runs, rounds sparred, how long he jumped rope, what he ate. It was hard evidence, as if his fight record wouldn't be self-evident. Is the ability to take a blow a talent or mental fortitude? And how would he, or anyone else, mea-sure the talent? It would be like bottling mist.

And of course, no matter what talent a fighter has or the commitment to hard work, the training is key. Andy has al-ways said that Floyd did a very consistent and solid job of starting people off. Like everyone else, Andy was given a little instruction and a lot of fights. No different than anyone else that came through the gym.

Longo disagreed with this. "Floyd was an incredible train-er. He taught some people with absolutely no athletic ability how to box."

When I talked with Alfie, he was more circumspect. "Ev-eryone he trained—he worked with them on the basics. He could tell if you didn't do your road work; he knew every fighter."

I am impatient with this whole debate in the boxing world. There are so many forces that shape success. Quality and specificity of training, of course, but also presence, loyalty, admiration, openness, determination, focus, dedication, men-tal health, physical health, opportunity, respect, camaraderie, even love... all tyrannized by this notion of talent.

From left: Alfie Bevier, Andy Schott, Danny Chapman, Floyd Patterson and Joe Walsh.
COURTESY OF THE ANDREW SCHOTT COLLECTION

Chapter Twenty-Seven

To the more inquisitive, each unturned rock or hollow log hides a world of its own. It is when one stoops close, nose to the water, that the Lilliputians emerge. Through the waters, the sun will cast its prism of light. This rainbow can reveal the dens of crayfish in their slow-motion world of altered dimensions. Here, crouched to the water, weeds and soil, lay some of my fondest memories.

– Brian Hurley, "My Impressions Upon Returning to the Woods of My Childhood," 1983

In the spring of 1979, after his loss in the Golden Gloves, Brian and Ti got an apartment together. I was glad he was leaving our house and intrigued by this living-together thing. My parents didn't approve of the general idea, but they were so relieved that he was paying his own bills and trying to set up a real life with Ti that they didn't say anything to him about it. Brian and Ti mustered furniture from friends and family and the local Goodwill. Brian even set up his fifty-gallon tank and went to buy fish for the first time in years.

"Brian and Ti invited us to dinner on Saturday night," my mother said to me.

"I'm supposed to go up to Andy's on Saturday," I said. "He doesn't have a fight this weekend."

"Well, I'm sorry," my mother said. "We've been invited and we're going. You'll have to change your plans."

"If we get done early, can I still go up to Andy's?"

My mother sighed. "Look. This is a big deal. Brian and Ti are really trying to make this work. We need to show up and be supportive. I don't want to hear you say a word about wanting to leave. If it works out that we leave there early, I don't care if you go to Andy's."

Brian and Ti's apartment was only a couple miles from our house, in a complex that was low and long, made of blonde brick and white wood framing. Each unit had its own doorway to the street. As we parked, I noticed tricycles and plastic toys at the apartment next door, a pot of basil sitting on the stoop. It was already dusk when we arrived, and the light was on outside the door. My father knocked. It struck me as odd, that a father was knocking to be let into his son's home. This was new territory for all of us.

Brian opened the door, and an aroma of something savory and roasting rushed out to greet us. His face was slightly flushed and sweaty, he had a dishcloth slung over his shoulder. There was an awkwardness to the moment that all of us recognized. My father stuck out his hand, and Brian shook it. Nora was the first in the door.

"Look at the tank," she said.

It was, indeed, something to look at. It filled the small living room with a watery glow that lifted the room, with its humbled furniture and scuffed walls, into a cozy appearance. The hum of its filtration and oxygenation system was like a background music of sorts. I smelled that odd watery scent, slightly metallic, from the days when Brian had six or seven tanks bubbling at one time in our basement. Now, it almost masked the faint mustiness of the old carpet beneath our feet. Tetras and angelfish flashed in and out of faux coral and live underwater plants. I could see a catfish scooching through the pink and orange gravel that lined the bottom.

"Wow," my mother said. "That looks great." I could hear the relief in her voice.

Brian closed the door behind us and waved at the couch and two easy chairs. "Have a seat," he said formally. "Ti's in the shower, she just got off work." He clasped his hands together in a way that reminded me of my father. "Can I get you something to drink?"

My mother and father glanced at each other, and I could see them wondering together, what does he mean?

Nora jumped right in. "Do you have Coke?"

Brian ticked it off on fingers. "Coke, ginger ale, milk, orange juice, water."

"Coke."

My father waved a hand. "Nothing right now." He sat gingerly on the boxy couch next to my mother, and I saw her put a hand on his leg to stop it from jiggling. Instead, he fingered the ribs of the gold corduroy, the worn-smooth spots.

"I'll just have some ginger ale, but let me help you," my mother said and began to rise.

"No, no, I'll get it." Brian disappeared into the kitchen.

"Hey," Ti said from the doorway into what I presumed was the bedroom. She was dressed in jeans and a T-shirt, long hair making a wet stain down the front of her shirt where she pulled it around from the back to wring it out. "I'm sorry I was in the shower when you got here. I had to work late."

My mother smiled at her. "That's quite all right. How is work?"

Ti sat on the arm of one of the easy chairs. "It's terrible, as usual."

"Tell them about the union stuff at the nursing home," Brian said from the kitchen.

Ti hesitated. "We're not supposed to talk too much about that right now. But yeah, there's a union effort going on. We need it."

Brian came back in with the ginger ale for my mother and Coke for Nora. As my mother took the glass she murmured,

"Thank you," and then, "I've been saying they need to unionize out there for years. It's not just good for the employees; it's good for the patients."

Ti nodded. "Baby." She smiled up at Brian. "Can you get me a big glass of water?"

I followed Brian back into the kitchen to see what was cooking. The table was set for six with mostly matching dishes from a set my mother got through Green Stamps at the grocery store. The table was Formica topped with chrome legs. I looked closely to see that it was the kitchen table and chair set we inherited from my grandmother's apartment after she died. The tiny kitchen was hot and steamy. Two pots were on the stove top, one simmering. Brian opened the freezer to get ice and nodded toward a cabinet over the sink. "Glasses are in there."

There were three more glasses in the cabinet and one in the dish drain. I realized he had exactly six, all matching, and wondered if he ran out just today to buy them. I put the glasses on the counter, and he plunked the ice in without saying a word. A buzzer reverberated in the close quarters.

"Excuse me," he said softly, stepping around me to get to the oven. He pulled the door open and bent over, grabbed the dish towel off his shoulder to use as a hot pad, to slide out the heavy roasting pan. It was a turkey, stuffing and all, even though it was March. The heat in the kitchen ratcheted up, and I was tempted to back out of the room, take my water with me. But I was fascinated by Brian's careful tending. He looked up at me, his eyes glittery from the steam rushing into his face. "There's a big serving spoon kind of thing over there in that drawer. Can you get it?"

I grabbed at the drawer handle, suddenly wanting to be a part of this effort. The drawer rattled as it opened. Inside there was the spoon, a long-handled fork, a spatula, a can opener. That was it.

He ladled the broth over the turkey for several minutes. It was amber in the low light of the single overhead bulb, a slippery mosaic of fat globules that quivered for not even a second before sliding off the crisping skin. Brian handed the ladle back to me, like a surgeon relieves himself of a scalpel to an assistant, shoved the whole pan back in, shut the door and reached to set the timer again. As he turned, he stopped short. I was standing right there, hadn't moved an inch. The ice settled with tiny plinks as it melted in the glasses.

He grinned at me and then reached over and rubbed the top of my head with his knuckles. I felt tingles run down my scalp and along the ridge of my shoulder blades.

"How's Andy," he asked and picked up the glasses to fill them with water.

"He's fine," I said. I didn't bring up Andy's quarterfinal fight in the Gloves, the decision that went the wrong way, in my opinion and that of the crowd's, who chanted bull*shit*, bull*shit* and stamped their feet, jeering and booing. It was so similar to the end of Brian's bid in the 1976 Gloves that I'd found myself just tired of the whole world of boxing. So much hype, so much hope, so many bad decisions. "Yeah, he's doing OK."

"Good." He gave me a glass of water and gestured with the one intended for Ti. "Too hot in here. Let's go in the living room."

As we walked back into the conversation, I felt as if I had turned the dial on a radio, tuned back into another station. Ti laughed loud and long at something Nora said and glanced up at Brian, "How's dinner, baby?"

"It's fine. Almost ready." He gave her the water and sat down in the easy chair next to her.

It was too late to go to Andy's that night after we left, and I really didn't mind. On the ride home I reached up to touch the spot where Brian rubbed my head and thought about how good the turkey tasted, even though he said it was a little dry.

Chapter Twenty-Eight

Everyone who knows me understands my determination. Even my girlfriend realizes how important it is to me. She knows I was boxing before I met her and she accepts the fact that I've got to keep on training if I'm going to make it as a fighter.

– Andy Schott, quoted by Mark Schwartz in
"Schott Does His Talking in the Ring,"
Middletown Sunday Record, May 6, 1979

There was my name, at the end of the ellipsis that connected me to the lead role, the beleaguered first-time teacher in *Up the Down Staircase*. I leaned my head against the glass display case in the front lobby of the high school and considered the call list. The other roles were filled with students who had many plays under their belts, some even in regional theater productions. How in the world did this happen? I had never been in the drama club before, had auditioned for a one-line part of an obnoxious student.

Andy stood next to me, and when he finished reading the list and the rehearsal schedule, he hugged me. "You better start learning those lines. There are a lot of 'em."

I couldn't sleep that night, not just for the thrill of getting the lead in the school play. How does one learn all those lines?

But I did. It was easy. For once, there was a script to follow, I knew just what I should say and do. I went to school, went to rehearsal and then went to work at the local Hallmark shop, sorting cards and ringing up purchases. Andy went to school, went to the gym, training hard for the Empire State Games, a path to the Nationals that would be held in May in Louisiana.

I loved going to rehearsal, even on days that I had no scenes to rehearse. The director was creative, adding dance and music in separate scenes that made us feel we were doing something unique. Andy and I watched the movie of *Up the Down Staircase*, with Sandy Dennis as first-time teacher Sylvia Barrett, delivering her lines with an overbite and a whine.

By April, Andy had won his way to a berth on the regional team headed to the Nationals in Louisiana. I was thrilled for him. And then we checked the dates. He would be gone ten days, if all went well. The first weekend of his trip was also that of my play, the second weekend was my junior prom.

I lay on his bed. "Shit!" I yelled. "This sucks!"

Andy looked at the calendar. "Hey, I can come to the Thursday night show. Opening night. That's good, right?"

"But I want you to come to the cast party at my house!" I grabbed at the calendar and examined it closely as if, somehow, we'd read it wrong. "And my prom. I'm not going to my prom."

Andy lay down on the bed with me and stared up at the slats of the top bunk. "I'm sorry about the cast party," he said. "But I'll see the play. As for the prom…" He hesitated. "You should go."

I snorted. No one went stag to a prom.

"No, really," he said. "You should go. Ask someone to go with you."

"That sucks!!" I yelled again. "I don't want to go with some-one else. I want to go with you."

Andy sighed. "All I am saying is go, ask someone else. Of course, I want to go with you, but I can't. Not if I am going all the way in the Nationals."

I was suddenly filled with dread. "Do you want me to go with someone else?"

"I thought I had taken care of all those insecurities," Andy said, smiling but with a bit of weariness. "No, I don't want you to go with someone else, but it seems selfish of me to say that you shouldn't go to your own junior prom. It'll be OK, really."

And so, we had a plan. Andy would come to see me per-form. Then, he would go to Louisiana while I was celebrating at the cast party. In Louisiana, Andy would knock out every opponent, win the Nationals as a middleweight and be right on track for the 1980 Olympics. And really, how did my prom compare to that dream? I would ask another boy to take me to the prom, explain the situation so that there was no misun-derstanding about the circumstances. I would go to the prom with this yet-to-be-named boy, have a reasonably good time, and most importantly, of course, avoid the slow dances. Then I would head home to bed, surely no later than midnight. Andy would come home the next day, victorious and inspired by my loyalty.

It was a good plan.

The high school auditorium was packed, compliments of a small town with little to do on a Thursday night. To be fair, the success of the previous year's production, *Bye Bye Birdie*, probably helped, too. We were just ninety miles from Broad-way and the locals took theater very seriously. I felt, as any actress should, as one with my character. Oh, the challenges she faced in inner city Calvin Coolidge High! Such poignant issues! Such brave efforts to change a system!

I got to say things like, "If you deny what you know, or what you are, or where you are, you deny the simplest part of being alive, and then you die."

Though I would never say this to members of my cast or to the director, I did relate to Sylvia Barrett and her confusion, her desire to help and fix. I was sure she was a middle child, too, with an older brother who was troubled and inaccessible, a family that was struggling to understand him. As Sylvia Barrett, I was the foil against which the humor and frustration played out. For most of the play I was just myself, letting the action and the characters swirl around me, thankful once again that there was a script and all I had to do was follow it. I even wore my own clothes, not a costume, as if my destiny was in my closet all along.

The night before we opened, I came home from dress rehearsal and found Brian sitting with my parents in the dining room. I was struck by how relaxed the three of them were. My parents watched him eat a bacon, lettuce and tomato sandwich and listened to him speak around the food in his mouth. He glanced up when I came in the room.

"Hey Jan." He reached for his glass of milk. "How goes it?"

"Hi honey," my mother said. "How was rehearsal?"

I sat down. "It was…good. I guess. There were some glitches, but Alice says that the dress rehearsal is bound to have glitches. Gets it out of our system for opening night."

"We're going tomorrow night," my father said to Brian. "Do you and Ti want to go with us?"

"Oh, well…" He studied a stray piece of lettuce on his plate and then popped it in his mouth. "I don't know if Ti has to work tomorrow night."

"Just come with us," my mother said. "Stop by after work and eat dinner with us and we'll all go together."

Brian stood up, plate in hand. "Yeah, yeah. That's cool. I'll just go out with you guys." He walked into the kitchen and slid the plate on the counter. "I gotta run. I'll see you tomorrow."

My mother leaned back in her chair to watch him head to the front door. "Come right after work, that'll give us plenty of time to eat. The show starts at seven."

"Sure, sure," Brian's voice lingered behind him as he went out the door.

I toyed with one of the placemats on the dining room table, rolling the coarse fringe between my thumb and forefinger. "Do you think he'll really come?"

My mother frowned. "He said he would, didn't he?"

Alice was right about opening night, most of the glitches from the night before were resolved. The cast was giddy backstage as the momentum built through the night, and it seemed everything would fall right into place. We heard laughter where we expected it and an attentive hush during the poignant scenes. The added dance and music received enthusiastic applause. In Act II, I walked out into the staged classroom and found that someone had scribbled "Clapton is God" in large white chalk letters on the blackboard. I stopped for a moment—Shit, what do I do now? This isn't part of the script—then walked to the board and erased the offending statement as I sighed and shook my head. My finest acting moment.

I saw Andy first thing when I came out of the dressing rooms. He leaned against the wall, and behind him I could see my parents and Nora, and beyond them, my employers from the Hallmark shop where I worked.

Andy grinned and hugged me tight. "I was so glad you didn't trip up there."

"Thanks for noticing my finer points."

"Naw, really, you did such a good job. My parents are waiting for me so I gotta go, but I'll call you tomorrow. Try and remember all the nice things people say and tell me about them!" He slipped a card into my hand and made way for my mother and father. "Don't read that until tomorrow!" Then he was gone.

My father handed me a bouquet of iris and yellow daffodils that he had been holding down at his side like a newspaper. My mother kissed my cheek.

"That was so great," she said.

"Very good," my father said in his formal coach voice. "That was very good."

He eyed the line of friends who were waiting respectfully to talk with me. "I guess we better get going, let you speak to your friends."

"Fans," my mother said. "We'll just wait outside in the car. Take your time."

I could have just left it at that, could have just lost myself to more congratulations from my friends. But I had to ask. "Hey Mom," I called. She turned, her face bright and smiling. "Where's Brian?"

Her face lost its sparkle. "Oh, well, you know, he never made it to the house. We waited, called the apartment, but he must have had to work late. I'm sorry, honey."

I waved her on. "It's OK. See you later."

She turned then, hurried to catch up with my father and sister, and I regretted asking.

I read Andy's card as soon as I got home and wondered how I'd gotten so lucky.

> First of all, I loved your play. You made me sooooo... proud.
>
> Well, now that it's too late to back out you want to know what I really think of you going to the prom with someone else? *@#**! No, nay, wrong. I am only joking. I really am glad you are going, I wouldn't have said to go if I wasn't. I can't impress upon you more my loyalty... I feel funny

leaving now… First, I'm gonna miss a lot of excitement that's gonna fill your life. Second, I feel this is a time in your life that will never return, a very memorable time, and I won't be a part of it. I want you to remember everything so when I get back you can tell me lots of good stuff. I can share the good times with you, a least a tiny bit.

Love you, Andy "The Cat"

I accepted the phone charges from Louisiana with relief. I was at home all that Sunday, waiting for the call, exhausted from the weekend drama, on and off the stage.

"Hey," Andy said. "How did the cast party go?"

I told him about the band setting up in my parent's living room, the parody re-enactments from the show, how I cried at the end. "How is it down there?"

"Good," Andy said. "Let's see, I have a cool roommate, Andre. He's a light heavy. I'm learning when to say y'all. I tried grits after saying no a hundred times. I was right. They're disgusting. And I have a little problem. I get five dollars a day for food."

"Five dollars?" At that point, Andy ate four or five times a day, burning through calories before he even swallowed them. "Call your parents. Call Floyd."

Andy sounded patient as he told me it wasn't Floyd's responsibility, that he wasn't even Andy's trainer because he was on the regional team. And that money from his parents wouldn't arrive before his first fight. "Don't worry," he said. "I got a plan. I met this girl from the kitchen, and she said I could peel some potatoes to earn some money."

"Peel potatoes," I said. "That's ridiculous."

And later, when I told my mother about it she said the same thing and added, "Floyd needs to do something. Why didn't he go down too? He certainly has the money to pay his way."

"I don't know," I said. "Andy's first fight is tomorrow. Maybe Floyd'll go down later in the week."

In school on Monday, I enjoyed the last of the attention from the play. The school newspaper said that I played the part of Sylvia with "caring and sensitivity," that I did "an excellent job with a complicated role." Friends stopped me in the hall to congratulate me. I sucked it all up like a greedy vacuum cleaner, used the crevice tool to get every particle. That afternoon I drove to a mall across the river to buy a pair of shoes for the prom. They needed to be high enough so that I wouldn't have to hem my dress but not too high that I would be taller than my date.

My date. Todd. After much thought and checking in with Andy, I asked Todd. He was in the school play with me, as one of the class members who constantly cut up. He was a dreamy sort, handsome, with deep brown skin, who wrote poetry along the soles of his sneakers with permanent marker. He didn't have a girlfriend, though there were several girls who followed him around much like disciples. Indeed, he seemed a bit above the usual high school romance scene, as if he had higher ideals. He was a sensuous boy, given to hugs and lying with his head in the lap of his friends. I thought he would be perfect. He would get the unconventional aspect of all of this, understand that I was asking for company only, and he was sort of a friend of Andy's. Sort of.

But he was also only slightly taller than me. I finally found a pair of sandals that I liked. They seemed a bit high but maybe not. Todd is a secure enough guy, I decided, he never cares what people think.

At the same time I worried over footwear in New York, I later learned, Andy climbed into the ring as his regional coach held the ropes wide for him in Louisiana. The crowd was light at the bouts that afternoon; it was early in the tournament. His opponent was nothing special, a boy from a small club somewhere in Tennessee, Len Boyd. He was a young white boy, a southpaw, already in the ring.

After the first round, Andy went back to his corner confident that he had won. He spit his mouth guard into the palm of his second, a member of his corner team, and listened to the trainer say all the usual things about southpaws. He nodded to let the trainer know he heard the instructions, took a last gulp of water, sucked the rinsed mouth guard back in and went back in for round 2. It was close at the end, and Andy hated the feeling that he didn't know if he had won it. Back in his corner, his trainer said that he had. Andy shook his head, felt suddenly very tired. There he was, after all those years of training, all those other fights and finally at the Nationals. Just two minutes left to keep it all moving forward.

The phone rang as I appraised the sandals with the prom dress in the full-length mirror in my parent's room. I clomped as fast as I could down the hall to the kitchen and grabbed the receiver before my mother could reach it.

"I accept," I said as soon as I picked up. I could hear Andy laugh as the operator stuttered, "Ma'am, I have a collect call from Andrew Schott. Do you accept?"

"Yes, yes," I said. "I accept."

"Little anxious to get my call, huh?" Andy said.

"Of course," I said. "How did it go?"

"I lost."

I didn't believe him. "Yeah, yeah."

"No really," he said. "I lost. It was a split decision. I could have fought better. He deserved to win. I was so tired by the end of the third round. It just wasn't my day."

"You didn't have enough to eat."

"Yeah, well, that's not it. It's OK. I'll be home soon as I can catch a ride. I'll call you when I get in."

I had no idea what to say. I leaned into the silence for a long moment. Finally, feeling foolish, I said, "Andy, I'm so sorry. So sorry."

"Yeah, well, I'm gonna go. I'll see you in a few days."

I sat down on the kitchen stool and cried.

My mother, who was cooking dinner, took the cue and shook her head. "Floyd does it again. He should have gone down there."

I ignored her, went into my room and closed the door. I didn't want to consider Floyd at that moment. Brian stopped by later that evening. I heard him mixing some chocolate milk in the kitchen. I hadn't seen him all weekend, not at any of my shows or at the house. In the face of Andy's news, though, my annoyance with him seemed petty. I opened my door. "Andy lost."

Brian turned, surprised. "Lost? How?"

"Split decision," I said.

Brian whistled faintly through his teeth, a habit of his when he was truly taken off guard by something. "Damn. I just thought he'd make it."

I saw the genuine dismay in his face. I could almost forgive him for not coming to my play. He finished stirring his milk, and then looked up at me again. "Tell him he'll make it. It's just a setback."

By morning, I had a more cheering thought. Perhaps now Andy could go with me to my prom. That day I watched Todd talking with some friends in the cafeteria. I kept thinking, now, now, just tell him. But I didn't. He was doing me a favor. How could I tell him I didn't want him to go? But surely, a girl with a boyfriend who wrote such a sweet letter, who was so supportive and constant, would do that in his time of need. Later, when I talked to my mother about it, she was unsympathetic to my anguish. "You invited Todd. He's probably rented a tux. You can't uninvite him."

When Andy arrived home from Louisiana, he agreed with my mother. "It's OK. It's really OK." We sat on his bottom bunk, our backs against the rough wood wall. It was the place we had all our serious talks. I stared at the calendar, where the week was circled, "Nationals" written across it in red, and then in smaller print, "Janet's prom" on the Saturday square.

I suddenly felt ridiculous. He just lost the Nationals for heaven's sake. Why was I bothering him with this? When I said this out loud, he answered, "You're probably more disappointed about the fight than I am." I knew that wasn't true.

I had to work on the day of the prom, selling pecan clusters and birthday cards until 4:00. My boss looked at me around 2:30 and said," What's the matter? You seem so sad."

"It's my prom tonight," I said.

"Why didn't you tell me?" she exclaimed. "I would have given you the afternoon off to get ready."

"It's OK," I said. "I'll have plenty of time."

"No, no, go home right now. I know how fun it is to get dressed up and ready for your prom. It's a big deal!"

I went home and called Andy. "I don't want to go."

"C'mon," he said. "It'll be fun. You'll see me tomorrow. Say hey to Todd for me."

It was the prom after all, with goofy dresses and the theme of "Imagine," which seemed a bit of a down song for a prom but did make for a good slow dance. Which I danced to with Todd, despite previous resolutions. And afterwards, at a prom party, surrounded by couples who were gazing into each other's eyes, there was the kiss that didn't seem out of place at all. But of course, it was. And so was the second.

Then, of course, there was that conversation the next day with Andy, when I tried to explain what neither he nor I could understand. And, of course, the follow-up talk, when he seemed mostly sad, not cold, but still distant. Followed by a note. About how he felt, at first, that the ties between us had been cut. That I'd just become a girl. The magic between us was gone. But as we talked, he'd started to feel unreasonable, started to see things in a different way. "For putting you through that, I am sorry," Andy wrote. "Now it seems as though the ties are mending, and maybe they'll be stronger now. I hope you feel better. I'm sorry I put you through such a tough time."

I felt out of breath from barely escaping my own misadventure and disloyalty, sure that I didn't deserve Andy's loyalty. I was no longer Sylvia Barrett from *Up the Down Staircase*, wise and just, but one of those capricious and thoughtless students. And I didn't have a script anymore to tell me my motivations or what to say.

In the middle of all of this, Brian came back to our house carrying a gym bag filled with dirty laundry. He told my mother that he and Ti were fighting a lot, that she kicked him out of the apartment. They could work this out, he said. Just had to give it a little time. Then he dumped his laundry in the hamper and went to lie down in his old room. He stayed there for two days, coming upstairs to get food and watch late-night TV. With everything happening with Andy, I hadn't paid much attention to any of this. Now, I could take a breath and wonder what was going on with Brian and Ti, just for a moment.

It didn't take long to find out. Light beams swung across the walls of my room as a car came down the hill and turned into our drive. One car door opened and then slammed shut. I heard Brian pound up the slate sidewalk and bang into the house. The screech of the kitchen stool as he sat down heavily sounded like a miniature car crash. His breathing was raspy yet soft and seemed to waft under the door to my room like smoke. I got up and cracked the door open to peer through the gloom. I could see Brian with his head down on his arms as they rested on the counter. His shoulders moved slightly as if he were crying. I closed the door and got back in bed. Sometime later, I heard him dial the phone and then a murmuring that rose and fell.

"I love you." Brian was suddenly loud and his words too carefully enunciated. "Just remember that while you are thinking about things."

I tried to stay attentive to the quiet that stretched from that point and finally dozed. Was it the sound of the pills on the counter that roused me again? The running of the tap water into a glass? Later, I wondered why I didn't get out of bed, run out and confront him, stop him before he got any of them in his mouth. But I was caught in a strange feeling that was equal parts disbelief, frustration, fear. When I did get out of bed, I walked right by him as he swallowed what I hoped was his first handful of… what? Sleeping pills, antihistamines, aspirin? I didn't know.

I opened my parent's door. "Brian just had a fight on the phone with Ti, and then I heard him dumping out a bunch of pills. He's taking them right now." I didn't consciously keep my voice calm—it just was, as if I were reporting that I'd finished my chores. I went back to the kitchen. Brian sat on the stool, empty pill bottles next to him. He didn't look up as I reached around him for the phone but turned his head slightly to watch me dial 911. He said nothing as he listened to me make the call, and nothing after. By the time we heard the sirens, Brian was slumped back against the wall, head resting at a slight angle, eyes half closed and shaking his head yes or no to my parent's shrill questioning. I opened the door to the

EMTs. Their official bustling and frank voices were reassuring and jarring at the same time.

Brian refused to go in the ambulance, shrugged off attempts by the EMTs to put a blood pressure monitor on him, swatted away the stethoscope that wavered above his chest. "Get your goddamn hands off of me," he snapped, and threw his arm backward, causing one of the rescue squad crew to stumble a bit. And because I was the one to set this all in motion, I cringed and felt responsible as I put out a hand to steady him.

The EMT I didn't know, a lovely woman who called Brian "honey" and "dear heart," told us they couldn't force him to go into the ambulance. She checked the bottles that Brian had emptied, felt pretty sure that the dose or combination wasn't lethal, though the fact that he had been drinking was a complicating one. "Don't let him sleep," she said. "Make him walk around, drink lots of water."

And so, we took turns, my mother, my father and I. Sometimes it took two of us to hold him upright. He didn't resist. He let himself be led back to life, muttering that he was nobody's honey and who did she think she was calling him dear heart? During those slow orbits of the living room with him, I remembered a day, not that long before, when I was so frustrated and angry about Brian that I'd told my mom that sometimes I just wished he were dead and felt immediately ashamed. To my surprise, she had nodded. Maybe because she knew I just wanted the pain to stop. For all of us. Now, walking with him, taking his arm again and again after he would shake my hand off, I forgave myself, finally. Because I so wanted him to live, no matter what.

At 7:00 in the morning, I said, "I'm going to take a shower so I can catch the bus."

My mother looked surprised. Brian sat on the couch, staring into space, hands loosely joined in his lap. She sat next to him. "You don't have to go in right now or at all if you don't want."

I nodded. "I want to. I have some things to turn in."

I found Andy pulling notebooks out of his locker and put my arms around his waist, leaned my head against his back.

"Hey!" He turned around. I kept my head down, leaned it into his chest. "What's wrong?"

I told it all to his solar plexus, as if wanting it to go straight to his heart. He kissed the top of my head, and I leaned against him and closed my eyes, so very, very tired.

Chapter Twenty-Nine

[1979]

Andy's birthday was in August, which made him a Leo. Perfect for a fighter with the ring name, The Cat. I headed downtown to Manny's Art and Supply store. It was a space that was devoted to art, not to shoppers. I squeezed through the aisles, finding the large sheets of cream-colored paper, the silver clasping rings, the stiff cardboard that I needed to make the cover for a scrapbook.

I'd made one for Brian years before as a birthday present, decoupaging the cover with photos of him cut from the papers. The paste mix had soaked through the clippings, ruining them. No reassurance from my mom could convince me to give it to him. This time, I decided, I would avoid the decoupage idea and just use burlap on the cover, use a permanent marker to draw a picture of a cat.

I made my purchases and started the walk back home, the big bag slapping at my legs, the crumpled edges at the top getting moist with sweat in the late July heat. I wished I had borrowed my mother's car.

P&G's, just a couple doors up from Manny's, was a local bar and hangout that had been around for decades. The wooden tables were carved so deeply with the names of lovers and the musings of barley and malt philosophers that glasses no longer had an even surface to perch on. I glanced through the windows and saw Brian sitting at the end of the bar. I walked on to the corner and stood there, adrenalin now heating my face far more than the sun. Someone muttered, "'scuse me," and stepped around me to cross the street. I watched the sneakered feet move by, unable to lift my eyes or say anything.

Brian was once again living with Ti, their reconciliation a quiet and private process after the public trauma of their breakup. Things seemed to be going OK in the months since Brian's suicide attempt, though it felt as if we were all holding a collective breath, waiting to see what would happen. Why wasn't he at work? I wondered. I turned and faced P&G's again. From this angle the windows were dark. I suddenly doubted myself. Maybe it wasn't him, I thought. I shifted the bag to the other hand and remembered where I was headed. It wasn't him, I decided, and turned around again, checked the traffic and crossed the street. At home, I didn't mention anything to my mother, headed straight to my room and put Brian out of my head.

That summer before my senior year, my family again went to the outer banks of North Carolina for vacation, this time without Brian and with an anxiety about what might happen in our absence.

We swung west into the middle of the state to Chapel Hill, to see the state university. In addition to the good creative writing program, which was my interest, my mother had gotten a graduate degree at the School of Public Health, back in the late 1940s. With the brick walks and old ivy-covered buildings, it just looked like the college I'd always assumed I'd attend. I decided then and there that this was the place for me. But I was an out-of-state student and getting in would be difficult. Even more reason to be perfect.

"Where else would you want to go?" Andy asked after listening to me talk about the campus when we got back. He had just graduated in June and was dedicated to training full time.

"I don't really want to go anywhere else," I said. "My dad wants me to look at the SUNY schools, and I guess I could. But I am not going to New Paltz."

Andy nodded, but not with agreement. "What if you don't get in down there?"

"I'm gonna apply for early acceptance. If I don't get in, I'll go to plan B," I said.

"You'll get in," Andy said quietly.

I shrugged. "I hope so."

That fall, I was in every advanced placement class the high school offered, took Spanish classes at the college three days a week, and was one of twelve seniors to enroll in a college freshman English class through Syracuse University that was held at our high school. It was all necessary, I thought. All I had to do was stay the course, make my parents proud, or, at least, not upset.

But inside I was slipping, down what slope and toward what end I didn't know. Panic and anxiety made me stop still for long moments in the hallways at school. Sometimes, I lay my head against the cool metal of my locker between classes and stayed there until the bell rang and I was late to my next class. This wasn't unnoticed by some of the adults at school, a couple who would invite me to eat lunch with them and then ask questions which had answers I couldn't share, not if I didn't want them to call my parents.

I felt like my life was split in two. On the outside, I was the straight-A high school student. At home as I set the table I would casually say to my mother, "Aced that physics test," or, "Ms. Evans said she had never seen an essay so well written." I told her stories about school to make her laugh, to reassure her that I was a good kid.

And, really, I was. Good at all the things I knew my parents wanted to see. Thanks to Andy, I didn't drink or smoke pot. I was president of the drama club, after my quick rise to local stardom with *Up the Down Staircase*. I raised money for the wrestling team, covered their matches for the local newspaper. My employers at the Hallmark shop adored me because I could charm customers with a perkiness I didn't feel inside.

I didn't know what to do for myself, but I had a list of things in my head that Andy would do if he really loved me. I demanded them of him before he could have a chance to even learn what they were and then was unsatisfied with anything he did.

I was jealous, that black-hole kind of jealousy where reassurance is insulting and denial is confirmation. I threw accusations about wildly, sometimes accompanied by objects. Once it was a giant lollipop, swirled with orange and blue and red. It was just the first thing I picked up during an argument with Andy in my kitchen, when I was at home with Nora. Maybe she'd brought it home and left it on the counter, still wrapped in cellophane. It had surprising heft, and I hurled it as I might have thrown an ax, with poor aim but great energy. It smashed against the wall and fell to the floor, small pieces of candy scattered from the wrapping. Andy regarded the mess for a moment, probably wishing he hadn't been late, or that he hadn't told me that he'd gone bowling with his friend Billy and a couple of younger high school girls. He bent to pick up the pieces, and I said, "Leave it. Just leave. Just leave."

I didn't mean it.

But I was too confused by my own actions to explain them to him. Instead, I went into the living room and turned on the television. After a moment or two, I heard the front door open and close. When I finally returned to the kitchen hours later, I found that the tiny pieces of lollipop were stuck to the linoleum. And they wouldn't sweep up. I filled a bucket with water hot enough to turn my hands red and then got down on my knees and scrubbed.

When I got my acceptance letter to UNC in early November, I let the letter sit on my bed without even mentioning it to my parents, sat through a dinner with them without saying a word. Didn't call Andy.

"Well... I am really proud of you," Andy said when I saw him next. "You'll have to practice your drawl so you can be a proper southern belle."

"I guess."

Andy sounded puzzled. "You've wanted this for a long time. You don't seem very excited."

"Oh, well, I am. It's a lot to digest," I lied to cover up a truth I couldn't discern.

My mother actually clapped her hands together when I told her. "I knew you would get in. That is just wonderful."

I went to find my father in front of the television. He smiled up at me. "That's great, Jan, just great."

Chapter Thirty

For Christmas, I gave Andy a boxing robe, black satin, trimmed with white, The Cat stitched prominently across the back. I drove to Kingston with my father to order it from a sporting goods store, plunking down the equivalent of over thirty hours of card sorting. Andy gave me a guinea pig, after listening to my story about losing a whole family of them to heat stroke when I was seven or eight, how Brian had helped me to bury them. It was cute, but I'd forgotten how much they squeal and poop. And it wasn't a ring, which I felt embarrassed to want.

On New Year's Eve, Andy and I ate dinner at a restaurant downtown and then went back to his house. Sitting on the couch in his family room, I thought about the year before and our shy distance in the beginning of the evening. This year, though we sat close and watched television to see the ball drop in Times Square, I felt uneasy.

"So, what do you see for this year?"

"What?" Andy leaned his head against mine. "I didn't hear you."

I got up, turned off the TV and came back, nestling in under his arm. "This year. What do you hope happens?"

He looked a bit puzzled and then said slowly, "It's pretty obvious. Gloves, Nationals, Olympic Trials..." He ticked them off on his fingers. This wasn't news to me. This had always been the plan.

"Is that it?"

He got restless then, shifting his shoulder so that I had to straighten up. "That's a lot, don't you think?"

"What about us?"

He sighed. "What about us? I don't know. You tell me. You're going to North Carolina in eight months. Who knows?"

It wasn't the answer I wanted, and he knew it. He got up. "Hey, come into my room, I have something for you."

It was a pair of earrings, lovely and glittering in the low light of the bedside lamp. Without saying anything, I exchanged them for the earrings I was wearing and shook my head to feel them hit against the side of my neck. Carefully, I put the lid on the box and sat down next to Andy.

"They look good on you." Andy pulled me back so that I would lay down with him.

"Thank you." I was unable to bring any sincerity to it. "They're really beautiful."

"What's the matter?"

"Nothing," I said. "Hey, what do you want to do tomorrow?" One more day before school started again for me.

"Have to train."

"All day? Can't you just take the day off?"

"No, can't take the day off. The Gloves are just like three, four weeks away."

I felt bad. "I know." And I did, knew that this year was the one he had been working toward since he was thirteen. The Olympics. It was all or nothing now. I shifted so that my back was to Andy and put my hands under my head, felt the earring there press on my fingers. I waited for him for to say, "But I can spend the morning with you," or maybe, "Later in the afternoon we can go to a movie."

"What's the matter?" Andy lifted himself up on one elbow and leaned over to see my face.

I turned it away. "Nothing. I'm not feeling very well."

Andy was quiet for a moment, assessing. Finally, he said it again, with less concern. "What's the matter?"

"My stomach. Just my stomach. It just feels weird."

He lay back down. "Oh."

"I just want to go to sleep."

The next morning, when I woke up, the sun was full on into those big windows, and my heart thudded a bit as if I had slept for days and missed a math test or something. I heard someone turning off the shower in the bathroom down the hall. A moment later, the door to his room opened, and Andy stepped quietly into the room. "You took a shower already?"

"Yep," he said cheerfully as he pulled a clean T-shirt from a pile on a chair. "In fact, sleeping beauty, I have already run to the gym, worked out, and sparred with Dorsey. Gave him a bloody nose by the way." He chuckled. "So now I am back here, with you. To spend the day. What do you want to do?"

"I don't know," I said.

Andy sat down next to me. "Hey, how is your stomach?"

"Stomach?" I thought back to the night before. It really had been queasy. I wriggled a bit. "I think it's fine."

Later that January, I was scheduled to cover a wrestling match for the local paper. It was the one Friday night I had off from the Hallmark shop in months, and I'd accepted the stringer assignment for the local paper, thinking that Andy would go with me. We were both so busy, me with work and school, him with training and work, that we saw each other only a couple of times a week, if that. Andy's first fight in the Gloves was just days away. I called him after I got home from school.

His mother answered the phone. "He's at the gym. He should be home pretty soon."

But he didn't call back by supper and I tried again.

"Just a minute," his father said. "Let me check, I just got home. Andrew!"

I heard his mother in the background. "He's not back yet from the gym."

"Sorry," his dad said. "He should be back soon."

"That's OK. Just tell him to call me."

"Will do!"

Before we hung up, I asked about a ride to Andy's first fight in the Gloves the next week, only to hear that his parents couldn't make it but would be happy to take me to the next one.

Andy called just as I was getting ready to ask my mother if I could borrow the car to get out to the high school.

"What's up?" he asked. It was his usual greeting and wasn't a real question, but that night I heard it as one.

"The meet! You said you'd go with me. I gotta be out there."

His voice lost its friendliness. "The meet doesn't start until seven."

"But I have to be there early so I can get the names of the other team and…" I looked at the clock. Really, I had plenty of time, but I was annoyed that Andy was pushing it. "If you don't want to go, then don't. Just make up your mind so I can ask my parents about the car."

"OK. I have made up my mind. I'm not going."

"What?"

"I'm not going."

"Why not?"

"Because I was gonna go, had planned to go but you make everything so difficult."

"What do you mean I make everything so difficult? What are you talking about?"

"You knew I was at the gym. I just didn't get home when you thought I should get home. But I can look at a clock. I knew I had time and we do. And…my dad said you were asking about a ride down to the city for the fight."

"So? They're not going anyway. I'll just ask Billy. You said he might be going."

"Yeah, well, it's always such a big procedure with you. It's a hassle. I don't care if Billy goes. But with you it's just a hassle. I don't want to deal with it."

I couldn't believe this. "Why…Why is it a hassle?"

He was quiet for a moment, as if surprised by everything he had said. "Well," he said slowly. "It used to be that when I did things for you, you were happy and surprised. Now it's like you expect things, like I have things I have to do, and it just makes me not want to do them. Nothing is ever good enough."

"But it is, good enough. I mean…" I leaned my head against the wall, the phone cord wound tight around my wrist. "I can't believe you don't want me to go to the fight."

"It's just that you make a big deal of it, right when I need to focus the most."

"But I won't."

"Look," Andy said. "I'm really tired. Just go to the meet and call me later."

"OK," I said and saw that now I really was late. At the meet, I was too preoccupied to take good notes and asked the scorekeeper for the score books at the end of the evening just to make sure I got my facts straight. Even as I regarded the scribbles that would tell me who had the takedown or the reversal, my mind was on Andy's voice in my head: but with you it's just a hassle.

I called him when I got home. His voice sounded sleepy and gentle. "Hey!"

I was relieved. "I'm sorry. Sorry if I do those things, expect too much."

"It's OK. I'm sorry I got so… stubborn, upset. I do feel like that, though, that I am always guessing what it is I am supposed to do."

"Then tell me when you notice it because I don't," I said. "I don't mean to do that." But I knew he was right, and worse, that sometimes I did notice, did mean to do it.

"OK," he said. "How was the meet?"

"We won." I was distracted by unfinished business. "So, do you think Billy would give me a ride to the Gloves? I mean, do you want me to go?"

The silence stretched long and thin. Finally, he said, "Look, come down later, after I win a couple."

"You don't want me to go," I said.

"No," he said. "I don't want you to go."

The night before the fight I ate dinner at Andy's, and we hung out for a bit in his family room. We didn't talk about the fight. I didn't mention that I had avoided Billy at school, thinking he must know that Andy didn't want me to go. Once, when I saw him at the far end of the hall, I thought, "I know more about boxing than he does! I've been watching boxing since I was eleven, for God's sake!" and then shoved my books into my locker so furiously that they fell back out into my arms. But I was calm with Andy. I had thought about bringing him something, a card, a talisman for good luck. I didn't.

He walked me to the door at the end of the evening.

"Well," I said. "Good luck."

He sighed, pulled me close into him and kissed my forehead. "I'll call you after, OK?"

"OK." All of my disappointment and humiliation left me, draining as quickly and completely as if I just pulled the plug on it. There was no peaceful moment though. Right behind it came the other very familiar feeling of anxiety about the outcome of the fight. As I drove home, I thought, It's just the first fight. Don't get so worked up.

My father was the one who answered the phone the next night, and he glanced at me as I came to stand in the doorway from my room into the kitchen. "Yeah, yeah, I'll accept the charges." A pause. "How'd you do?" He looked down at the counter as he listened. "Well, I'm sorry, Andy. There'll be other fights. Janet's right here; I think she wants to talk with you."

I felt as if I were in seventh grade again, listening to my father take the call from Floyd about Brian. I didn't want to talk with Andy. If I didn't talk with him, I wouldn't know, and it wouldn't be true. My father handed me the phone and left the kitchen. "Hey," I said. "What happened?"

Andy's voice was low. "It was a good fight. I thought I won it. The crowd thought I won it."

"Who did you fight?"

Andy laughed without humor. "This guy Mike Martinez who is probably one of the best in the city. I'm not sure why they paired us up right out of the gate. Usually, the best fighters meet toward the end of the tournament."

"I know," I said. I thought about all the favoritism and the politics that were behind the Gloves. "Maybe they just wanted to get Floyd's guys out of there early."

"They took a big chance then."

"Yeah, they did. Are you hurt?"

"Nah, well, I have some swelling around my eye. But it's OK."

"I'm really sorry, Andy." I wished I knew what else to say.

"Yeah, well, so am I. Be glad you didn't come. You woulda been really mad about the decision. You know how it is."

"Yeah, well, I am mad." But I wasn't. I was just tired and sad and not quite believing.

"OK," Andy said. "I'm gonna ride home with Billy. I'll call you tomorrow."

I called him from school the next day. His voice was still low and strained. "I'm just hanging out," he said when I asked him what he was doing.

"Should I come see you later?"

"That would be good." There was no change in his tone.

"I saw the newspaper this morning. It said you were robbed. You didn't tell me it was a split decision."

"You know, when I was at the diner with Billy last night it really hit me. None of that mattered. I lost. I was the loser. 'Should have won' doesn't really matter. Doesn't really matter what people say. I lost."

I'd never heard this flatness in Andy's voice before, and I searched for the right words. I thought about all the hours and hours of training, the notebooks where he tracked it all, the confidence he had as he came into the new year. This was supposed to be his year. It wasn't just a loss. It essentially took him off the entire Olympic track. I could feel the weight of his disappointment in my chest, and for a moment it was hard to breathe. "Well," I said. "I'll see you this afternoon."

Sometime in the following weeks, Andy came home from the gym feeling extra tired, a bit feverish. He woke up the next day with chicken pox. I had them as a child, didn't remember it very well and was unprepared for how sick he was, how completely listless. But as the pox disappeared, his good humor re-emerged and so did his optimism. I felt as if we had been in the murky depths together, and now, he was swimming strongly up and to the surface. As much as I wanted to, I couldn't follow, as if my legs were wrapped in seaweed and I couldn't kick free.

Chapter Thirty-One

Funny how
in this civilized
intellectually and
emotionally
oriented society,
it is physical pain—
the primitive irritation
of nerve cells
that is finally
the only acknowledgment
of being real.

– Janet Hurley, February 1980

"I didn't do a great job of wrapping." Andy placed the package on my lap. We sat on the couch in his family room on our second Valentine's Day together. It followed weeks of arguments, most at my provocation, with long discussions and letters between us filling the time we should have just been having teenage fun. So, I was surprised, on Valentine's Day, when Andy handed me the package.

Two boxes of cracker jacks. Ah. I shook them, close to my ear, played along. "What could be in there?"

He shrugged and pointed. "You have to open them in order." I saw the one and the two in permanent marker on the side of the boxes. "You have to eat the cracker jacks to find out what's there."

I laughed and thought, Everything must be OK. It's gonna be OK.

My tongue was gluey with caramel by the time I finished. Box 1 gave up a small plastic monkey riding a bicycle. Box 2 harbored something wrapped in masking tape. A ring. It was simple, a gold band with an opal. I slipped it on and looked up at Andy to find him studying me. He reached over and turned my hand, palm up. "What's this?" he pointed to the scabby red line that edged out from under my watchband.

On the other wrist, I wore a thick leather bracelet to hide the scar there. I snatched my hand away. "It's nothing," I said. "Thank you for the ring. It's beautiful."

"It doesn't look like nothing."

"I'm fine." I was embarrassed. "Just believe me. I'm fine."

How could I explain? The first time I cut my wrists, it just happened. I'd opened a drawer in the bathroom to search for a hairclip and saw a gleam under the hairbrushes. Why the manicure scissors caught my eye on that particular day, I don't know. I felt more curious than resolute as I put a blade to my left wrist and pressed a preliminary line across the blue criss-cross there. I must have known this would be ineffective, but it served some purpose, a calmness, for just a moment. A small beading of blood made me hastily wipe the scissors on my pants and tuck them away in the drawer. I washed my wrist, and the blood barely tinged the water as it swirled away down the drain. I kept the cuff on my shirt down for the next few days so that no one could see the welts. And then, whenever I wielded the scissors, I used my watch and bracelets.

Andy didn't believe I was fine. He checked my wrists every time he saw me, and for a while, the lines faded before my compulsion led me to the bathroom drawer again.

"I'm worried about you," Andy wrote in a card that he left in my room one evening. "I worry about how you drive too fast, and the scars and I don't know what to do. It seems like stuff that Brian would do and that isn't like you. But I am here for you. Whatever it is, I am here for you, right behind you."

At the very least, I found myself thinking, he worries about me. And then I would look at my ring, my sweet opal ring, and feel the enormity of my depression, need and insecurity.

I told my parents nothing. I didn't want to be like Brian, who called on them to bail him out of everything. I would handle this, I said to myself, they didn't need to worry about me. So I told my parents nothing. And neither did Andy, though one time he came to my house with my best friend Brenda, and they tried to talk with me, asked me to tell my parents. I remember being furious with them both, feeling excluded from their banding together, saw them exchange glances with each other that seemed to me to say, I told you so. I told them to leave. Which they did. Which tripped me from anger to despair.

I entered the contest, as did every other student in Mr. Masson's poetry class. He probably intended for this assignment to motivate us to write and rewrite. In the end, however, I sent in the poem I wrote for Brian after his accident. I was completely surprised by the award when Mr. Masson congratulated me at school. The County Arts Council, sponsor of the contest, hosted a reception for the winners at the same local community college that Brian had intermittently attended over the years.

That evening, as I set the table I said, "I won a county award for a poem."

My mother turned from the oven where she was checking the broiled chicken breasts. "That's great! What poem? I didn't know you had entered a contest."

I shrugged. "It was something we were supposed to do for class. Enter a poem. No big deal."

She shook her head and closed the oven door. "It is a big deal. What poem?"

"Just a poem," I said. She raised her eyebrows at me.

Unexpectedly, I wanted her approval for something besides doing well in school, for not drinking or smoking pot or not getting pregnant. Approval for the one thing I felt sure about. "OK, I'll get it for you." As I went into my room, I said over my shoulder, "The award ceremony is Sunday." I came back in the kitchen, handed the sheet of paper to her, and began rummaging noisily for forks and knives.

"An award ceremony and everything. How fun!" my mother said. "Sunday is so soon. Do you know where it will be?" She glanced down at the paper and read the title, "For My Brother." She fell silent then. I could see the words in my head as she read them.

Before I could finish the poem in my head, my mother looked up at me, her eyes filled with tears. She blew her nose three times. "You should show this to Brian."

"No."

"Why not?"

"Just don't want to."

She studied me for a moment. "It would do him good, I think, to know how much you care."

"I wrote this five years ago," I said.

"But you still care."

I chose to go to the award ceremony alone.

As I rounded one of the last inclining curves that led to the community college, I had a feeling of regret so intense I pulled off on the shoulder of the road and found my breath coming in short and quick bursts. Why did I want to come alone? It had seemed imperative just hours ago. Now I couldn't get that image of the hurt on my mother's face out of my mind when

I'd told her. She'd covered well, but it was there, a crinkling around her mouth and eyes. I had the impulse to turn the car around and go get her. Then I thought, I'll call from the college and ask her to come. But there were only minutes before the ceremony. The community college was forty minutes from our house. Either plan was pointless. In the end, I drove on, parked and joined the stream of other award winners and their families going inside the cafeteria.

The ceremony lasted longer than I thought it would. I didn't have much time left before I had to return the car, so I drove back to New Paltz in a hurry to get to Andy's house. I took the road that followed the river, a winding rural highway that also ran parallel to the mountains. I let my foot sink down on the accelerator, leaned into the curves and then felt the two wheels on the right side of the car lift, just for a breath, just for a small slurping moment in my stomach and a buzz of adrenalin that made my hands tighten on the wheel. I slowed down, until I saw the next curve approaching. This time, I couldn't keep myself in the right lane as I went around, came close to the edge of the road on the other side, thought for a moment I would go off and then corrected. I slowed down again. I promised myself that I wouldn't do it again, and as the next curve approached, I kept my speed exactly at the speed limit, expecting at any moment for my foot to press down in uncontrollable impulse. But it didn't, and I felt an enormous sense of relief at the knowledge that I did, truly, have some authority. Sometimes.

When I got to Andy's, he was outside playing tug of war with Kayo. The hair that often fell over his forehead and into his eyes was pushed back and dark with sweat though the end of the day was cool. From his sweat suit, I guessed he was just back from running.

As I got out of the car, he called out, "Hey! How was it?"

Kayo ran down to me, wriggling and wagging his tail, leaving strings of drool on my jeans as I pushed past him. Andy's demeanor was much more cautious, but as I got close, he held out an arm and ushered me in next to him, gave me a kiss that tasted salty, then lifted me up and twirled me around.

I laughed. "It was good. Fine."

He looked at me closely. "Yeah?"

"Sure. It was fine." I hesitated. "I wish you had been there."

Andy's arm dropped and he sighed. He spoke with a bit of an edge to his voice. "I would have been."

I wanted to snuggle back against him, felt the missing arm weighing heavy across my shoulders, making it hard to breathe. "I am an idiot," I said finally.

Andy picked up the knotted rag that served as Kayo's toy. The dog bounded forward and snatched one end, sinking his teeth deep and already jerking backward, legs braced against the grass, muscles quivering. Andy shook the rag and growled, which made the dog shake his head furiously. After a moment, he looked up at me, his face serious but now gentle. "You are not an idiot," he said. "I don't know what is going on with you. But I do know you are not an idiot." He let Kayo go then, and the dog bounded away gleefully. Andy held out his hand. "C'mon. I'm starving. Come in and eat with me." He turned my arm and glanced down at my wrist.

I held up the other to show him the faded scar. "I've stopped doing that." It was true. The urge that came on me so suddenly and inexplicably months before was now just as suddenly gone. The fast curves had taken its place.

Chapter Thirty-Two

The school play the spring of my senior year was *Guys and Dolls*, a musical. I'm pretty sure no one noticed my poor singing in the night club numbers where five or six of us in hot pants and Betty Boop blouses backed up Adelaide, the rough torch singer with the heart of gold. Beautiful voices floated past me into the lead roles. I was philosophical and took on my lesser roles of "hot box girl" and a dancer in the tradition of Carmen Miranda. I cha-cha'd onto stage with a turban full of fruit, trilling and swaying my hips, trying not to fall off my four-inch stiletto heels. Today, I shake my head while thinking about all the ways in which the *Guys and Dolls* play and these parts were so wrong, especially when filled by a white, blonde girl in upstate New York.

While I considered the challenges of turban-wrapping, I also considered the attention I was getting from a handsome boy recruited from the football field to play one of the gamblers. He was a year younger, shy despite his good looks. He was sweet, I thought, and most importantly, didn't know me. Didn't really know me.

Brian was coming out the front door just as I went in. He held the door for me and said, "Nice ride. Who was that?"

"A guy from the play."

"A guy from the play." Brian nodded knowingly. "Hey, do you have five bucks I could borrow?"

I pushed past him. "No, I do not have five bucks."

He followed me back in the house. "I can pay you back Friday."

"With what?" As far as I knew, he wasn't working. He'd come to live at home again. He and Ti were on the outs, and they lost the lease on the apartment. I didn't ask many questions of him or my parents. Since he moved home, he constantly begged money, from me, from my parents, even from Nora. After a couple of ten-dollar bills went missing, I kept my money hidden in the hollow part of a lamp in my room. Brian had also started stealing. Jewelry from my mother, mostly, including pieces she'd inherited from her grandmother. I knew about this because she'd asked me first if I had borrowed them. I'd helped her look in her drawers, listened to her come to the conclusion that she should ask Brian. Yet another late-night, low-voiced talk at the dining room table. He'd apologized for pawning them, she told me. And also confessed that he'd pawned the old pocket watch my grandfather had used as a dining-car conductor. "I'm going to try and get them back," she'd said. "He told me where to go. He felt terrible about it." But nothing was ever recovered.

Now, I shook my head at Brian's request. "You were gonna pay me back last time."

"I know. But I will."

"Yeah." I went to my room, and though he didn't follow me, I could feel him lingering there near the front door. I returned in a moment with the five-dollar bill. He flattened it out between his palms and bowed slightly to me.

"I'll pay you back," he said as he went out the door.

"Yeah."

That evening, I called Andy. Just before ending the conversation, I said, "Stephen gave me a ride home today."

"Oh yeah?" Andy's voice was relaxed. "How's he?"

"He's fine. He plays one of the gamblers in the show."

"Yeah, I think you told me that."

"Brian's been asking me for money again."

"Did you give it to him?"

"I wasn't going to, but I did," I said.

"Why did you do that? You won't get it back. He never pays you back."

"I know. I just... I had my mind on other things, and I just wanted him out of my face. Call me tomorrow, OK? I have to work after rehearsal, so not until late."

"OK." There was a tiny note of surprise in his voice, but he didn't pursue it. "Talk to you tomorrow."

Andy said little when he came in the door the afternoon I ended our relationship. Or thought I ended it. I could see he had pulled himself behind a wall of indifference, a wall built by two of us surely, but most of its height created by my own actions. Maybe in those moments, had I reached out to touch him and confessed my confusion and fears—about my own depression and anxiety, about going to North Carolina and leaving him, about how I missed the friendship we let get buried under our teenage lack of perspective—the afternoon might have gone differently. But that's what I was, a teenager with wildly unwieldy feelings and little perspective. And he was a teenager with real feelings and a perspective that had a distinct horizon point, the Olympics. So, I said, "Let's just get out of here. Go for a drive."

We drove to a parking lot at the college and sat in silence for some time. I had written him a letter detailing all the reasons as to why we should break up, omitting only the small part that I had been swept off my feet by someone with no other distractions except a distant season of football, which I would miss anyway, being at school in North Carolina. The letter was my practice run for what I wanted to say to him. But at the last minute, I lost my courage and just handed it to him, tears already sliding. He read it through once, folded the pages, and started the car without a word. I cried as he drove me to my friend Brenda's house. He didn't turn off the car when he pulled into the driveway, and I finally looked directly at him as I opened the door, put a foot on the ground, reluctant to leave.

"I hate this," I said. "I just think—"

He held up a hand, his voice as neutral as the white noise of an air conditioner. "It's the best thing, really. You said it all in your letter."

Unlike the plot of *Guys and Dolls*, where the gambler ends up with his girl in true love, my relationship with the handsome boy ended fairly quickly. And not long after the curtain came down on all this drama, I went to a party where parents were conspicuously absent. One of my new friends from the show was with me and, after the bottles we'd brought were empty, we decided to mix up cocktails from the odds and ends of liquor bottles that we found in the cabinet over the refrigerator. After not drinking during my relationship with Andy, I felt like I was reentering the real world of teens, where fifths of Seagram or cheap vodka were copious, easy to procure for seniors like me who were turning eighteen, the legal drinking age in New York at that time.

I walked outside for some fresh air to see Andy standing at the edge of the yard with Billy. I was shocked to see him, hadn't seen him or spoken with him since we broke up. I stepped back into the house.

My friend peered into my face. "What? What's the matter?"

"It's Andy," I started to cry, tasted the bizarre mix of whiskey and crème de menthe in the back of my throat.

"Well, go talk to him. You're obviously not over the boy."

I did. I could see his arms cross his chest as I walked up to him. I looked at Billy. "Can I just talk with him?" Billy moved off, not too far. I turned to Andy. "I need to talk with you, I—"

"I don't want to talk."

I put a hand out to him, and he pushed it away. "You're drunk. Hey, Bill, c'mon, let's get out of here."

And they left. I sat down on the grass and sobbed.

I threw up. Sobbed some more.

I saw a lot of Andy after that, in the newspapers. I didn't know the stories behind the stories, not until years later. Didn't know that he'd added an injured elbow to his list of setbacks for the year. Didn't know that he went to a club match just to support his teammates, not intending to fight, and at the last moment was asked if he wanted to get into the ring when someone else didn't show up. Didn't know that he borrowed trunks and shoes and gloves and won that fight by knocking out one of the best amateur middleweights in the state, impressing the organizers of the regional team and gaining a berth in that tournament. I read about the two knockouts there, which sent him to the Nationals in Las Vegas.

I cut out all the articles, and as I was trimming the news about the Nationals, Brian walked in the dining room. My mother had told him about my breakup with Andy, but he never said a word to me about it. If he missed talking about the fights with Andy when he came over or missed his humor or was glad to have him gone, I couldn't tell.

"Hey," he said. "I didn't get to read the paper yet! What are you doing?"

I slid the article toward him. He sat down to read it, holding his forehead, fingers disappearing into his long curly hair. I wanted to knock on his head, in that old child's game my mother played on us. Knock on the head, peek in, lift up the latch, walk in. What was he thinking? When would I ever know what he was thinking?

He looked up at me after a moment. "That is very cool. I knew he was just having a downturn for a bit. I knew things would turn around. Good for him. He could really do it. Go all the way."

"Yeah." My voice sounded shaky, and Brian regarded me for a long moment. I could feel the flush percolating under my cheekbones and wouldn't meet his gaze. I took the article and placed it in the stack with all the others. Please, I thought, don't ask me how I am feeling about Andy.

"Hey," Brian said. "Can I get a couple of bucks? I can pay you back tomorrow."

I couldn't believe it. "No. Don't have it."

He must have heard the finality. "OK, not a problem."

In the end, I sent all the articles to Andy. Not that I thought he didn't have his own clipping service of friends and relatives. I just wanted him to know that I was glad for him.

When the postcard came, I had already read about the outcome of the Nationals, news services being a bit faster than the post office. But the card was more than a boxing update.

Here I am in Las Vegas and staying at Caesar's Palace. Not a bad joint if you like rich elegance. But I'd rather be home wrestling the fuh-doggie. I lost last night but at least I got a berth in the Olympic Trials. Thanks for the card and the articles, I appreciated them. Well, TTFN. (You know what that means).
– Andy "The Cat"

I felt a relief not unlike the kind one has after a power outage when the refrigerator suddenly starts humming and life returns to normal. At least we were connected again.

Andy lost in the semi-finals at the Olympic Trials in Atlanta. Then he learned that he would go to the Olympics as an alternate at 165 pounds. But a world away from the dream that was finally taking its form for Andy, Russia moved its military into Afghanistan even while preparing to host the summer Olympic Games in Moscow. After months of diplomatic considerations, President Jimmy Carter called for a US boycott of the games. And there were no Olympics for Andy.

Chapter Thirty-Three

[1980]

That summer, after I graduated from high school, I sat behind a boy on his motorcycle as we rode to an Italian restaurant. After a nice dinner and a fun conversation, Jake and I went to a bar downtown. When we walked in, I spotted Brian at the bar with Ti. They were back together again for the umpteenth time and not sober, though Brian was still living at home. I caught his eye, and he nodded to me. We were always awkward around each other these days. He didn't approve of my barhopping, that I was drinking, so our disregard was mutual in nature. And he didn't approve of the boys I'd dated since Andy. Boys like Jake.

Jake moved to New Paltz from New York City. He was older than the rest of my senior class, a boy who could recite entire paragraphs of Dostoyevsky in the voice of a wise guy. He walked with a swagger that suggested he once had plenty of reading time in a juvenile detention center. He was a thug with a brain, and I was intrigued by the combination. It was worth one date, at least.

Jake and I found a booth and sat to drink our gin and tonics. Not moments later, a man came in carrying a motorcycle helmet and came straight to our booth. He pulled up a chair without acknowledging me and said to Jake, "Goddammit, I just slid the bike."

Jake shook his head in disbelief. "What the hell?"

The man's agitation filled the air around us. "I know, I know. This guy, this motherfucker pulled out in front of me. The bike's a mess." The guy looked at me. "Yeah, hello."

Jake put his arm around me and introduced us. "Freddie came up from the city." He smiled at me and then turned back to Freddie. "Do you have it?"

Freddie reached into his coat pocket and pulled out a gun. He actually laid it on the table before Jake snapped, "Put it the fuck away."

Why was I here? I wondered. Jake obviously planned this meet up with this Freddie person. Why did he bring me? I felt a little sick to my stomach, unsure of what to do.

"I have to go to the bathroom," I whispered in Jake's ear.

He stood up to let me out of the booth, kept a scowl directed at Freddie. "You are the dumbest fuck," Jake said.

I willed Brian to still be at the bar. He was. I put my hand on his shoulder and he turned, surprised at the touch, more surprised that it was mine. "Can you walk me home?"

Brian looked at Ti and then back at me. "What?"

"Can you walk me home?" I said again. "Jake's friend over there brought him a gun. I just want to get out of here."

Brian whistled through his teeth, laughed, and shook his head. "Well, Jesus Christ," he muttered. He turned to look at the booth where Jake and Freddie were still in deep conversation. "I told you he was a punk."

"You never told me he was a punk."

Ti put up a hand. "Stop, stop. The boy has a gun; go walk her home."

Brian stubbed out his cigarette and stood up.

I went back to the booth where Jake and Freddie sat, silent now, the gun out of sight, told them that my stomach was feeling weird and Brian would take me home. Jake looked behind me at Brian. He liked Brian, saw in him a jaded street wisdom that he praised often to me. "I'll take ya home."

"No. Really. I don't want to interrupt here. Thank you for dinner, it was great." I moved backwards as I spoke, turned and, with Brian behind me, left the bar.

We didn't talk. I was afraid he was going to lecture me. Maybe he was afraid of that too. The dark side streets felt intimate. Our breathing and footsteps syncopated into a reassuring percussion. Brian walked so close to me the smell of him filled my nostrils and I could taste it on my tongue: a mixture of beer and cigarettes riding on top of sweat and Herbal Essence shampoo, all sweet and stale at the same time. When we reached the top of the hill that led down to the deadest-end cul-de-sac and our house, he stopped. "You'll make it the rest of the way. I don't want to keep Ti waiting."

"Yeah, thanks." I ran down the hill, the slapping of my feet on the asphalt an unnerving sound. At the bottom of my driveway, I turned and looked back up the hill. I could see the glow of his cigarette brighten as he took a drag.

A Sunday. 11:00 a.m. When I woke up, I felt awful. Hung over, stiff, and my elbow hurt. I reached my arm up and bent it several times. I must have banged it. I rolled over in bed, felt my pajama top pull across my chest. I fingered the light cloth, felt down to find I was wearing the matching shorts. I couldn't remember putting them on. Nor could I remember getting in the bed. Or coming home. My summer had been full of hung-over mornings and disappointed parents, but this felt like something worse. I walked into the kitchen with visions of cool glasses of water. I drank two and then heard my father's voice. "Jan, we need to talk with you."

My parents sat at the dining room table, the Sunday paper and dirty dishes spread around them. I joined them warily. With a week to go until I went to college, I was hoping to avoid any major conflict with them. My father's voice was serious but not angry. "Where were you last night?"

I thought a moment. "I went to Tom's for that party." I hesitated because I remembered sitting on the couch at Tom's house and saying, "Let's head downtown." I couldn't remember anything else. "Then we must have gone downtown."

"Have you seen your face?" My mother touched her own as if to guide me.

I reached a hand up.

"Your forehead."

As soon as I touched it, I pushed away from the table and hurried to the bathroom to look in the mirror. Over my right eye was a huge knot, already purplish blue with lines of nubby brown blood edging a shallow gash. I looked at the elbow that was sore, another gash. And on my knees, my upper arms, rising bruises.

My mother came to the door to tell me that she'd gotten up when she heard me in the bathroom the night before. She'd been worried because I was in there so long. She found me standing, looking into the mirror, and asked what I was doing. I'd turned to her, eyes wide, pupils huge. "I'm waiting for my roof mates," I'd said. "They always send you roof mates you know."

"This wasn't beer, or just beer, or liquor," my mother said now. "And this morning, when I walked the dog, I found your underwear on the road. And a sock."

I felt sick. When I returned to the dining room, my father cleared his throat a couple of times. "Do you think you … does it feel like … do you think you need to go to the hospital?"

I stared at him for a moment as the implication became clear, and my stomach filled with a churning mixture of embarrassment and fear. "I don't think so, Dad." Though really, I had no idea. He nodded, obviously relieved. I could see his jawline soften a bit, even as my own grew rigid.

Brian came upstairs from his bedroom and through the dining room without looking at me. I heard him murmuring with my mother in the kitchen.

She came to the doorway. "Brian says he heard you come home. He said that he heard a car come up the drive and then drive away. He says you were outside so long that he went to see what was happening. You were just coming up the walkway, very slowly, and you wouldn't talk with him when you came in the door."

"Whose car was it?" I asked.

Brian called out, "Never saw it before."

I went again to the bathroom, pulled my pajama shorts down and turned slowly in front of the mirror, holding the shirt top up around my waist, craning my neck to see. Wide stripes of raw skin led up from my buttocks to the small of my back. They were already scabbing and looked like carpet burns. Feeling shaky, I sat down to pee, and winced as the urine trailed away onto more sore flesh. The sting brought tears. I sat there for a long time, cupping my hands over my eyes, fingers pressed tightly into my forehead. The tears continued to roll down onto the heels of my palms, over the scars on my wrists and down my forearms.

I called my friend Tom. I told him the whole story, summarizing the physical details, and he said, "Jesus Christ. I kind of remember that you were going to leave. But then you were gone, and I didn't actually see you go. I don't know who you were with."

"Do you think someone could have slipped me something? My mom said I looked like I had taken something, not like I was drunk."

"I don't know. I don't know who would do that."

"Can you find out for me?"

"I'll try," he said.

For the next day or so, my parents and I moved around each other quietly, all of us extra polite, as if we could bury what happened under talk of the pending travel to North Carolina. This gave us something to focus on at dinner. The gash on my head and elbow, the bruises kept me at home just when I wanted to say my last goodbyes to friends, to New Paltz itself. But I was too ashamed for anyone but my family to see me.

Tom did try to find out what happened, and a few others joined the search. But it would take another year before a boy I'd gone to school with since kindergarten confessed to our mutual friends. And they told me, in halting voices, wondered what I wanted to do. It was an ugly story as they'd heard it, even without the details that accounted for the raw skin and bruises and gashes. He was really sorry, they said. I never told my parents, never told Brian.

As I waited to head south, I renewed that promise I'd tried so hard to keep all through high school. I would go to college, get straight A's, pay as much of my own way as possible, not be another burden to my parents. Make it all up to them, somehow, for this summer, for this bump on my forehead. I would recommit to being perfect.

When Brian came home early to watch television with my parents, a couple nights before we were to leave for Chapel Hill, I didn't think much of it. I stayed in my room and read the list of what I should bring for my dorm room for the hundredth time, pondered what my roommate would be like, this girl who wrote me a note in cute cursive to tell me she could bring a chair and some curtains for the room and then signed it with, See you soon!!!! Sandy.

The next morning, I saw that Brian was asleep on the couch. My mother and I went shopping for all those last things I thought I might need for a dorm room. Brian was still at the house when we came home, stayed for hamburgers and TV with my dad, and fell asleep on the couch again.

The next night was my last night at home. The car was packed with my suitcase, a box of linens and towels, and

another box that had my high school yearbook and scrapbook, tapes, some photos. My bike was rigged onto the back.
Nora was scheduled to stay with a friend for the five days my
parents would be gone. Everything was ready.

But Brian hadn't left the house. Not once. I could sense my
parents growing more and more uneasy, questions seemed to
quiver right behind their lips whenever they looked at him.
His posturing of good cheer made them wince. They were already worried about leaving him in the house during our trip
south. After a subdued dinner that night, with halfhearted
discussions of the routes we would take, the places we would
stop, I cleared the table and settled with a book in the living
room.

"Brian," I heard my Dad say, "Let's go into the TV room
and talk."

"What?"

"Let's talk, OK?" my mother said.

I saw Brian's shoulders slump downward. "Sure."

I stared at the page in the book. I considered going into my
room, but as always, I was caught between wanting and not
wanting to be in the know.

The conversation dribbled out to me after some moments
of what I imagined to be a murmured confession from Brian.
What was it this time?

"Jesus Christ," my father said. His tone was sharp and
angry.

More murmuring, a shushing from my mother.

"Do you know how much money we have spent on you
over the last couple of years?" My father wouldn't be shushed.
There was silence. After a beat, my father said, "Twenty-five
thousand. Getting you out of jail, getting you lawyers, paying
for therapy and college you never finish, cars you wreck. It all
costs money. *Money.* Twenty-five *thous*-and dollars. We can't
even help pay for college and expenses for Janet. She had to

take out loans because we spent all that money on you."

I sat up and moved closer to the edge of the couch. When we filled out the student loan applications, my father's hand had shaken as he signed. He didn't live on credit, paid cash for everything he could out of his modest salary.

From the silence in the other room came Brian's voice, low and vicious and desperate. "I know, I know. But you know what? Janet is a slut. She is nothing but a slut."

My father exploded. "Don't you ever, ever say anything about your sister like that again. She is your *sister*."

My mother's voice was shrill. "Sit down, Bill."

I heard the sliding glass door roll shut, as if someone just noticed that their voices might carry, might invade other rooms, might assault others. I had to get out of the house. I jumped up and made a straight exit out the front door, thinking if I could just move fast enough, close the door quickly enough behind me, I could shake that word. But it shot through after me, dogged me as I headed down toward the woods where we'd played as kids, stuck with me no matter how hard I kicked and screamed at it.

I came back an hour later, sweating, breathing hard from the effort to not think about it, that word. I sat on the front steps of the porch as the evening pulled itself down around me. My mother was in the kitchen. The sounds of dishes clinking and the tap being turned on and off floated out over the sink, through the window to where I sat. They were normal sounds, regular sounds. Anyone listening would think: just a family engaged in its daily chores. I considered how I might just live on that porch, not ever have to go back in.

I finally did, slowly, shutting the front door and locking it, hesitating before going into the kitchen. I took a seat on the kitchen stool and waited.

"We aren't leaving tomorrow." My mother turned to face me. "Brian owes some dealer a lot of money. He hasn't left the house because he's afraid to be in town anywhere. This guy is threatening him, and Brian says it's real."

"How much does he owe?"

"Two thousand dollars."

I felt that zing in my veins, my heart supercharged by the rush. After some moments I said, "So, Dad is going to give him the money?"

"He has to be able to walk around town, has to be able to leave the house. What would you have us do?"

I shook my head. "Let him deal with it."

"He is our son," and that word came out of the back of her throat, guttural, primal, unarguable. She didn't ask if I'd heard what Brian said. I didn't tell her that I had. And I never told Brian either.

I lay on my mother's bed and watched her pack her suitcase. We said little. My father had been gone a long time. I tried to imagine it. Tried to imagine what it was like for my father to drive down by the river and walk up to that old white two-story house with chipped paint and a dog tied to a once-elegant balustrade, my dad knowing that inside this house was a man who was threatening to hurt his son. My father didn't trust Brian to take all the money to this man, didn't trust that this man wouldn't hurt Brian right then and there even if the money were paid. So my father went alone with $2,000 and came home without it. At the time, we all thought it would just be that once.

Part 3

Now the ring is in sight, lit up like a shrine. About the ring it is dark, and the spectators fade off into the mist and shadows, all intent. In the light now, you duck under the ropes and spin in one quick motion to face your corner. Always know your corner. It is imperative that you do this before you survey the rest of the ring. This is so that you may locate yourself during the fight under any conditions.

> – Brian Hurley, "The Other Side of the Ropes,"
> *The Huguenot Herald*, New Paltz, New York,
> June 23, 1976

Chapter Thirty-Four

[1980]

My dorm was a modern, pale red brick high rise on the south campus, Hinton James. My roommate, Sandra, was pretty with brown hair, Heidi-like skin and wide blue eyes. She declared her heritage as "Americun" with family that had lived for generations near Shelby, a small town outside of Charlotte. A smart girl, she was at school on a scholarship and work-study loans with plans of med school. She told me that she was still in love with her high school boyfriend. His name was Tony, which she pronounced, Toe-nee. More ee's when she was annoyed with him, which was often.

We attended my first pig pickin' together on the grassy lawn behind the dorm, where a pig was smoked in a huge barrel cooker. I learned the best way to eat barbecue was to pile it onto a bun and top it with coleslaw. The other first year students and I chewed and listened to extra cheerful upperclassmen tell us how to fit into the campus life.

But it seemed to me that I would never fit in.

Everywhere I looked on campus, I saw young women with add-a-bead necklaces and incongruous combinations of pink and green. Izod alligators snapped over their hearts, and they often wore, of all things, skirts. As they passed me, I heard chatter about which sororities they were pledging. My usual outfit was a pair of jeans and a T-shirt, and I thought sororities had gone the way of the poodle skirt. Or should have. At a first-year orientation dance, I watched couples do an anemic version of swing called shag dancing. As far as I could tell, the main point of the dance was to be so smooth as to never spill a drop of the beer each dancer held in their free hands. I often had the urge to change the tape and let Bob Marley blare. I wondered if somewhere in this student body of 25,000 there was another Grateful Dead fan.

In the student store poster sale, I found one of an iconic painting by George Bellows, depicting Luis Ángel Firpo sending World Heavyweight Champ Jack Dempsey through the ropes during the first round of their 1923 fight. I defiantly stuck it up on the concrete walls of my dorm room with adhesive putty, but no one ever asked me about it, not even Sandy.

As orientation to college life continued, culture shock gave way to an obsession with making amends to my parents for my behavior during the summer. I took a job at the south campus cafeteria so that I could cover the cost of my own food. I served on the line, but eventually ate at the salad bar, trying to avoid the starches and fried food that already had made some of my pants too tight. Every night I had to take a shower to get rid of the odor of grease and dirty mop water. But I liked the women who worked with me and my manager. He was a heavy-set Black man, an old army guy we called Sarge. He and I had talked boxing one night as I hauled trays in off the line, and he'd invited me to see some bouts in Durham with him. I declined sincerely, having too much schoolwork.

Schoolwork. I devised a chart for studying that accounted for all my time in fifteen-minute increments, 7:00 a.m. to midnight. Sandy went home every weekend to see Toe-nee so I spent Saturday and Sunday in the dorm room doing homework. During the week, she spent hours on the phone arguing with him about the state of their relationship. I found an isolated desk, way back in the stacks of the old graduate library where southern archives were carefully guarded. It became my refuge, and I sometimes emerged at night feeling like a bat, blinking and shaking out my wings.

When I called home, I often couldn't speak for moments when my mother answered. She learned to wait before she asked, "What's wrong?"

"Nothing," I'd say. "I'm just homesick," and then would tell her all the good news I could think of. She did the same, though I could tell she was often not telling me something else. It usually came out by the end of the conversation. Lately, the stories about Brian involved Gino, who he first met in Little League Baseball and who wrestled on the team with Brian during high school. I remembered him as both a big Black guy with a broad face and nose and an easy smile and as a little boy, running to home, winning the game, crowded by his mostly white teammates cheering his name. Until the ref said Gino hadn't stepped on the plate. Watching him slink away with his parents to his car, jeers still ringing around us all, my mother had been angry with the ref, with the other parents. "It's just a game," she'd said. "He's just a child." Now, according to my mother, he was to blame for the drinking and drugs in Brian's life. I knew better than to argue with her.

Conversations with my father were always brief. "Everything under control?"

I knew my line: "Yeah, it's OK."

On the rare occasion that Brian picked up the phone, he immediately said, "Hey Jan, looking for Mom?" I was relieved that he passed me on so quickly

I took a general drama section, taught by an eager MFA student, Derrick, who had the physique of a wrestler, intense blue eyes, and the hair of a medieval knight, long and golden.

I thought he might have been perfect in the pro-wrestling leagues. But he was sincere, and it was the one class I looked forward to during the week.

In class one Tuesday, we worked on scenes in pairs. My partner was a young Black woman, slender with a wistful long face and hair pulled tightly back into a small bun. Sherrie and I had worked together in this class before. We had a nice feeling between us, though when we left the building, we always went in opposite directions. Derrick chose us to be first. Our scene was a tight dialogue between two friends in the middle of an argument. We stood up and squared off, spoke our lines with the bit of movement we'd carefully blocked out.

Derrick was impatient. "That's great. You guys have it memorized. But you aren't in the lines. I have to shake this up for you guys. Jerry, come help me with this." He ran over to the other side of the old ballroom-now-classroom, with the student following apace. Together they pulled a heavy claw-footed table into the middle of the floor. Derrick gestured to Sherrie. "Climb aboard. Lie down and be still."

Sherrie looked at me and shrugged, slid up onto the table and turned her head slightly so that she could see me. Derrick took my elbow and positioned me so that I was next to Sherrie but still somewhat facing the other twenty students.

"Now Janet, I want only you to say your lines. I want you to look at Sherrie and say those lines, starting about halfway through." He sat down cross-legged on the floor.

Obediently, I turned to Sherrie and cleared my throat.

"Oh wait." Derrick waved his arm. "Sherrie, you're dead. So close your eyes."

I started. "She's dead?"

He smiled. "Yeah, let's see what that does to the lines."

I took a deep breath and focused on Sherrie. I could see the pulse in her neck as she laid there, eyes closed but barely. "I have tried so hard to love you." I stopped when I saw a slight smile plump up Sherrie's cheeks. I felt ridiculous. I tried again. "I just can't do this anymore with you."

"Stop!" Derrick jumped up. "OK, OK. This isn't it. OK, Sherrie. You are still dead." He looked at me for a long moment. "This isn't a lover. Or a friend. This is...your brother. Do you have a brother?" He put both hands on my shoulders and peered at me. His hair fell and curtained a private space between us, as if we were in a confessional booth.

I stared at him for a moment. "Yes."

"Good, then say those lines from that place," Derrick said. "What's your brother's name?"

"Brian."

"Then use it. OK, I won't interrupt again."

I looked at Sherrie, could still see the pulse throbbing, her lips were parted slightly, eyes closed firmly now, with lashes curling slightly on the full cheeks. "I have tried so hard to love you...Brian." A pause. And then it came out of my mouth, "Brian, I have tried so hard to love you."

Sherrie's eyes opened. I never took my eyes from hers as I continued with my lines. A tear slid across the bridge of her nose, beautiful and silvery on her dark skin. My throat closed up and tears, en masse and indelicate, ran down my face.

"I can't do this." I grabbed my backpack near the door just as Derrick began to protest. I was gone before he could call me back.

Chapter Thirty-Five

During that first college holiday break, 1980, I went down the stairs into the heart of a party hosted by one of my high school friends in New Paltz. It was one of a long line of parties scheduled, gatherings of returning college freshmen anxious to share real or made-up success stories about their first semester away from home. I stopped on the bottom step when I saw Andy on the edge of a couch, deep in conversation with one of my former classmates. He looked up, caught my eye and smiled. We were still talking hours later as the party dwindled. He was now a student at the college in New Paltz, though fighting was still his focus. Finally, he looked around the room. "Looks like the party is over."

I nodded and said impulsively, "Hey, I need a ride, maybe we can stop for coffee."

He didn't hesitate. "Sure."

In Dunkin' Donuts, we sat at the counter, drank coffee and watched the lone waitress struggle with the late-night crowd, stoned and anxious for sweets. Andy cleared his throat. "It's good to talk with you. I've missed this. Our friendship." He cocked his head to look into my face. "Are you OK?"

I kept my eyes lowered, checked about inside to see how I was with regards to him and us. "You know. I am, OK. So, let's try that out again. The friendship. How does that sound?"

"Sounds good."

"That means letters."

He laughed. "You gotta write first. But I'll write back."

I didn't see him again while I was home. I got swept away by a boy I knew in high school who I met again over that break. It was a welcomed distraction from a Christmas short on merriment and long on my mother's heavy sighs when Brian holed up in his room for the day. I discovered that ignoring him was so much harder when he was absent than when he was right at the table with me. I stayed out of the house as much as I could, and the weeks slipped away. Before I knew it, I was heading back to North Carolina.

I received a letter, full of Andy's news and humor. He'd won the Empire State Games and was invited to train with the USA Boxing Team at the Olympic Training Center in Colorado Springs. There he won a box-off and headed to Louisiana to represent the US in the North American Championship. After a technical knockout of his first opponent, he faced Gomez, the Cuban champ, best in the world—though in the ring, Andy said, he didn't seem that good. Until he broke Andy's jaw with one blow, caught him again and broke it in another place. Andy wasn't staggered, didn't go down, but his jaw hurt a lot, and he was glad the ref stopped the fight.

"I have to have my jaw wired for 4-8 weeks," he wrote. "I'M HUNGRY! I have to eat through a straw. Besides that, everything is pretty good. I can walk, talk, have sex, and even clean myself. I'm working and taking one class. I missed so much school that I had to drop the others."

He wrapped up the letter with good wishes and a friendly tease about Chris-of-the-Christmas romance. And then added a postscript: "I'm going to the Nationals and then turning pro in June."

As I folded the letter up, I had a mix of feelings. Glad he

was OK. Glad he was writing to me. Worried about the turning pro part.

I went home to New Paltz for the summer and got a job at the local bargain department store. I quickly fell into the routine of working, then heading out with friends or Chris-of-the-Christmas-romance (who turned out to be not so fun for summer romance) to the bars until the wee hours. I deserved it, I thought, after how miserable I was at school, how hard I worked. I thought my parents were unreasonable with their repeated requests to come home "at a decent hour." Couldn't I be just a little less perfect in the summer? My late-night habits seemed paltry compared to the troubles they had with Brian.

They'd convinced him to go into a rehab center in New England somewhere. The night before they would all drive there, I found Brian alone in the dining room when I came home. It was late, or early, really, maybe 2:00 am? My parents and Nora, of course, were in bed.

Brian was smoking a cigarette, looking at a roll of gray-green khaki on the table in front of him. I got a big glass of water and sat down, still tasting gin and tonics, even after the third gulp.

Brian glanced at me. "What's up?" He took a drag.

"Nothing," I hoped my voice sounded normal, if slow. "What are you doing? Aren't you leaving first thing tomorrow?"

"Yeah." Brian unrolled the fabric. It was stained, dirty. There was a tiny, clinky noise, and he cleared his throat. "I was just thinking."

I saw the spoon with the bent handle, the hypodermic, the rubber tubing, the lighter being slowly revealed, like some sort of striptease act, and any impulse to speak left me. Brian touched the spoon tenderly, ran a finger along the hypodermic, gently lifted the length of rubber tubing and let it dangle a moment before setting it back. I wanted to feel these things myself but, instead, clasped my hands in my lap. I looked up at Brian's face, caught a glint in his eyelashes when he glanced up at me and then down again. "It's over." I heard the true regret in Brian's voice as he folded the cloth back up. "I can't do it anymore."

I was horrified and fascinated as he rerolled the khaki and kept one hand on it, while he lifted his cigarette with the other.

A few days later, I was in my room, adjusting my outfit one more time for an evening out with friends, when the phone rang. Alone in the house, I ran to get it, thinking it might be one of them calling. It was Brian.

"Jan?"

"What?" I was immediately wary.

"Are Mom and Dad there? I need to talk to them. I can't stay here."

"No, they aren't here." I wished they were. My father had returned only the day before after taking Brian. He and my mother were out to dinner, trying to relax in the brief relief of feeling like something might actually change for their son. They had no idea that they would look back and call this his first rehab.

"You can come and get me," he said now.

"I am not going to come and get you."

"Jan, you don't know what it's like here. It's a prison. It's awful. Please, if you love me, take the Volkswagen and drive up to get me. It's like four hours or something."

I looked up at the Volkswagen keys hanging on their nail beside the kitchen cabinet. What would it be like? What if I did it? I imagined pulling up in front of an ominous and low-slung building. Brian would be waiting in the shadows, and I would see the glow of his cigarette, showing me where to go. I would slow just a bit, and Brian would run alongside the rolling Volkswagen, opening the door and jumping in. I would drive off with a squeal of wheels, and we would hit the dark country byways, bound by complicity and bravado. And for a short four hours, in the dark, in that moving car, we would talk and laugh, and Brian would be grateful and realize how much I loved him. And then, of course, he would reconsider his ways. No, no, I knew he wouldn't change. That's how much I loved him. I would go get him and ask nothing of him and then he would really know, and we would be connected. It would be worth all the trouble, all the recrimination from my parents, if I could be the hero of Brian's life for just those four hours in that tiny car.

"Jan? You gotta talk to me. I left. I walked to this gas station, and I don't have much money. What are you going to do?"

"No," I said. "No. I am not coming to get you. Go back. It's the best thing. That place will help you."

"I am not going back. So, either drive up here and get me or I'll hitch back."

"I guess you'll have to hitch. But I love you. I just want you to be OK."

"Yeah." He hung up. I listened to the buzz of the phone line for some moments more, reluctant to put the receiver back in its cradle.

When I went out that night, I looked for Andy. Somehow, I thought he might understand why I had almost driven up to New England to get Brian. Or help me to understand why I didn't. I didn't find Andy. He'd been scarce that summer, training hard, as usual. I'd only run into him once. He'd won his first pro fight with a knockout in thirty-seven seconds. He'd told me that as he raised his arms in victory, he looked out of the ring to see Brian, also with arms over his head, wearing a huge grin that cut through the noise of the fight crowd, told me how, a few days later, he saw Brian on the street in downtown New Paltz. Brian had shaken Andy's hand and held it just a tad too long, too affectionately; he never acted like this when he was sober. "Your fight was great," he'd exclaimed. "You have a great future ahead of you." And then he mentioned that he was thinking about heading back to Floyd's himself. Andy told me he tried to be neutral, not too negative about that idea. And just thanked Brian again for being at the fight. "Yeah, of course," Brian had said to him. "You think I woulda missed that?"

That report had filled me with frustration. Going back to the gym? And now, he'd shown he couldn't even stay at the rehab, do what he had to do if he ever wanted to go back to the gym.

When I told my parents what happened with Brian calling from the rehab, they called the center. Yes, he left against medical advice. But there was no way they could force him to stay. We waited. He didn't show up for days, finally just walking in as if he had never been gone. My parent's late-night discussions and bedtime murmurings resumed. Brian ignored me, and I wasn't surprised. "The next time," I wanted to say. "The next time, I'll come get you."

Gino

[2005]

Gino now lives on Springtown Road, a couple of miles down from Floyd. He cautions me about the flooding Wallkill River and suggests I should take the "Doug Road way." Even though I haven't lived in New Paltz since 1982, I know exactly what he's talking about. Gino's house is an old, dark wood-shingled house, built close to the road, with the river flowing just behind, but a safe distance below.

Gino answers the door, and I'm surprised. While Alfie, Harold, Longo, Andy, and Sammy have all been familiar despite the years, Gino looks nothing like I remember him. He seems shorter, his shoulders hunkering forward a bit. His face is smaller, it seems, and a bit paler. His hair is cut short with gray creeping up from his temples. He smiles, seems shy and a bit awkward, and I feel reassured by the warmth in his eyes. It helps to steady me.

"Ya found it OK?" he says and looks out at the rain, shaking his head as he gestures for me to come in.

"It wasn't a problem," I answer, taking care to wipe my muddy feet. The room is warm and cozy, a kitchen-living-room combination with a big wooden dining room table. It hosts a platter of cheese and crackers and fruit.

A slender white woman gets up from one of the small couches. She has long blonde hair, blue eyes and seems older than Gino. There is some mother energy about her that I like immediately, and I wonder if she is responsible for the snacks.

"This is my girlfriend, Hope," Gino says, and I shake her hand.

She gestures to the table. "Please sit. It's really nice to meet you."

Gino and I both take a seat, and she goes back to the couch. It's a clear deference to the conversation I want to have with Gino, as if she is there just for moral support. Later, when she pipes in with her own memories of Brian, I'm startled and intrigued, regretful that I didn't include her sooner.

"I told my mother you were coming out to talk about Brian," Gino says. "She said she remembered Brian was a really nice guy. He used to work on the bus that took kids to the center." His mother is the longtime director of the Migrant Childcare Center and knows my mother too.

I nod. "Yeah, with Andy Schott. That was early or mid-80s, I think. Andy drove, and Brian kept the kids under control."

Gino chuckles. "Yeah, yeah, that's right." He shifts as if he is uncomfortable. "You know, I don't know how helpful I'll be. I'm not sure I have memories of Brian that will be any good for you. I've been clean and sober for a long time, and there's a lot that I just don't remember from those years."

"Well, we'll just talk and see what comes up." I say this as I am rustling through my bag for my tape recorder and a tape. "Did you hear from Alfie?"

"Yeah," Gino says. "He called. He's still coming. I told him to go up and around too."

It was Alfie who gave me Gino's number, and I invited him to join us, just in case he had more memories to share. And because I want to see him again, know he'll bring a depth and calmness to the conversation.

"What about Sammy?" Sammy now works occasionally for Gino, doing construction.

Gino shakes his head. "I left him messages."

From her post back on the couch, Hope says, "Several."

I make my voice chipper. "Well, maybe he'll come out. I left him messages too. I tried to see him the last time I was up."

Gino nods. "Yeah, Alfie told me about that."

I sense a bit of exasperation in Gino's tone with regards to Sammy, but I know better than to capitalize on it. Their relationship is probably as complex and tenured as Sammy's was to Brian, to Alfie, to Floyd. I leave it be. Just as we are talking about the Little League game that both Gino and Brian played in, Alfie arrives, wearing his tam and green army jacket. He stoops to come in the door and stamps his feet.

"Sorry I'm late," he says. I get up to hug him, my affection for him even stronger, knowing that he just drove thirty minutes in the pouring rain to join us.

We talk. Eat crackers and cheese. Pop off grapes and roll them around in our fingers as we consider the life of my brother, share stories.

One of my favorites that Brian always told was about a time he and Gino were at Ti's apartment under the nursing home. They were stoned or drunk and had no money. Which of them decided to kill one of the chickens in the nursing home petting zoo for dinner wasn't clear. When Gino and Brian finally caught one of the birds, they first tried to wring its neck, then to drown it in the small pond. At some point, Ti just came out the door of her apartment, completely exasperated, and chopped its head off with a cleaver. They roasted it with potatoes and carrots, and they were the only things tender enough to chew.

Gino and Alfie laugh as I finish the story. "I don't remember that at all," Gino says. "I remember that Ti lived out there and we'd go there. But I don't remember that at all."

We talk about the gym and boxing and Alfie tells stories, and Gino, though he went to the gym only a couple of times, tells stories too. And one that I have never heard, not about the gym, but about Brian's fish tank. The one set up at the apartment he shared with Ti, the one that had bubbled so much hope and possibility.

Gino had stopped by the apartment to pick Brian up—it was mid-morning, and the door was slightly open. He stuck his head in, called for my brother, heard something and stepped all the way in. Brian was on his back, snoring on the sofa, one bare foot on the floor, which was covered with glass and small pieces of brightly colored fish tank gravel. And fish.

As Gino stepped over it all to shake Brian's shoulder, he felt the squish in the carpet. When he finally had Brian roused, Gino gestured at the mess. "That's a shame, man. What the hell happened?"

"Yeah, oh yeah." Brian rubbed his hands over his eyes. "I went out last night and got fucked up. Just so fucked up. But!" He waggled a finger at Gino. "Ti said be home by nine, and I was home at nine. I think. But when I came in, I just lost my balance and fell on the tank."

"I can't believe he wasn't cut," Gino says now. "But he wasn't. I helped him clean up best I could. But I let him flush the fish."

There's not much to say after the sibilance of this whispers through the room, and we are all quiet for some moments.

The phone rings. Hope answers it and holds a hand over the mouthpiece to say in a low voice, "Gino, it's Sammy."

As Gino gets up, I ask Alfie, "Did you ever reach Sammy?"

He shakes his head. "No, I left four or five messages. I told him I thought it would be good for him to come."

Gino says into the receiver, "Where are you?" and angles the phone so that we can hear Sammy's response.

His voice hasn't changed, loud and reedy. It carries easily across the room. "I'm down at P&G's. I just want to come out and get my tool belt."

"Your tool belt?"

"I left it in the truck."

"Well, come on out. Brian's sister Janet is here."

"Well, thanks a lot!" The exclamation is almost a squawk.

Gino frowns. "What are you talking about? I told you she'd be here. I left messages all week. So did she." He sees Alfie raise a hand. "And Alfie did too."

He turns away from us then, clamping the receiver tight against his ear. "What are you doing at P&G's, man? It's only two in the afternoon! Yeah, yeah, well. Whatever. Come on out."

He listens for a moment more. "OK. Well. You gotta do what you gotta do." He hangs the phone up and sits down heavily. "He's not coming."

Alfie shakes his head. He's leaning forward, elbows on his knees, holding that pointy chin in the palm of his hands, long fingers stretching up toward his eyes. "He needs to come out, man."

Gino nods.

Alfie continues. "He's gotta talk about this. I think it's why he's so stuck. And why did he call out right now? He knew she'd be here. So, if he didn't want to come out, why did he call?"

Gino shakes his head slowly. All four of us are silent, as if we are all picturing Sammy at the bar in P&G's, willing him to leave there, to come and talk.

"Well," I say. "I have to give up on that, talking to him. I tried; you guys have tried. I think I have to let it go."

Alfie stares at the floor. Must still be seeing Sammy at the bar. "He's really got to talk about this."

And I know that, at this moment, he isn't concerned about what I have to let go.

Chapter Thirty-Six

[1981]

My parents encouraged me to go back to school without the idea of getting straight A's. I just couldn't bring myself to do that. As the weeks wore on, walking to class while pondering what was happening at home was like moving through a sludge that caked my feet. My legs, my body were heavy, exhausted. Even talking was an effort. My body seemed to have pulled all my energy into my core like it would shunt blood to my vital organs to protect against a freeze.

My mother urged me, in letters and on the phone, to get out and have some fun. She'd taken a new job at Manny's craft store. It would help with the bills, she said, so I didn't need to worry as much about money, could maybe quit the cafeteria job and find something a little less tiring. I couldn't bring myself to do that either.

My new roommate, Gwen, was a slender Black girl from Fayetteville, North Carolina, a year older than me. She wore glasses and her hair pulled back in a bun during the day. She had dimples when she smiled, which was often, though I was so self-absorbed that I didn't notice that right away. She was a serious student, with a habit of pulling on her hair as she studied, and our evenings were quiet, devoted to scholarly endeavors. She didn't have a boyfriend, so the phone was free for me to call home often. I kept my head down on my arms to muffle my conversation, so that she wouldn't hear me crying, know that I was so homesick or sick of home, whichever the prevailing feeling was at the moment.

I didn't know what she thought of the despairing phone calls. I didn't ask, she didn't offer. During one of those with my father, he said, "Jan, look. If you are so unhappy, I'll drive down tomorrow and get you. I'll call in sick, get in the car and come get you."

He let me think about that for a few moments.

"No." I felt so guilty. "I don't want you to come get me. I'll be OK. I'm sorry I've been complaining so much." I didn't hear my father sigh with relief, but I'm sure he did. Just before I hung up, Gwen brushed by me on her way out the door.

Late one afternoon, I called home to find out that Brian had hepatitis.

He had returned home to be nursed by my mother after living in his car or in Ti's apartment for some months. My mother reported that he was extremely jaundiced and had bled from his nose and rectum before knocking on their door. I hung the phone up and sat back down at my desk, pretended to study the Krebs cycle for my biology test.

"Hey," Gwen said. She hesitated. I knew why. The protocol of the tiny dorm room demanded that eavesdropping would go unmentioned by either party. She'd certainly heard plenty so far.

I turned around. "What?"

It wasn't an invitation, and Gwen said simply, "You OK?"

"Yeah," I glanced at the alarm clock on my dresser. "I gotta get to work."

The smell of the cafeteria food hit me as I opened the door, as it did every night. It covered me like a uniform. As he passed me, Sarge said, "Hey now, all chins must be up before shift starts."

I looked up at him and smiled and then began to cry. He was surprised and embarrassed. He pointed to the little alcove that served as his office. "C'mon in there and talk to me, girl."

In a chair facing him, I couldn't stop crying. He leaned back in his chair and waited. Finally, I said, "I have to quit."

"Quit?" He shook his head. "Don't want you to quit now."

I nodded. "I know, I know. I just have to... you see... my brother is dying."

"What?" He leaned forward in his seat suddenly and put his huge forearms on the desk. "What is it? Cancer?"

I stared at him for a long moment. I wanted to tell him the truth, tell him about the phone call. Tell him no. Tell him, no, my brother's a heroin-and-whatever-else-is-handy addict. I imagined how his face would slowly close up, how he would lean back in his chair, move away from me.

"Yes, cancer. He's very sick."

He nodded. "I understand. Baby, I am so sorry. But listen, you just take all the time you need, and when you want to come back, come back."

I went straight to my dorm and opened the door quietly. Gwen was still reading, finger caught in her hair. She looked up, must have seen the look on my face and decided to barge in. "Let's go ahead and talk about this. You don't have to go it alone here."

When I told my parents that I quit my job at the cafeteria, my mother sounded relieved. "I can send you money every week," she said. "It won't be that much, but now that I'm working again, too, we can do that. Don't go out and find another job!"

The next week, I got a letter saying that Brian seemed stronger and that he'd appreciated the card I'd sent him.

As Brian got better, my spirits lifted. I thought, Surely this is it. Maybe turning yellow will turn things around for him. Wouldn't it be hard to be that sick and not think twice about picking up another needle? Apparently, according to my mom, it was. Brian had been drug-free for a month and had an up-coming interview to get into another rehab center.

"Brian has gotten to the point where he can be concerned about other people," my mother wrote. "He asked me how you were doing."

It was easy to maintain hope some six hundred miles away. I packed it along with everything else and brought it home for Christmas. Brian came in the front door late on my first night home as I watched television with my parents. I stood up when I saw him, but he just nodded from the door of the family room and said pleasantly, "Hey Jan."

I sat back down. "How are you feeling?" In the dim light he looked just as white as ever, with the jaundice no longer an is-sue. But his face was leaner, making his mustache look too large. His clothes fit a bit too generously, pants sagging on his hips.

"I'm good, I'm good. Much better. I'm... gonna make a sandwich."

On Christmas morning, I was surprised to find a small wrapped square with my name. My name in Brian's writing. A fold of cash dropped into my lap as I opened the package. And a note, which said Brian and Ti had looked for the Neil Young album I'd wanted and couldn't find it.

I glanced up at him. He sat at the dining room table, not quite a part of the activities. I held up the money. "Thanks, Brian. I really appreciate it."

He nodded. "Sorry I couldn't find it."

"It's the thought that counts." And I let it. Count.

Back at school, I relaxed more in my friendship with Gwen. I learned about some of her family struggles. She was amazed that I knew Floyd Patterson, though her opinion of him wasn't high. She said, "No offense, but he acted too white." This was something different than Ali calling Floyd an Uncle Tom. I was surprised to learn that she felt the same way about Sidney Portier and had her doubts about Bill Cosby. Brian and I had listened to Cosby for hours when we were kids.

"C'mon," I said. "Don't tell me you don't love chicken heart eating the New Jersey turnpike, ba-boom."

She laughed and said, "Well, I didn't say he wasn't funny."

When Gwen dismissed many of the Black television actors and sports stars as being too white, I started to think of racial identity as sort of like a suit, like a space suit, worn at will or through attribution or force or, as in my case, with unknowing privilege. When I argued that many of the stars she mentioned didn't really have a choice given the times in which they were acting or playing ball, she countered with Muhammad Ali. When I pointed out that he had a white trainer, she said that proved her point, that you didn't have to be white to work with whites. All of it was new territory to think in for me. I kept tripping over the subtleties of racism that I'd never had to consider, having grown up with parents who decried overt racism, who supported desegregation and equal rights. Eventually, I would understand that Black people had been watching the fights during the civil rights movement of the late '50s, '60s, and early '70s with infinitely more at stake. That the deep issues and divides about strategy and progress in the movement were reflected in which Black fighter was wearing the heavyweight championship belt.

It was the first of many such conversations for us. Gwen confessed that she thought my depression during the first months of school was about her, that I was so unhappy with a Black roommate I almost went home. I felt my face flush with the shame of knowing that she was a casualty of my struggles, much as my parents or I were casualties of Brian's. I confessed that I'd never really had to think about being white. She was unsurprised, of course. We kept talking. It was the beginning of a lifelong journey for me, to understand my whiteness, its impact, my responsibility.

Gwen and I spent less time studying together and more time just being friends. I hung with her over the edge of our dorm balcony to watch the step dances of the Black sororities and fraternities, most of which were housed in the same building. And when Michael Jordan made his famous at-the-buzzer basket during the NCAA tournament in New Orleans, we went together to the main street of Chapel Hill, where we painted our faces Carolina blue and held up our index fingers—NUMBER ONE! —to any photographer.

Gwen and I applied to be roommates again for the following year, and she made it back into the dorm via the lottery that the university held every year to distribute the limited number of dorm rooms. I didn't. I found an apartment through a woman I knew, gave her my deposit for the fall, and hoped for the best as I headed up north for what would be my last summer at home.

Chapter Thirty-Seven

Brian had gotten into the rehab he'd interviewed for and stayed the whole month. He was still living with my parents and doing well by all appearances, made it to a job at a warehouse every day, stayed home in the evenings to watch football and boxing and Johnny Carson with my father.

He also had a new plan: to go into the army. He was worried that his hearing would keep him out. All those childhood ear infections had eaten away the cartilage in his right ear. Surgery in his late teens failed to repair it, leaving him deaf on that side. Apparently, the recruiter needed to make some quotas because he passed Brian on through. I thought maybe, just maybe, he had turned the corner, even though the thought of the army made me shudder.

The day before he was due to report, I saw Brian going into P&G's as I drove past. I headed straight to my parents.

"Mom?" I called as I came in the front door. "Dad?"

"We're in the dining room," my mother answered. "What's the matter?"

I sat down with them, suddenly hesitant. My father stubbed out his cigarette. "What?" His face was carefully arranged into its pre-storm look.

"I just saw Brian going into P&G's."

My father closed his eyes for a moment, and my mother said, "I can't believe this. I can't stand this."

"He was with Gino," I said. "I'll go get him."

My father shook his head. "I'll go."

"Let me," I said. "Just let me try."

My father parked a block from the bar, and we sat for a moment regarding the sign. Even in the afternoon, a bouncer sat just outside, enjoying the sun. "I'll be right back," I said. My father nodded, lit a cigarette, and then grabbed the wheel with his free hand as if to steady himself.

The bouncer was a local boy, and he waved me through.

"Is Brian still here?"

He nodded. "Yeah, him and Gino are in the back there."

After my eyes adjusted to the dim bar light, I saw Brian and Gino standing near the foosball table, awaiting their turn. They each sipped a drink as they watched the game in progress. Brian was good at foosball, even better when he was a little stoned or drunk and had a good rock and roll beat smoothing his moves. His back was toward the door, and as I approached, I saw Gino spot me and nudge him. My brother turned. "What's up," he asked, not unpleasantly.

"You gotta get out of here," I said in a whisper.

Brian leaned his head into me. "What?"

I grabbed onto his arm, feeling the bicep still strong despite the years away from the gym. "C'mon. Please Brian, you have to leave. You can't be here. You know that."

He pulled back from me. "Like you won't be in here every night this summer? Forget it. It's not a big deal."

"It is. It's a big fucking deal and you need to come out now. Dad is waiting in the car."

"Dad? Why is he out there?"

"I saw you come in here and I told him and we came down to get you."

Brian pursed his lips and glanced at Gino, who was doing his best to study the foosball match and had even turned his shoulders a bit to pretend that he wasn't listening.

"Please," I said. "C'mon."

"All right, all right." Brian took a big gulp from his glass and set it down on a nearby table. "Gotta run," he said to Gino, who looked back at us over his shoulder and lifted his chin in acknowledgment.

I reached the car first and slid on to the back seat. "He's coming," I said to my father.

Brian opened the door and stooped down to look at us. "Dad, everything is fine, really."

My father started the car. "Get in."

"Jesus Christ." As Brian sat down, he turned his head to glare at me.

"That is the last time," I said.

"The last time what?" Brian asked as if he could care less what my answer was.

"That's the last time I am ever going to go after you." My voice was low with the effort not to cry. "No more. That's it."

Brian saw my tears and bit his lip for just a second before he nodded and turned to look out his window. "Good," he said. "Glad to hear it." He left the next morning.

Brian enjoyed the rigors of army boot camp. He called home every week to entertain my parents with the character studies he was so good at making. He was approached by an officer about boxing with the army team after he got stationed. With just a week to go before he got his orders, he failed to respond to an officer. "Are you deaf, private?" the sergeant bellowed.

"Yes, sir," Brian answered. "In my right ear, sir."

He received an honorable medical discharge and headed home.

I learned about this when I came home from my summer job at a local discount department store, something akin to Kmart. I was tired and hungry and knew I was a little late for dinner. When I came into the kitchen, I saw an open packet of ground beef on the counter. My parents and Nora were already eating in the dining room. Not talking. I knew that something had happened with Brian.

"Hey, Jan," my father said. "We're eating hamburgers. You can make yourself one."

"And French fries," Nora added, waving one in my direction.

"What's going on?" I didn't want to ask.

My father sighed and told me.

My mother said nothing, just chewed as she looked at her plate.

I washed my hands and took a handful of the ground beef, molding it into a patty of sorts, slapping it back and forth in my hands as I got more and more angry. Not at Brian. So much of our lives focused on "fixing" Brian or, for me, trying not to be a problem to be fixed.

"I am so tired of this," I said. "I just want a mother who isn't depressed all the time."

My mother finally lifted her head, looked straight at me. "Oh, that's what you want? Who was it who took all those calls from you when you went to college? Who listened to all that crying?" She shook her head as if incredulous. "And now you don't want a depressed mother. And you get to leave at the end of the summer. You have no idea."

The phone rang then, and my dad, who hadn't said a word, picked it up. "Yeah, hey Bri. Yeah, yeah, we'll be there. At the gate." As he set the receiver back, he said to my mother, "Flight gets in at eight. We should leave pretty soon."

Whats

[2005]

My mother rarely dated her letters, which I now find frustrating. I need to place them all in chronological order so that the progression will be like a coat rack, and I can hang my memories on the appropriate hooks. But really, what happened when is only sometimes relevant. There were so many "whats" about life at home and Brian: horrible whats, slightly better whats, great whats, this-could-be-the-time whats, sarcastic whats, doing-worse whats, hopeful whats. From various references to personal, local or world events I can roughly surmise the letters that came to me during college and the years after. There is no progression, no pattern, so I can only pick and choose, try to match Brian's whats with the mosaic of my own.

Sometimes the letters remind me of other events in Brian's life. Like the one about him and Ti going to the Solidarity Rally in DC. The fight to unionize the nursing home where Ti worked was intense and drawn out. Eventually, she and other workers went on strike. Brian joined her to sit on the picket line, day after day, to watch vans of temporary workers roll by.

Brian had his own experience with picket lines in the early '80s. While working in the kitchen at Kentucky Fried Chicken, he witnessed the manager throwing yet another job application from a Black man into the trash. He called the state human rights commission and the labor board but got no satisfaction. He confronted the manager then and quit. He and Ti sat outside KFC with signs for several days, waving at cars from their lawn chairs. They didn't know it was a trial run for the nursing home, which at least was more successful.

Sometimes the letters challenge what I held to be true for so long. I've always said, my mother never apologized for anything. But this isn't true.

"I really didn't mean to lay all that guilt on you that you talked about in your letter," my mother wrote. "We don't want you to be dependent on us and I'm glad you have been able to deal with problems on your own. As you know, everyday life is extremely stressful here… We are very proud of you and what you've accomplished under difficult circumstances. We know it hasn't been easy, so I'm sorry if I made you feel bad."

I don't know exactly what I had written to her, but I suspect that it had to do with the usual dinners out with my parents when I came home, when they would talk about Brian. And I would listen and offer supportive sounds and then tell them funny stories about school or work or my dog. What had prompted me to finally put that hand up? … to say, I can't hold this for you anymore? I don't remember. I do know that hand lowered quickly, so unskilled and unsure.

I'm struck by how many letters my mother wrote, almost all ending with, we love you. And how many letters even now provoke a familiar frustration, like a residual taste after twenty-five years. There are the double-edged notes: "We are so proud of you making Phi Beta Kappa. Of course, we're proud of you for many other things too! When I told Brian he said with real enthusiasm, Excellent, excellent! So, you see, he cares."

There are the letters almost serrated with bitterness that make me feel like I have to hold them with extra care, most of them focused on reports relayed to her through Brian from equally bitter sources about money and Floyd. One about

Andy and Floyd's relationship that I know to be untrue. The rest had to do with fees that Floyd received for bringing his fighters to match bouts and making his image available for promotion. I wonder again, why was it wrong for Floyd to monetize his celebrity? Didn't we see Olympic stars on cereal boxes? I remember Brian talking about becoming a million-dollar commodity if he were to make it into and do well in the Olympics—and he wasn't talking about pro purses.

I revisit the letters like I first read them, as a daughter or sister who wished that my parents would consult the normal-family instruction manual and make different choices. But instructions in our family looked like this: "So, when you come home, I know you are going to go the extra mile and do your best to make this a comparatively happy time," my mother wrote. "You will be leaving in a week, but we will be staying. Conflict and unpleasantness only add to our tension. Dad and I try not to look back and not to look forward but to deal with each day as it comes. Brian is living a life of misery, most of it his own making and he knows this. But, at the moment, he is not capable of standing on his own two feet."

It's this line that makes me go back and reread with mother-eyes: "Dad and I don't know that what we are doing is right, but it's the only thing we know to do."

I have the luxury now to use their experience and my own as I parent my children, to look back and second guess. I now know how addiction renders its own family map, with no key, no distance markers, with dragons fierce at the edges. But what of all the other situations a parent can face? Who might second-guess me? Still, even that compassion is accompanied by a wondering: why did my parents persist all those many years without a guide? No therapists for them, no family counseling, apart from obligatory rehab sessions for them and Brian. After one of those, my mother told me, "Brian was so angry. I asked him, why are you so angry?" When I was a sophomore in college, my mother encouraged me to visit student counseling services, to deal with my depression and anxiety, and I did. When I found the first psychiatry resident too clinical, I asked around and found another service with a psychologist named David, a kind listener who I saw for the remainder of my time at Carolina. And by the time I turned thirty-four, I'd spent almost as many years in therapy as I had living with my family in New Paltz. I'd started taking antidepressants, which, for me, were life-changing, providing a foundation, not a fix, for all the personal and interpersonal skills and awarenesses I needed to learn and maintain. The more I learned about brain chemistry and depression, the more I wondered if Brian had ever considered medication. I know from experience that many Twelve-Step groups frowned on this at that time. And certainly, as a teenager, this wouldn't have been an option for him.

My mother did start going to Al-Anon at one point, quickly taking on a leadership role and, just as quickly, deciding it wasn't for her. When I asked her why, she said that she understood the serenity prayer about accepting the things she couldn't change and courage to change the things she could, but she just didn't get that part about the wisdom to know the difference.

Amidst the hundreds of letters from my mother are just a few from my father. Though he dates his letters, the whats are of a completely different nature.

11/19/83

Dear Jan,
A little business to take care of before you come home.
Read the small print on the contract—30-day limit.
Mom
Says
I

Should
Send
You
Longer
Notes.
Looking
Forward
To
Seeing
You
At
Christmas.

Love
Dad.

Chapter Thirty-Eight

My mother wrote to tell me that she and my Dad, and presumably Brian, had watched Andy fight on TV. "It was pretty neat because they interviewed him too. He has become a much more aggressive and interesting fighter."

By the time Andy turned pro, he had ten years of training, 128 amateur fights and was ranked as one of the top amateur middleweights in the country.

Floyd was now on the New York State Athletic Commission, which regulates the rules and laws pertaining to wrestling and unarmed "combative" sports—like boxing. As a paid commissioner, it would be a conflict of interest to be in Andy's corner, though Andy could still train in Floyd's gym. There was no question in Andy's mind who could do the training and be in his corner: Longo.

But Longo and Floyd were at odds. Andy didn't quite understand all that was involved, but after some of his earnest cajoling, they agreed to meet. It didn't go well. And it didn't go well fast. They never made it into Floyd's house or into the gym. The conversation started in the driveway, probably right where Longo and his buddies greeted Floyd all those years ago. And it ended there, with both Floyd and Longo shouting about who had done the most for Andy and Longo simply getting into his car and roaring down the driveway. Floyd and Andy were quiet as they watched his car turn right at the bottom and head back to town.

"Andrew," Floyd said as he turned to go back into the house, "it's him or me."

Andy shook his head. "That's not the point. It doesn't have to be this way."

Floyd had nothing more to say.

Of course, Andy stayed at the gym with Floyd. But in his first pro fight, the one where he looked out to see Brian grinning at him, he had an old friend of Floyd's in his corner and his own roommate as his second. Floyd was at the fight but couldn't advise him. Andy made $250 for that fight, gave $60.00 to Floyd per their agreement and shared some with the corner guys as well. Despite his win, he knew that he needed so much more: more management, more training, more sparring, more. More to make a real pro career work.

Some months later, he got a phone call from a guy who was a cousin of a good friend. He talked big, this guy. He was a lawyer who had backers out of Texas and money and talked visions of a well-equipped gym, focused training attention, a weekly salary into Andy's head. Just one catch. They'd want to do the training and managing themselves. No Floyd.

Andy drove up past Floyd's, past where his parents and he had lived for so many years, to a small parking area. From there, he hiked in on a trail he ran every morning when he was in high school to a granite outcropping with a vista of the Hudson Valley. It was there, in the quiet, that Andy decided he had to take this chance. And he had to leave Floyd to do it.

The guy who was a cousin of Andy's friend congratulated him on a decision well made. "Look," he said. "I'll just call Floyd right now and talk with him."

Andy was quiet for a moment. Tried to imagine how he would even broach the topic. After all these years, what would be the first words? Maybe if this guy called Floyd, it would give him some time to think, react. And then Andy could talk with him.

"OK," he said to the lawyer-cousin of a good friend during a phone conversation. "Call." Later, when he thought back on this, he knew that fear and grief and maybe a bit of embarrassment had muddled his thinking.

He hung up and drove immediately to Floyd's. Andy found Floyd in his kitchen, at the table. As Andy slowly eased the screen door shut behind him, Floyd smiled up at him. "Hey, Andrew. I was just talking about you." He nodded to a chair. "Sit down. Tell me what you're thinking." His voice was calm and his face relaxed. Andy felt a bit of the tension ease from his shoulders as he sat down.

"Yeah, Floyd, well, I just gotta give it one more shot. These guys seem like they have everything I need." Floyd nodded, as if he agreed. Andy hurried on. "You know if I make it, I'll give back to the gym, to you. You know that, right?"

Floyd nodded. "Sure. Sure. Well, Andrew, I wish you the best." And he smiled.

After a moment, Andy realized that the conversation was over. "Yeah, well, thanks Floyd." He stood up, not sure what to say. "I'll see ya."

Andy wasn't surprised to hear that Floyd said different things, showed different feelings to other people and sometimes to the press, about his decision, that he was upset about it. But he and Floyd never talked again while Andy was fighting, and it was years before they saw each other. And by then, time had restored a measure of goodwill; there was always a big hug between them.

And it wasn't surprise that Andy felt when the backers from Texas disappeared. It was something deeper and more motivating. He set up a small gym in the attic of his apartment building, called Longo and asked him to be his trainer, and they found an experienced manager out of Yonkers, Mike Vetrano, to set up the fights.

My mother sent me the articles: "Schott Launches Pro Ring Career with Quick KO," "Schott Wins Second Pro Boxing Match," "Schott Wins Third Bout," "Schott Still Unbeaten," "Schott Wins Seventh."

Years before, after his loss to the Cuban champion who broke his jaw, doctors told Andy that his wisdom teeth should be pulled before fighting again. But he had continued training, even while his jaw was wired, and felt strong enough to ignore that advice. And so, the tooth sat in his jaw like a wedge waiting for the blow of a mallet, or in this case, a well-placed blow in his eighth professional fight in the Felt Forum in New York City. When it came, Andy's jaw split like a log. He came back to his corner and hissed through clenched teeth to Longo, "My jaw is broken."

"Shit. Whaddaya want to do? I'll stop it."

Andy shook his head. Longo sighed. "You're ahead, you're winning. So, if you can just keep that guy away from your face, I think you could pull it out."

The next time Andy returned to the corner, Longo said, "You're winning, you're winning. Stay away from him, move, box—don't exchange."

In the sixth of an eight-round bout, Andy was against the ropes when he saw an opening to take a clean shot. He pulled back his arm. It tangled for just a moment in the ropes. His opponent sent the punch to Andy's jaw that changed all the plans. From where he sat, Longo could see the shock of it go through Andy's body as he went down and then was back up on his feet instantly. Longo told me, years later, that he thought of the fights they had scheduled in the coming months, a big-time fight in Las Vegas, big with money, big with opportunity to get to a middleweight title. But he felt that blow for Andy. He thought about the promise he'd made to Andy's father that he would take good care of his son. Longo jumped up screaming, "Stop the fight, stop the fight."

The ref yelled at him too. "What are you doing? You can't stop the fight."

"He has a fucking broken jaw," Longo yelled. "He's been fighting with it since round 2. This fight is over!" He grabbed a towel, jumped up on the apron of the ring to wave it, and the fight was stopped with Andy ahead on the scorecards of all three judges.

My mother sent me the article, "Titles and Broken Dreams."

Not long after Andy's last bout, he came up behind Brian in a convenience store just as he was paying for a pack of cigarettes. Brian stepped back and almost on to Andy's feet.

"Hey, oh, hey, sorry. I didn't know you were behind me." Brian's manner was subdued. He gestured with the cigarette pack toward Andy's broken jaw, still wired. "I hate that, man. You don't deserve that. After all that fucking work. What are you gonna do?"

When Andy shrugged and slid his milk onto the counter, Brian said, "Yeah, yeah, sorry. I forgot you got that mouth wired. Just makes you realize that shit happens. I keep thinking I am gonna go back to Floyd's or go back somewhere, some gym, and give it another try. And then shit like this happens… you realize that anything could happen. And you think, is it worth it?" Shaking his head, he backed out of the door. "Take care of yourself, man. You got a whole life ahead a ya."

Andy nodded, grabbed a straw for the milk and was glad he had a good reason not to get further into this conversation. He knew it would take his heart a lot longer to heal than his jaw, and he was in no mood to talk with Brian about his comeback longings or about the life that Andy had ahead of him. The doctor told him that he could fight again if he had the wisdom tooth removed. Winning seven fights in a row was a great distraction from the realities the broken jaw now made him face. He was still training in his attic. Didn't have many sparring opportunities. Longo didn't have the time to give him the training he needed. He just couldn't find the passion it would take to continue.

For the next two months, Andy sipped milkshakes and looked around at that world, huge and empty without boxing. He knew he had to fill it up with something. He re-enrolled in college, filled his calendar with class schedules and work obligations, made up study plans not unlike his old training schedules and followed them with his usual unusual diligence

He wrote to me about his new life the following April. "Andrew 'The Cat' Schott, once promising middleweight, gave up boxing to chew food on a regular basis, drives a bus for the migrant childcare center in order to acquire the food he likes to chew on a regular basis." He wrote he was doing well in school, and so many new directions appealed: teaching, coaching, psychology, sports announcing, physical therapy, training fighters. "I'm happy, proud, a little shocked, but I have no regrets. I thought I needed boxing, but I am finding that I don't. Only time will tell."

Over the following years, he later told me, thoughts of a comeback surfaced once, twice, then slipped into the deep and were gone.

Chapter Thirty-Nine

[1984]

> Boxing comebacks are built on the allure that every fighter might just get that one shot, that one punch that could fell an opponent 10 times as talented or experienced.
>
> – Andy Schott, email to Janet Hurley, 2004

Late in the summer, Andy got Brian a job as an aide on the migrant daycare bus. While Andy drove, Brian looked sternly at any rambunctious child and shushed the babies who fretted at the bumpy ride. Andy wrote: "Brian is doing fine. He is learning to wipe little noses with great proficiency, and his patience and understanding of children has risen to a point just below mediocrity. Just kidding, he's doing great."

Andy and Brian had long conversations every day, interrupted often by the picking up and unloading of children, but always continued. The "comeback" was a frequent visitor to their musings.

One day, Andy heard more than just a longing and regret in Brian's voice. Brian was showing up consistently for work. It had been a while since he was in a rehab or jail or living out of the back of someone else's van. Andy knew Brian was still smoking cigarettes and who knew what else, though he mentioned Narcotics Anonymous (NA) meetings often. He thought back to those early days at the gym when he admired

Brian without reservation. During the ten years of boxing he had under his belt, Andy never saw another fighter who could bring as much heart to a fight, who could continue to move forward and go for a knockout no matter the level of exhaustion. Not even himself. He thought maybe Brian was in a place to really go for it and brought it up.

"Jim and Melio down at the gym in Beacon looked at me when I went pro," he said one day as he closed the door behind the last child they picked up each morning. "But you know, after I left Floyd, Longo was part of the deal for me, and they just didn't mesh. I think they are good guys though."

Brian smiled at the little boy and patted the seat next to him, inviting him to sit. "Yeah. I think I might do that."

Andy let the clutch out, and they rolled forward. "Just go on down there. Tell him I said you should check them out and they should check you out." He looked up in the rearview mirror and saw Brian nod.

Jim Fredericks told me that he was skeptical when Brian first came into the 5 Star Gym in Beacon. Brian hadn't fought in five years. But Jim was willing to look at Brian if Andy Schott was vouching for him. Jim said he'd felt awful when he read about Andy's broken jaw, the end of such a great amateur career, after such an auspicious start to a pro career. So, he had said sure, send Brian on over. He kind of remembered this Brian from some years back, good amateur record, might have chased a title. But something happened, and Brian had dropped off the radar screen.

Brian was thinner than Jim thought he would be, with a wild mass of curly hair and a mustache. He came in the gym door and stood politely nearby while Jim worked with another fighter. When Jim was finished, he wiped his hands on the towel around his neck and offered one to Brian.

As they shook hands, Jim was glad to see Brian looking straight at him, confident and courteous at the same time. "I appreciate you taking some time with me. I've heard a lot about your gym."

Jim nodded. "Yeah, well, Andy said take a look. No harm looking, right?" He could see Brian's shoulders relax a little. He pointed to the gym bag. "All right. You got your stuff. You can start right now."

That first workout was rough. After just a round of shadowboxing in the ring, Brian was winded, and sweat stained the neck of his gray T-shirt. Still, Jim was impressed with the technique that seemed stored in Brian's muscle memory. He climbed into the ring with a pair of punch mitts and called out a few shots. Even without much breath, Brian could still deliver something.

Brian sucked in air. "I know I gotta lot a running to do."

Jim nodded. "Yeah. But for right now, just hit the jump rope, do some sit-ups. You know the drill."

Brian nodded and climbed out through the ropes. He was doing sit-ups when Jim's cousin, Melio Bettina, walked in the door. He was Beacon's favorite son, light heavyweight champion in 1939. A short man who looked much like Jim, stocky, balding, with a round belly and dark tufted eyebrows, he liked to dress in much nattier attire. He nodded at Brian. "Who ya got there?"

"Brian Hurley. Remember him? Used to be at Floyd's."

Melio thought a moment. "Yeah, yeah, I remember him. He was good."

"Yeah. Brian had a good record. Never knocked out. I remember people talking about him."

"So what happened with Floyd?"

Jim shrugged. "Who knows? You know how it is. Shit happens. But he says he wants to make a comeback, and Floyd's a commissioner these days, so I guess that's why he's here. Andy Schott called me about him."

Melio nodded. "Worth a try."

"Worth a try."

I had just graduated from college and was working, short-term, for a political advertising consultant in Chapel Hill. Nora had just graduated from high school. Julie had gotten a master's degree in speech pathology and audiology and was working up north. My dad had just retired after thirty-six years at Kingston Schools Consolidated and was in the beginning of planning a business with some of his cronies from the sports world and army reserves: day trips and short overnight excursions for senior citizens. He was also planning to take a class in making stained-glass art, which he'd talked about for years. My mother had just started volunteering at Val Kill, the estate of her beloved Eleanor Roosevelt, across the Hudson River. She would eventually take a job there with the national park service, as an interpreter, wearing what we would call her Smokey the Bear outfit.

We were all trying to move our lives forward.

But it was this new opportunity for Brian that became the focus. "These men are willing to try and put together a pro package for him. I just hope it works out," my mother wrote.

When I got this letter, I couldn't believe it. Brian was twenty-six now; he hadn't boxed since 1979. Five years. Since I'd moved south, I'd managed to put a little distance between myself and the roller-coaster ride of Brian's life. After all the rehabs and lost jobs, stolen money and faith, I wasn't about to get back on that ride for a nebulous comeback scheme. What was it with comebacks and fighters anyway?

"Brian is training every day," my mother wrote some weeks later. "These men really like him. They are going to pay him a salary to train so he doesn't have to work. They are even going to build a gym in one of the men's backyard so he doesn't have to train at that old school where the gym is now. Brian hasn't had a drink or anything in months. And guess what, he's not smoking."

I couldn't believe this letter either. Brian had smoked since he was thirteen. And build a gym just for him? Who were these guys? Why would they need to build a gym for Brian? Pay him a salary? After he was out of boxing for five years? Maybe it was real. But so what? How long does a pro career last? And in Brian time, what would that get whittled down to?

The gym was more of a garage, as Jim and Andy later described it to me. And it wasn't built specifically for Brian. Jim had plans for it already. His hope for Brian's career motivated him to actually build it. It was small, with the ring predominating, much like a king-sized bed in a cheap motel room. With a few heavy bags, one speed bag, a small bathroom with a shower and a little floor space for calisthenics and jumping rope, Jim thought he had everything he needed to train a good fighter. He plastered the walls with clippings of fighters he'd trained or admired and liked working with Brian under those watchful eyes. Jim saw Brian arrive every day on foot, though he knew he lived across the river, some fifteen miles away.

"You don't have a car?" he asked him one day.

Brian plopped his gym bag onto the bench outside the bathroom. "Nah, I don't have a license right now. But I will soon. I just hitch over. It's not a problem."

Jim nodded. He didn't want to ask too many questions. He was just glad that Brian got himself there and when he was there that he worked as hard as he did. He had stamina, that's for sure. And such a nice guy, he told me years later, such a philosopher! Later that day, after three rounds of shadowboxing in the ring, three more on the heavy bag and the speed bag, Jim left Brian to finish his workout with calisthenics while he went into his house to make a phone call. When he came out forty-five minutes later, Brian was still doing sit-ups. Jim couldn't remember the exact conversation, but I imagine it went something like this:

"Whoa there, tiger," Jim said good naturedly. "I think you deserve a break."

Brian came up in a crunch and blew out wet air, like a whale spouting at the surface. Before he lowered back down, he said, "Strength and beauty."

Jim bent down. "What?"

"Calisthenics. It's a Greek word for strength and beauty," Brian said from the floor.

"Oh yeah? What's the Greek word for 'take a shower and go home and get some sleep'? I lined up a sparring partner for you tomorrow."

Jim watched Brian in the ring with a former Golden Gloves champ who sometimes sparred with that formidable kid Mike Tyson. Jim had signed a manager's contract with Brian some weeks before, and as he watched the sparring, he knew for certain that he was right. He was sure that the backers who were paying Brian a weekly salary to train would be pleased. It was all there, technique, power, heart. And something else. There was an edge to Brian's keen focus. He had seen it before. It was desperation.

"I think Brian could really do it this time," my mother wrote. Brian was going to NA consistently, and Jim and Melio treated him well. They'd also lined up a fight for him the next month in Albany. The poster had already come out, with Brian's photo on it. "He looks good." My mother's pride fairly radiated off the page. "There's a guy named Mike Tyson who is the headliner. Everyone says he is really good and that this should be a good show."

As I finished that letter, there was that feeling in my stomach again. A *maybe*, another goddamn *maybe* erupting from a little cocoon I didn't even know was there. I couldn't help myself. I sent Brian a card. *Good luck! I'm rooting for you from all the way down here in North Carolina!*

The Egg was a sports and entertainment venue on the Rockefeller Plaza in Albany. Designed in the late seventies, it could have been from the set of the sci-fi movie *Blade Runner*, gray and hulking.

Jim held the door open for Brian. To the right of him, in the big glass case that clung to the outside wall, was the poster heralding the fights of the evening, with Mike Tyson as the main draw. He was stirring lots of speculation that he would best Floyd Patterson's distinction as the youngest man ever to win the World Heavyweight Championship. Beneath that, with smaller photos, were the undercard fighters. Jim had taken Brian's photo with a small Kodak behind the gym in Beacon. Brian said he didn't like it, wished he'd cut his hair, which curled out in a crazy bowl shape, but at least he looked lean and in shape, like someone to be reckoned with.

Jim took a deep breath. Brian had worked so hard these past few months. Seemed hard to believe that there was a time at the gym when he wasn't there. This Tyson guy was getting a lot of notice. Cus D'Mato, Floyd's first manager, was working with him. If Brian did well on the undercard, he could get noticed too. Jim had high hopes. Brian was a natural. And he was a helluva nice guy.

"C'mon," Jim said and smiled at Brian. "Time to do this thing."

Jim finished taping Brian's hands, turned them over to check his work again. The inspector, standing behind him to watch, said, "Looks good. Good luck," and moved off to the next pair. Jim could feel the charge in Brian's arms, that mix of anticipation and nervousness that every fighter needed. He let them go and slapped Brian on the shoulder. "There ya go. Let's wait on the gloves for a bit. You're not first on the card or anything."

Brian nodded and stood up from the wide wooden bench where his gym bag and clothes were piled. He rolled his head and shrugged his shoulders to loosen up, squeezed his hands into fists. The wraps looked extra white in the gray cement room. "They feel good."

The high ceilings doubled the thrum of last-minute admonitions between trainers and fighters. Jim knew a lot of them, some of them came through his gym at one time or another.

A white guy in an ill-fitting suit and dress shirt, open at the collar, came into the locker room. Jim knew him as one of the New York State boxing commissioners, though they had never formally met. Now, he looked around the room, caught Jim's eye and headed toward him. The fights were about to start. There were maybe fifteen minutes, what was he doing here?

"Hey." The commissioner didn't waste any time. "I need to talk with ya." He used a thumb to point over his shoulder without acknowledging Brian. Jim followed him a short distance away. He glanced over his shoulder to find Brian staring after them with a puzzled expression. It matched how he felt inside.

"Listen." The commissioner put his face close to Jim's and unbuttoned the front of his suit jacket as if he were suddenly hot. "Your fighter there, he didn't pass the EEG. I was just checking all the paperwork, and he didn't pass."

"What the hell are you talking about?" Jim was sure this was a mistake. The fight opportunity came up quickly, and they'd had to rush all the requirements for the pro license in New York State. Jim had been too busy to check the mail these last days. But everything went like clockwork, from the physical to the brain scan, the EEG, the test that made sure the fighter's brain didn't show abnormality that might be exacerbated by blows to the head. He hadn't worried about any of it. Brian had never been knocked out, had won most of his amateur fights, he was sure he hadn't taken many blows to the head.

"Your boy there," the guy hissed, "he failed his EEG. I can't let him fight."

"There's gotta be a mistake," Jim hissed back. "He's in great shape. There ain't nothin' wrong with his brain. Jesus Christ. He's ready for this fight."

The commissioner shrugged. "Yeah, yeah. I know. It's a shame. But have him do it again. Sometimes those tests are screwed up. Do it again, you might get different results. But I am tellin' ya, I can't let him fight tonight. Look, I gotta figure who can fill out this card now, and I got a million other things to do. I'm sorry. There's nothin' I can do for ya." He moved off then, hailing another trainer.

Jim turned around. The fluorescent lighting made Brian's freckles look as if they were tiny leaves floating on a white, white lake. His green eyes were steady as Jim walked toward him.

"What is it?" Brian's voice was quiet.

Jim couldn't speak. He looked up at the ceiling for a moment, with a scene in his head of the last time Brian sparred, confident and effective. He looked back at Brian. "Ya can't fight."

Brian nodded, looked down at his hands as if he knew that this would happen all along. "Why?"

His voice was so low, a whisper really, that Jim almost didn't hear it. "What? Oh yeah. Why? Jesus Christ. It's the EEG. Ya didn't pass it. But we'll go to another hospital, have 'em do it again. Those things can be totally wrong, the doc who looks at it could be totally wrong. I think it's just a mistake."

Brian nodded again. "Sure. It must be a mistake. But I can't fight tonight."

"No," Jim picked up one of Brian's hands. "They coulda least told us before we wasted all this gauze and tape, eh?" The chuckle he meant to be reassuring came out as a raw gargling sound. He gave up talking, and with his other hand, rummaged through his own gym bag to find his scissors. They were shaped much like a hockey stick, with short sharp blades meant to cut through bandages or clothing. Jim held Brian's hand steady with one hand and cut with the other, let the pieces drop on the floor.

When I heard the news from my mother, I wondered what it must have been like to be upstairs in the arena, waiting for Brian to come up and fight and hear that the fight was canceled. My dad was there, in a ringside seat, but I couldn't bear to ask him. My mother was too nervous to go. By then, Ti and Brian were completely finished, and she was living in Connecticut. I don't think there was a woman there to cheer him on. Andy, he wasn't there either. After his last pro fight, he found he had to go cold turkey. No boxing. No going to fights. No training other fighters. No boxing. No exceptions. Who was there? Not me.

In mid-October, my mother wrote to tell me about the skull series and CAT scan scheduled for Brian at the end of the month. "He's holding up pretty well but not being able to box is a terrible blow. He continues to go to NA, and I think its reinforcement helps him."

Ten days later, Andy wrote that he "ran into Brian of the Hurley variety." After asking me not to mention this to him, he continued that Brian was drinking heavily and very depressed. He told Andy that he wasn't going to drink during the week, just once in a while. "Thursday is the big day, he takes his CAT scan." I could tell that Andy wanted to end on a hopeful note. "Maybe after Thursday, everything will be straightened out."

Brian, 26, photo
taken for first
pro-fight poster.
COURTESY OF THE
JIM FREDERICKS
COLLECTION

Brain Maps

[2005]

Jim Fredericks lets me in the door with a big smile. His is a modest apartment building, four units. He lives in number three. He wears a pair of dark slacks and a short-sleeve polo shirt, though it is early January in Beacon, New York. He is thick in the way of a man who was once an athlete, with large, tattooed forearms and a belly that is now cautiously venturing beyond the line of his belt. Balding and gray, his eyebrows are still dark and heavy, guarding equally dark eyes that are at the same height as mine. He asks anxiously if the directions were OK. I assure him that they were. Mrs. Fredericks comes to take my coat and exclaims, "My goodness! So young! I thought ya'd be an old lady!" She's slender, a little shorter than her husband, with blondish coiffed hair. She wears a pair of slacks and a floral-patterned shirt, has taken care with lipstick and a bit of rouge.

Mr. Fredericks snorts. "I didn't say she was an old lady. She's Brian's sister. Younger sister. You remember Brian."

Mrs. Fredericks tsks, "Sure. I remember Brian."

We move into the small kitchen where Mrs. Fredericks has set out lunch: cold cuts, buns, cheese, lettuce, appropriate condiments. We all take a seat, chair legs scraping on a high polished linoleum floor. Mrs. Fredericks urges me to make a sandwich and wonders if I drink coffee. When I say I do, she happily gets up to start her machine. Over her shoulder she says, "Take two pieces of turkey, hon, you are so skinny."

Mr. Fredericks slides an article toward me, apologizing before it even reaches my fingers. "It's all I have. I'm so sorry. I looked through all my stuff."

We look at the article, browned with twenty-one years of being stuck in a folder, which heralds Brian's amateur record (40–9, with twenty-four knockouts); his new contract with Jim and his cousin, Emile; Brian's upcoming first pro fight at the Albany Civic Center and former pro boxers Dom Yovella and Carmine Fatta both referring to Hurley as being "very impressive."

"He had everything," Mr. Fredericks says. "He got in the ring, and I was so excited. He had everything. He was a natural. And he loved boxing."

I ask Mr. Fredericks about the EEG as I finish making my sandwich and take a bite.

"I told him he should go to these two other hospitals. They didn't pass him. One was so close...but you know, I don't really know what they measure anyway. I couldn't understand it." Mr. Fredericks spreads his hands wide on the table, pushing down on the last joint of each finger until they whiten. "He was never knocked out as an amateur. New York State said they preferred he didn't fight, that maybe Connecticut would let him fight." He lifts his eyes up and looks into mine. "But I couldn't take the chance. I felt so bad. Brian loved boxing, and he was a great guy. I think about that to this day. He still comes up."

My mouth is full of bread and turkey; I can feel mayonnaise on my lips. Before I can chew and wipe my mouth to ask why, he answers. "You know, just in that way you talk about good fighters. If there was a Hudson Valley Boxing Hall of Fame, Brian would be in it." Mr. Fredericks sighs and finally reaches for the platter of cold cuts. After he makes his sandwich, he puts the knife down and sits back in his chair. "I thought he coulda been a champion; I really did."

It is a statement heavy with cinematic allusion, Marlon Brando seems to beckon. But I push him away. This is Mr. Fredericks's life, with real regret. Who am I to dismiss? And why would I want to?

That night, I look up EEG on my laptop. I type in "EEG Boxing." Hundreds of entries appear. I scroll through several. I learn that electroencephalograms are widely used in the boxing community even though they aren't a very good test for evaluating chronic brain injury. In fact, studies have shown that the EEGs of at least half the boxers studied were not different from the EEGs of non-boxers.

I go back to Google and type in "EEG Substance Abuse." Once again, hundreds of entries are listed. I scroll. I learn that EEG measurements enable researchers to create colorful maps of the brain that clearly and dramatically show the damage caused by drug abuse. That EEGs have been shown to reliably predict drug and alcohol relapse potential.

Where are those "colorful maps" of Brian's brain? I wonder. Are they archived or thrown away each decade? I could find out. I could find out that somewhere in Albany there is a map of my brother's brain. If I were a mystery writer, I could send my sleuth back into the past to find the map, to read it with all the scientific knowledge we have today, to save the day! But I am not a mystery writer. I know I won't call the New York State Athletic Commission. Because I can't be sure it matters. And because, in the end, maps have always been subject to the vagaries of interpretation and human will.

Jim Fredericks, Brian's pro trainer and manager.
COURTESY OF THE JIM FREDERICKS COLLECTION

Chapter Forty

[1984]

[Schott] said he could correct his jaw with surgery,
but it would be expensive and time-consuming.
"There's no sense in doing that," he said. "Unless
I'm ready to come back. But I don't know. The jaw
is prone to breaking. Not eating for three months
doesn't thrill me. And there's a lot of things about
boxing I don't miss. I miss the dream. I don't miss
the reality."

– Paul Hurley, "Titles and Broken Dreams,"
Poughkeepsie Journal, May 16, 1984

"It's weird," I said as I watched Andy take a drink of his beer.
"I have never seen you drink before."

He laughed. "Yeah, all those years."

The bar we sat in was oddly well lit for the time of night.
Some eight months after the break of his jaw, Andy's face
looked none the worse for the wiring. His hair was cut shorter than the last time I saw him. He looked as if he had never
stopped training. I was sure he hadn't, not really.

"You were a good influence on me when I was in high
school," I said. "Shit, if we had stayed together, I might remember a lot more of what happened the summer after I graduated."

"Yeah, well, after my pro career was over, I had to go
through what other people go through in high school, finding out how much you can drink. You know. All that stuff. I

remember the first time Brian saw me in a bar with a beer. He was so amazed. It was funny really."

It was late summer. Brian was in the beginning of his training with Jim Fredericks. We didn't know yet that all his efforts would be thwarted by a large donut-shaped machine that would inspect his brain and find it unsatisfactory. At that point, we were all hopeful. But Andy and I didn't linger on the topic of Brian. After another beer, Andy said, "You know, when you broke up with me, I was devastated."

I stared at him. He had never told me this, not in letters or the occasional short visits we'd had when I came back to see my parents. "Really? Why didn't you ever tell me?"

He shrugged. "I was angry. I felt betrayed. And I just have this thing: why would I want to be with someone who doesn't want to be with me?"

Now that is a policy I should adopt, I thought, after too many relationships based on chasing a guy until I lost interest only to have him turn around and chase me. The night took us into other topics: my new job in Chapel Hill and my doubts about my current relationship, Andy's thoughts about studying psychology and his breakup with his girlfriend.

"But I did want to be with you." I had to go back to this. "I mean, after I broke up with you, I tried to let you know it was a mistake. You didn't seem like you cared."

"I know. I was a cold prick, wasn't I?" He nodded. "I guess I was just...angry. I just wanted to move on. I was kind of relieved because I just wanted to focus on my boxing." He smiled. "But it didn't last long, did it? I mean, looking back, maybe a couple of months or so. I've always wanted this friendship with you. You've always gotten letters, haven't you? Well, got them at least occasionally, right?"

"Yeah," I said. "Often enough."

Not long after I returned to North Carolina, I got a short note from him. He was really glad that we'd gotten together, he wrote. "We shall endure and our friendship will last longer than a Sears Eveready DieHard battery."

That fall letters found their way between New York and North Carolina on a regular basis. We shared our respective lives with a familiar honesty, detailing the humor and frustrations of relationships, from roommates to romantic interests.

I wrote to him about the trailer I lived in outside of Chapel Hill. It was small, secluded with a surround of blackberry bushes. From the attached deck, I could watch horses grazing in the field next door, laugh whenever my golden retriever Riley climbed into the horse trough to cool off. I wrote about the ups and downs of my waning relationship with my college boyfriend and about flirtations with other men. I was twenty-two, in my own place, with my own money. And life was too large to guess its eventual shape. Sometimes I wondered how Andy might fit into it beyond letters and phone calls.

I drove up I-95 for my annual Christmas visit in New Paltz with Riley riding shotgun. Brian's EEG results and CAT scan were final. He wouldn't be able to box in New York. I imagined what Brian might say if I asked him about it. I felt guilty for not believing in his comeback from the beginning, as if my faith would have yielded a different brain scan. I wondered what Christmas dinner would be like, if he would even be there.

"Andy?" My mother was puzzled when I told her I was going to see him one day.

"We're just friends, Mom. It's not a big deal."

"Yeah, well, I'm not too keen on Andy these days."

"Why not?"

"Brian says Andy buys him drinks."

I felt a rush of frustration. "But Brian is in the bar. Brian takes the drink. Andy isn't his keeper."

"Well, Brian said when he refused the drink, Andy kind of made fun of him. He's obviously not a friend."

"That's ridiculous. How do you know it's true? That Andy buys him drinks?"

She looked surprised. "Brian told me. He wouldn't lie about that."

"My mother says you are buying Brian drinks."

Andy frowned. We sat on the couch in his apartment in downtown New Paltz, which he'd been living in for several years. I filled the silence with a nervous qualifier. "I mean, I don't believe it. It's just that she brought it up to me."

"We've been out a couple of times," Andy said. "I didn't buy him drinks. I was drinking and he was drinking. He's been depressed since the EEG results came back, but lately it didn't seem like he was drinking too much. I'm not his keeper anyway."

"I know. That's exactly what I said to my mom. I don't know why Brian told her that."

Andy shook his head. "I don't know. Hard to know what goes on in Brian's head sometimes."

I nodded. "Let's just forget about it."

Brian was watching the fights with my dad in the family room when I got home, his face pale and bluish in the light from the screen. His hair was cropped close to his head, the mustache gone. His cheekbones were pronounced enough to make shadows on the skin below. He moved over to make room for me on the couch. "Hey Jan. How's it going?" Didn't turn his head when I said, "OK."

"Damn!" Brian sat up straight. "That musta hurt."

My father nodded. He leaned forward, elbows on his knees, hands clasped together as he watched. "Yeah, it hurt him. I don't think he's gonna make the next round."

I ran through all the things I might make conversation about during the commercial. Didn't want to bring up the CAT scan or Andy or what Brian's plans might be. Talking about my life seemed like a bad idea: the contrast of whatever I said, good or bad, with what was happening in Brian's life could be heard as insensitive or irrelevant. I finally decided that I would just ask about the fight right in front of us. But it didn't matter. When the commercial came on, Brian jumped up. "Gotta make a phone call."

Andy's letters never failed to arrive without an update on a long philosophical conversation with Brian as children whined or giggled about them on the bus. There came a point when I was disappointed if a letter didn't include some tidbit about my brother, though sometimes, I felt an odd irritability after reading it. I was almost, but not quite, jealous. Why couldn't I have these conversations with Brian? It was so long since we really talked. Had we ever really talked? But after so many years of news filtered through my parents, I was glad for this connection to him through Andy. Once again, he was the bridge to Brian. Even when I was exasperated to read that Brian proclaimed that he would get back to training and fight amateur for a while and maybe go to another state to turn pro. "Like North Carolina, where the boxing commission consists of a retired fireman and a farmer who sells moonshine on the side. We'll see…" Though the last part made me smile, I thought, Please Brian, move on. Give it up. And please don't come to North Carolina.

In another letter, about the kind of jobs he and Brian wanted, Andy reported that Brian saw himself in an office somewhere, wearing nice clothes. "I told him he had to get that application into school if that's the case. He just laughed. He's a funny guy, your brother."

Brian never asked me about my job. A job in an office where I had to wear nice clothes. I now worked in advertising sales for a company that produced magazines for large shopping centers. I traveled a good deal with the job, visited accounts along the Eastern Seaboard, and some in the Midwest. I did well, made decent commissions, but most of all, felt like I could take care of myself, pay my own way. I always had the distinct impression that Brian found my corporate life distasteful, but now he wanted a job in an office.

"Well," Andy replied to my feelings about this. "He did say that he thought you would do anything to get ahead. Wait, wait, don't get mad. I told him he doesn't really know you, doesn't know what your life is like, what's important to you. But you gotta realize, Brian sees it as: my little sister is doing better than I am. Think about it; it would be hard. After everything he's been through, and you were always off making good grades and now you have a good job and it probably sucks for him to think about."

In the spring, I organized a thirtieth wedding anniversary dinner for my parents, just family. I had a promise from Brian that he would show up for the anniversary dinner at the right time and in the right clothes. He was still living at home, but I knew his comings and goings were often like a raccoon's, nocturnal, secretive.

On the day of the dinner, I headed to my parent's house with a corsage for my mother and the hope that Brian would show.

And he did. Early. He wore a dark blue sports coat and was even willing to let Nora take pictures of us in our going-out-to-dinner finery. At dinner, he sipped a Coke and presented my parents with a glimpse of his old sense of humor as if it were a gift. I couldn't quite identify how I was feeling about this when I went to the bathroom. I was having a good time with Brian, but wary. And then I thought about how wrong I was about him showing up. I stripped away the caution, left it behind me as I went back to the dining room.

I forgot my purse in the car after we returned home and went back out to the driveway to get it. Brian came out of the basement door and stopped as he saw me. "How much do I owe you for my part of the dinner?"

"About twenty-five dollars." I hesitated. Knew I shouldn't. "But I know money is tight for you, so whatever you can do is fine."

He nodded. "OK. I'll get it to you before you leave." He turned to walk down the drive.

"Hey." I stepped after him. "Aren't you coming inside? I think Mom and Dad thought we were all going to hang out here for a while."

He shrugged out of his sports coat. "Nah, I gotta meet some folks downtown. Take this inside for me will ya?"

I folded the coat over my arm as he walked away. Folded it slowly and carefully, though I wanted to throw it on the driveway pavement and stomp on it.

Sonia, Janet and Brian before the thirtieth-anniversary dinner.

A few months later, home for a summer visit, I sat with my mother in our dining room. The fun of the anniversary dinner, the surprise of Brian's participation, had long dissipated. Because, really, what had changed? Brian was still living at home, and she lived and breathed his hopelessness right alongside him.

"When is your flight back tomorrow?" she asked and then bit into a sandwich made with one of my dad's homegrown cucumbers.

"It's at eight. In the morning, but I asked Andy to run me down," I said this as casually as I could. I just knew she wouldn't want to hear it. Knew in that way a daughter knows. "I'd have to be there by seven, which means you'd have to get up so early to take me."

"Andy!" My mother exploded, bits of her cucumber and mayo sandwich erupted from her mouth. "Let me tell you what he did to Brian. He told Brian that he was never very good at boxing, that he would never have made it anyway even if the EEG was OK. He told him that he should just get over the boxing thing, move on. Just get on with his life the way that he, the great Andy Schott, has. As if things are so simple. Brian came home and he was… destroyed."

I sat absolutely still. I felt like a squirrel in the middle of the street, frozen with the sudden awareness of the metal immensity bearing down. "There is no way—"

"You don't know. You get to go back to North Carolina. You get to live your life. You don't know what it's like day to day here. And just when we think Brian is doing a little bit better, Andy destroys him."

I tried again. "I don't—"

My mother put up a hand. "Go ahead. Have him drive you down to the airport tomorrow. But what I am saying is that Brian is your brother. And what I am saying is that I… *hate*… Andy Schott." She chewed furiously, eyes filled with tears.

I spent the rest of that day not calling Andy. I couldn't imagine hearing his voice and not having the whole story fall out of my mouth. I couldn't bear repeating it. What if he told me it was true? Was it true? It couldn't be true. I knew that my mother expected me to make a choice between Andy and Brian, Andy and my family. That for her, my friendship with Andy was a betrayal. I just couldn't do it. Have her think I would betray her. Or Brian. By the next day, I had tumbled the matter over so many times in my head and heart that both felt scoured and empty. Andy lived not a mile from my parent's house. I didn't walk there, didn't drive there. Didn't call. My father drove me to the airport.

"Janet, let's see. You were supposed to call, I was supposed to write…" Andy's letter included another one he'd planned to send. "I figured I would just give this to you when I saw you. Here's where you come into play—I didn't see you. Why? It's a mystery but perhaps the solution will be uncovered in another chapter."

But the next chapter was far from honest. Even with the distance of miles and time, even on the phone with his voice as familiar and dear as ever, I could not bring myself to tell Andy about the conversation with my mother. I let phone calls and letters drift before I answered.

Instead, I waded into parties and relationships, drink in hand and, more often than not, got in over my head, which at least kept me from thinking about Brian and Andy.

One morning, I woke up with a nauseous stomach from too much gin the night before and suddenly remembered that Andy's birthday was the following week. I spent an hour picking out a card, trying to find just the right one. In the end I chose a light unsentimental birthday card and signed it simply, *love, Janet*.

Finally, I got the letter I expected from him, about drifting apart, about wondering what was going on in my life, about not knowing what to say.

It's for the best, I wrote in my journal. A few months later, Andy sent another letter, telling me that he was back with his girlfriend, things with her and with classes were going well, and he felt good about the future. He didn't mention Brian.

I wrote back about my hectic work life on the road, selling advertising, about the guy in Tennessee and the one in Washington, DC.

Within weeks, I would meet a man with skin as pale as Brian's, long, dark hair, blueberry eyes and lips that were full and tender. He called himself Jack when he played rock and roll with his band, the Cadillacs, and Michael when he crooned bluesy ballads about love and addiction and reckonings just around the corner.

Confession

[2004]

I start at what seems the most natural point, Andy's admiration for Brian when he was first at the gym. It is familiar territory; we have discussed this before. I like hearing this story.

"But in the end," Andy concludes, "You know, he was really ... average."

"Average?" This isn't part of my story. I shift the phone to my other ear, thinking I haven't heard it right.

"We all were. When I look at who really made it out of Floyd's, there is only one fighter—Tracy Patterson. He was unusually talented from the beginning. He won the NYC Golden Gloves twice, the only one ever to do that from Floyd's. Tracy never gave up. He was one of the best in the world."

"So, if Brian had trained and really worked at it, he could have been a champion. Maybe?"

I can tell from the silence that Andy is thinking about this, in that logical way of his, adding up the information, looking at the data he has recorded in his brain. "Well, I know Tracy's success makes it seem like a championship was possible for the rest of us. Maybe we could have made it. I gave it ten hard years. You know? I had one of those top amateur careers with over a hundred fights, Olympic Trials, US Boxing team, etc. But I only had eight pro fights. I never came close to a championship. I wasn't at that top level."

"But what if Brian had passed that EEG and got to go pro and—"

"But he wasn't even close yet. All fighters have that dream… all young fighters think they have a shot. It's like that kid with talent in the small little league puddle. He's dreaming about the big baseball ocean, but the dream isn't based in reality until you begin to get close. You have to fight the fighters who are at the top to know if you are one of them," Andy says this all easily, almost cheerfully. He's totally unaware that I'm struggling.

Finally, I say, "I hate this discussion. My brother and father had it all the time. Who had talent and who worked harder and what was more important, talent or hard work, and with hindsight, I guess it's easy to judge. And does it matter?"

There is quiet on the line while Andy considers this and finally clues into what I am feeling.

"You're right—it doesn't really matter about Brian's talent. It was real at the time."

After I get off the phone and think about Andy's love of a good analysis, his eschewing of emotion in favor of data, I put the pieces together. I go back twenty years to a conversation that must have happened with Andy and Brian. I can almost hear it. I imagine them on the bus, just the usual morning stream of consciousness between them.

"I know I fucked up," Brian says. "You know, if I had just trained and stuck with it, back then, back at Floyd's…"

Andy pumps the air brakes to bring the bus to a stop in front of an apartment building where they will pick up small children. He opens the door for them. "Yeah, but you have to look at who is making it now. It's Tracy. Next to Tracy, you were average. I was average. Even if you had worked your ass off, which I did, you might not have even gotten close. If you had wanted it bad enough, you would have trained more, stopped smoking. But you didn't, lots of people don't. You have to move on, get on with your life. That's what I had to do. And I'm doing well. I'm here to tell you, there is life after boxing. Really. C'mon, now, what are you doing? You haven't even sent in that application for school. You just have to move on."

Andy glances up in the mirror at Brian, thinks he is stating the obvious, as exasperated friends do when someone has been mired down and needs to get pulled out of the muck. He doesn't think much of it when Brian doesn't reply. There are kids to soothe, noses to wipe, they'll just pick up on the conversation later.

He has no idea that Brian is struggling. That what he has said left his mouth with one intention and arrived in Brian's ears with an entirely different meaning, that the words would be rotated, turned around and upside down, with their new arrangement confirmed by my mother. This had happened so often as to be de rigueur in my family, intention and meaning never clarified, assumptions becoming monstrous and ugly in the mind of one of us while another walked blithely about and had no clue until punishing silence became so loud or a secondhand version was relayed by an intermediary, months or even years later. Maybe by a different family member. Maybe not.

With this awareness and reconstructed scene in my mind, I have to confess. In another phone call, I tell him. I tell him what my mother said, and I say it, though it feels disgusting now in my mouth. "She said, 'I hate Andy Schott.'" I pause so that he can respond. He doesn't. "Did you and Brian have a fight? Do you remember this?"

Andy takes a deep breath and tells me about a night when he and Brian were drinking and playing pool with a friend and that Brian and the friend got into a "weird thing." Brian went after him, and Andy had to break it up. The next morning, when Andy went to pick him up for the bus route, Brian didn't come out to the usual beeps. Andy just assumed he was too hung over.

"But I don't remember this thing about boxing," he says. "We didn't talk boxing that much on the bus. Not after the whole comeback thing. But maybe. Maybe we did. If we did and he got upset, I didn't know it. He never told me."

"I'm sorry," I say. "I should have told you. Back then. I shouldn't have just built that wall. I shouldn't have made that choice."

Andy chooses his words carefully. "I'm sad that your mother felt that way. But I really don't think… I think Brian and I were OK. We kept working together, he moved in with me for a while. I don't think… it's a long time ago. I think we were all doing the best we could, you, me, your mom, Brian. You don't need to apologize."

But I do.

For years, I remembered the flicks of white bread that my mother spewed out as so much yeasty venom. Now, I can see it was desperation. It wasn't that Andy took Brian's place as the golden boy at the gym, or that he had the amateur career Brian always wanted, or that he got to turn pro. The real sin was that Andy was able to leave boxing behind him, move on, take on the next challenge. He could look back with a realistic eye and no regrets. And then, to add insult to injury, he had my trust and confidence, something Brian had squandered so many years before.

When my mother laid down the gauntlet that day, I think she intended for me to choose between Andy and Brian, for Brian's sake. I thought so, too, and that it was about loyalty to what the family needed. But as time went on, Brian continued to work with Andy, moved in with him and had the friendship with him that I gave up. Deep down, I think I knew my connection to Andy would endure, like that Sears battery, no matter the length of time between letters, despite the different paths we needed to take. But Andy's letters and phone calls had offered me a peek into Brian's heart and mind, and not finding them in my mailbox, not hearing the stories, was a loss I felt every day for a long, long time. And for this, I could never quite forgive Brian. Or myself.

//////////////////////////

Part 4

//////////////////////////

You are a little more comfortable now. You know what your opponent has and how to counter it. Your rhythm pervades his and takes over. The punches land solidly now, and you can sense it down to your toes. He's staggered. The punches land consecutively now. Faster. Faster, faster. Speed is power. Faster, faster, faster, STOP! The last punches passed through thin air. Look down, there he is. Sprawled awkwardly on the canvas. Eyes glazed he is down, down in the resin, the mud, in the gutter among broken whiskey bottles and dreams.

– Brian Hurley, "The Other Side of the Ropes,"
The Huguenot Herald, New Paltz, New York,
June 23, 1976

Chapter Forty-One

[1985–1986]

And if that's what love means to you
it should come to you as no big surprise
that everything I thought I ever knew
could be reflected in your baby blue eyes.

– Michael Kelsh, singer-songwriter,
"Baby Blue Eyes," *Steel Blue Ballads*, 1992

I first saw Michael in my rearview mirror. My friend Matthew had asked if we could pick up someone as we headed to see REM play in a small auditorium in Raleigh.

I'd said sure, then later, as we bumped and scratched over a muddy, potholed dirt road back to an old log cabin, I wondered why I'd been so agreeable. I waited in the car, engine idling, as Matthew picked his way around the puddles and banged on the door. A moment later, Michael got into the back. Just before the overhead light went out, I looked into my rearview mirror, into eyes that were bluer than mine. I later found out that his ex-wife called them blueberry eyes in her more affectionate moments, eyes with dark, long lashes to match even darker, even longer curly hair.

"Hey!" Michael said. "Thanks for the ride."

"Michael's a musician," Matthew said. "He's got a band called Jack and the Cadillacs."

"Cool." I shifted gears and slowly negotiated the ruts and bumps out to the highway.

On the way home, Michael sat in the front passenger seat, and we talked the entire way, ignoring Matthew. He told me to stop at the beginning of his drive. "Save the bottom of your car." He got out and leaned back down to look at me. "Hey, is it OK to get your phone number?"

"It is."

I was still living in the small trailer seven miles outside of Chapel Hill, surrounded by fields and blackberry bushes and horses that snorted in the early mornings. I was still a sales representative for the company that published shopping and trend magazines for large malls. I often went into the office with mud clods clinging to my Nine West pumps, a jean jacket thrown over my official business attire of skirt and blouse. This was my first long-term job, and I was part of a team that was building a new company for a larger consortium of publications. It was the mid-80s, and the company was in high gear. Within two years I became a sales manager, within four I was promoted to vice president.

I used my success to subsidize my new love. Though our first date was a chicken and rice casserole dinner made by Michael in his rustic kitchen, I paid for dinners out and usually drove. His Cadillac, with the license plate *Jackandthe*, was more of a piece of yard art than transportation. His log cabin was dusty and cold, full of records, guitars, amplifiers, and cats he'd found or that found him. Helping him haul his instruments, going to watch him play, and immersing myself in the burgeoning music scene of Chapel Hill was intoxicating. As were the ever-present alcohol and drugs.

Within months, we decided to move in together and found an old farmhouse to rent. It was some twenty miles outside of Chapel Hill, in Hurdle Mills, which boasted a post office, baseball fields and rolling miles of country highway named for whichever church anchored it.

My mother was unenthusiastic about our decision to live together. "Don't kid yourself. If you break up, it will be just like a divorce. Not that I'm saying you should marry him. I'm not saying that. He's already been married once, right?"

"Yeah." I wasn't sure what that had to do with anything. Michael was seven years older, and I knew that bothered her too. "I know living together isn't something to be taken lightly."

She sighed. "Well, you're going to do what you're going to do."

My father got on the line. After he listened for a moment, he said, "Well, Jan, we're just old-fashioned, I guess."

"You didn't have a problem when Brian lived with Ti."

"Well, that was different. Look, you're a smart girl. We've told you what we thought. We just want you to be happy."

I arrived at Michael's log cabin the night before the move. He lay on the bed, smoking a joint and watching his tiny black and white television without the sound. As I stepped in the door, my ears were filled with the rock and roll of Lone Justice and my nose with the ammonia smell of cat pee. Another reason to get him out of there, I thought. That cat pee smell will never go away. I lay down next to him. He curled his arm around me and kissed my forehead. I sat up, turned off the television and said, "Ready to live together?"

"Ready." Michael got up off the bed, changed the cassette to Jackson Browne and held out his hand to me. I joined him to sway slightly, bodies pressed together as tight as we could. "Hey," he murmured into my neck. "Let's not get weird."

"Weird?" I asked.

"Yeah, you know, let's just be in love. Let's not get weird."

Our house, on Walnut Grove Church Road, fronted eleven acres of overgrown fields, with 200 acres of hardwoods beyond. I was entranced by the farm pond with its rickety dock and fringe of grasses and wildflowers. Small tobacco barns hunkered here and there. Square hewn logs, weathered to a rich mahogany, were plastered together with what looked like smeared toothpaste. There was also a large barn that might have been used for animals or tractors, a chicken coop and a small shed. The house itself was small, four rooms downstairs, two on the second floor, reached by a rainbow-painted set of back stairs. My landlady told me that she'd just been trying to use up old cans of paint. The second floor was cozy, under a tin roof that came down sharply so that I could only stand in the middle of the room. The windows came up just to the tops of my knees. There was not one closet. The screen porch on the back, a relatively recent addition, was as large as the first floor of the house. The front porch boasted a swing that could get tangled in the enormous forsythia bush just behind it. Michael sat on it with his guitar and crooned to the fireflies across the road. His cats settled into the shed out back. I took Riley down to the pond for a swim every night after coming home from work. A friend who helped us to move said, "This is a good first place for you two."

Most of this relationship, I knew how to do. I knew how to love someone who was stoned most of the time. Michael came from a family rife with alcoholism and addiction too. I knew how to listen, how to be sympathetic, how to reassure. I could stay out at the bars until three or four a.m., after watching Michael play, and then go full speed at work. I thought that if I could just create a situation where Michael could play his music, just pay for everything as he sought his success, just help him achieve his dream, then everything would be OK. This was my specialty.

What I didn't know how to do was the rage that kept spilling out of me. One night, after an argument with Michael, I broke every windowpane in the second story bedroom. When moths and other bugs flew in to dance under the light, I swatted at them with the low-grade frustration left after such an explosion.

Michael lay on the bed and said mildly, "If you're gonna break all the windows, we're gonna have bugs."

I turned off the light to make them go away.

On a colder night, with Michael out much later than I thought he would be, I threw all his clothes out the window of the second floor. They crumpled onto the front porch roof, beaten down by icy rain. The next morning, as I left for work, I saw the frozen pant legs hanging over the edge of tin, a plaid sleeve crooked a few feet further, as if a body were lying there. I considered what the neighbors might think, then decided I didn't really care.

And condiments, in glass jars. They made for great emphasis in an argument, first the sound and then the sight of mayo or mustard or ketchup sliding down whitewashed walls. Hell to clean up, but it was something to do after the anger dissipated and before we would inevitably make love and new promises: to cut back on the drinking, cut out what we called "occasional drugs," to stop being weird.

I took Michael home to New Paltz over a Memorial Day weekend. We didn't see Brian the first couple of days until my mother called him and invited him to go out to dinner with us. "He said he'd come." She shrugged. "You never know."

He did come, wearing a tan three-piece suit left over from the seventies. He was thinner than I had ever seen him, his hair close-cropped; his skin looked stretched tight like canvas over a bone frame. He drummed the fingers of his right hand constantly, first on the dining room table, then on his leg when we got in the car. We went to a nice restaurant on the Hudson River and made small talk as we looked at the menu. Michael asked Brian about boxing and Brian asked Michael about music and I felt a pinch between my shoulders, as if there were a drawstring being tightened on a big bag of awkwardness and anxiety. The waitress came for drink orders.

My parents ordered martinis, one up, one on the rocks. It was a rare drink for both. I ordered a glass of wine, and Michael ordered a rum and Coke. Brian hesitated, then ordered a Coke. My mother leaned forward, put a hand on his forearm. "It's OK," she said in voice low and smooth with collusion. "You can have a drink if you want one."

Brian didn't hesitate for a second. He clicked his fingers to stop the waitress. "A rum and Coke like my friend here," he said and nodded at Michael, who glanced at me to confirm that he was feeling the same shock that was flushing through my chest and up to my face. I got the sense that my mother was so entwined with my brother at this point that she was speaking aloud his internal struggle, as if she knew what was best for him. I could feel that rage pushing up into my throat and forced it back down with food and sips of wine. Michael finally moved his drink away from his plate, half finished. Brian switched to vodka tonics. Later, I wondered, just briefly, why Michael and I had ordered drinks at all.

Some weeks later, my mother told me that Andy had moved to Virginia for graduate school after subletting his apartment to Brian and two other men. And not long after that, my mother called to say that Brian put a pot on the stove when he was drunk and then fell asleep. No one was hurt in the fire, but the landlord kicked all the renters out. Brian told my mother that he was drinking a fifth of vodka a day. He thought it was time for another rehab and wondered if he could come home to live again until he could get into one.

"What could I do?" my mother asked.

Chapter Forty-Two

[1986–1990]

Some of the causative factors of drug abuse are:
• escape from self.
• escape from problems.
• lack of goals.
• lack of effective role models (parents).
• boredom.
• peer pressure.
• today's propagandized lifestyle, i.e., immediate gratification, immediate release from mental or physical pain, unreal life situations presented on TV programs and commercials.
• desensitization to violence and even death.

– Testimony of Sonia Hurley, Coordinator of Drug Abuse Prevention Program, at the Poughkeepsie Public Hearing before the Temporary State Commission to Evaluate the Drug Laws, November 8, 1973

In December, some eighteen months after we moved in together, Michael and I hosted a holiday party at the farmhouse. As we cleaned up together, I had no idea that he was in the middle of making a decision. Maybe it was the sheer number of beer and empty liquor bottles, seeds rolling out of album covers as we put them away. Maybe it was finding the small square mirror that had tiny traces of powder not caught by a licked forefinger trying to get the total bang for the buck. Whatever it was, he sat down on a kitchen chair and said, "I'm done. No drinking. Nothing. I gotta be done. I am never gonna make it with my music if I'm high every day."

I didn't believe him.

Days later, he went to his first NA meeting and picked up a white chip, a tiny plastic disk not unlike a checker piece, only thinner. He soon found a sponsor to help guide him in his struggles to stay clean. At the same time, he signed a yearlong contract to play lap steel with a successful regional band.

I was still sure our relationship hinged on Michael's success and happiness with his career. All would be good between us. I was sure of it. So, I started to sit in circles of people myself, going to Al Anon, sometimes to listen to speakers at AA or NA meetings. We both went to a counselor Michael met while visiting his brother in a rehab. We were supported by Michael's sister, a recovering addict. We had a new lexicon, saying words like recovery, enabling, co-dependent, addictive behaviors, working the steps. It all became second nature to us. We could refer to the "Big Book" of Alcoholics Anonymous by page number and fiercely defend the twelve steps and traditions.

This was what I was waiting for with Brian, a true commitment to life without drugs and alcohol. The "if only he could…" of my relationship with him was transferred to my life with Michael. Somehow the reality was different than what I had imagined for Brian. In my scenario, Brian got sober, went to college, found a job and a woman he loved, even had his own place and a reliable car. His ability to have relationships, handle the difficulties of life would be automatic. I assumed the same with Michael and me. But what I discovered was that for Michael, indeed for anyone living with addiction or an addict of any sort, getting clean and sober was just about arriving at the ring.

"Don't get anything for Brian," my mother said when I called her from North Carolina about Christmas gifts. "You know he won't get you anything. He doesn't have any money."

This had been true for so many years that I decided finally to heed her advice. Michael headed to his family for the holiday, and I headed to mine with presents for everyone except Brian. On Christmas day, Nora, my parents, and I opened our gifts to each other. A pile remained under the small silvery artificial tree my parents had taken to putting up. They were from my parents to Brian, practical items like clothing disguised with wrapping paper as fun surprises. My mother said he'd been sober since the rehab and attending AA and NA meetings. We didn't know if he would arrive for dinner or, indeed, where he was. It was the unspoken theme of the day, and I almost wanted to hum with the constant refrain in my head, When will he come? When will he come?

Long after the dishes were washed and the gold-bordered Christmas tablecloth stripped from the table, Brian came in, slamming the front door behind him. He found us in the family room watching a rerun of *Cheers*. Still in his winter coat, freckles hidden by the blood summoned by the brisk December wind, he said, "Sorry I missed dinner. I have some presents." He looked good, healthy, cheeks plumper, eyes clear.

My mother immediately clicked the television off with the remote. She and my father stood to give him a hug. Nora and I were not so fast to jump. I stared at the darkened screen for a moment, wanting to just turn it back on and stay put.

But we followed into the living room where Brian proudly put a gift in my lap, another into Nora's. He put a large box in front of my parents. My mother gestured to the pile under the tree. "Open yours first."

He shook his head. "No, no, you first."

Smiling, my mother tore open the paper, and my father stuffed it into the fire. The box held a toaster oven with all the bells and whistles.

"Thank you," my mother said as if it were a set of the finest jewels. "That will be very useful."

My father and brother lifted the oven out of its box and my father adjusted his glasses so that he could read the instructions. Brian glanced at me. "Open yours."

It was a book. *The Natural Way of Writing*. As I turned it over to read the back, he said, "It looked really neat; I thought it might be handy."

"Yeah. It looks great. Thank you." My voice was low, and I couldn't look at him. I told myself this didn't change things, that he couldn't win me back with just one present. But the image in my head of Brian leafing through the book at the store and thinking I would like it, finally, after all these years, choosing something just right for me and buying it even though it would serve him no function, well, that image was irresistible. I didn't want to know where he got the money to buy the gifts. As I watched him unwrap his packages, a sense of dread filled me until I had to leave and go to the kitchen. Would he notice that there was no gift from me? He came in a few minutes later to make himself a sandwich from the Christmas dinner leftovers.

He placed the toaster oven on the counter and plugged it in. "The directions say it might smoke a little when it first heats up. So don't get freaked out."

"I won't," I said. And then, " Thank you for the book, I am really, really happy with it."

He nodded his head, stooped to watch the elements grow red behind the Plexiglas door. "Yeah, it looked good."

"I didn't get you anything. I'm sorry."

He glanced up at me and shrugged. "Yeah, well, that just makes us even. Don't worry about it."

I took my new book to my room, at first feeling relief. But as I lay down on my bed, I wondered how one well-chosen gift made us even.

I went back to North Carolina and tried to detach, detach, detach, as I was learning in Al Anon, and encouraged my mother to join again. Instead, she stocked up on all the self-help books she could. I couldn't help but wonder if she was looking for the magic sentence: It's not your fault.

Brian picked up the phone one evening. "Oh, hey Jan, you're looking for Mom?"

"Yeah." These days, my conversations with him were often measured in words, not sentences.

He called out for my mother. "She's coming. She was outside."

"OK," I said and then uncomfortably asked, "What have you been up to?"

"Not much... Hey, I went to Andy's wedding last weekend." Brian's tone was questioning, as if wondering if this would be OK to talk about.

"Yeah? I heard he and Tina were getting married. How was it?"

"Oh, it was good, really good. It was down on Huguenot Street, in that little church. Oh, here's Mom. Well, catch ya later."

"OK." After I got off the phone, I sat down at my kitchen table and took a deep breath to replace the air that was knocked out of me. I had heard through a friend that Andy was getting married, and I let the news float right past me. Now, it made the thinning of that connection painfully obvious, that he didn't write to me himself. What was even more painful to think about was that Brian went to the wedding, that they shared this, that I was once again the odd person out.

It seemed fitting that Michael and I made the decision to get married on an early December evening. We met in that month, he declared his sobriety in that month. Why not go with the flow? I knew my parents wouldn't be happy. In the three years since I'd moved in with Michael, they visited only once, when we had broken up for a short time.

At first, the visit had gone well. They'd brought me some boxes of things stored from my childhood, which were like time capsules, provoking laughter and "aww" as I pulled out little dolls and class photos from second grade and set them on my kitchen table. And then my mom told me she'd need to take back the microcomputer that she'd originally bought for Brian, and when he didn't use it, gave to me. It was a TRS-80, or trash 80, as it was known at the time. "He could really use it now," she'd said. "You have computers at work." When I'd protested that I couldn't use those for my writing, she'd pressed her lips together, stood up suddenly and went up to my bedroom, where she and my dad were sleeping.

I couldn't figure out how we'd gone from laughing to this. "Dad," I said. "Can you talk to Mom about this? Brian is never going to use the computer and I will."

My dad stood, quiet for some moments, and then said, "That woman up there…" He gestured to the ceiling. "That woman up there is your *mother*." He shook his head. "But that woman up there is my *wife*." And he left the kitchen to join her.

I lay awake on the couch all night, chilled by the clarity of my father's statement. We didn't talk about this the next day, or ever. When they packed up and drove away, they didn't take the TRS-80 with them. And, soon enough, it started to malfunction, and I never took it in to be fixed.

My parents never expressed dismay that Michael and I got back together. But I knew they were still hoping I would move on, never entertained the possibility that we would get married. Even though they knew he was a year clean and sober and we were working on our relationship with a counselor. In fact, we were working so hard on having a healthy relationship and detaching from unhealthy relationships that the thought of going home for the usual Christmas stress felt overwhelming. We decided that if we were engaged, we should spend Christmas together. We'd go to Michael's family and then later to see my parents, say, in January, skipping the whole will-Brian-come–home-and–will-he-be-sober-for-Christmas routine. I took a deep breath and called home.

"You're getting married?" My father's voice sounded even, though surprised. "Well, I don't know what to say about that."

In the background I could hear my mother's reaction. It was punctuated by the slamming of pots or something equally as clanging. "Married? That's ridiculous. She's not marrying that man."

My father tried to shush her. "Jan, why don't we talk about this when you come up for Christmas?"

"Well, that's just it, Dad," I said. "I'm not coming up for Christmas. I'm going to Michael's family, and then we want to come up after the holidays to see you."

"Not coming home for Christmas?" My father's voice took on a harsher edge. "How can you not come home for Christmas?"

Behind him, my mother's voice pitched higher. "Of course, she's coming home for Christmas." More clanging.

"Dad…" I felt miserable and angry and confused. "Dad, this is my home. Here. I've lived here now for eight years. And sometimes it gets so stressful on Christmas with Brian and everything."

My father was quiet for a long moment. "Do you want to talk with Mom?" His voice came from that place where tears were held hostage.

I thought about it for an equally long moment. And let my tears go. "No, Dad. I really don't. I love you. I'll call back when Mom isn't so angry."

The next day I came home to a message from my mother on the answering machine. "Janet, please call home so that we can tell you how angry and disappointed we are with you."

I knew I shouldn't call. Of course, I did. When I didn't change my plan for Christmas, she hung up on me.

I called again on Christmas day. My father answered the phone. He sounded glad to hear from me, but we stuck to safe topics like the forecast for snow. "Well, glad everything is under control," he finally said. "Want to talk with Mom?"

"Yeah."

I heard him call out to my mother, once, twice. "Gee, Jan, she was right here, but Nora said she went for a walk. I'll tell her you called."

I felt sick to my stomach. "OK. Merry Christmas."

"Merry Christmas."

I wrote them a letter full of earnest Twelve-Step Program phrasings, reaffirmed my right and desire to marry Michael, and offered a wish that we could love each other uncondition-ally. My mother's reply was swift and in writing.

"If we didn't love our kids unconditionally, we would have disowned you all long ago."

After a few weeks of feverish mulling, I called home to talk with them. Brian answered the phone.

"They aren't here."

"Oh." I was relieved. "What do you think about all of this?"

"All of what?"

"About their being mad at me for marrying Michael."

Brian's voice was guarded. "I really don't know anything about that, Jan."

"You don't?"

"Look, I'll tell them you called."

They didn't call back. I didn't call again. Months passed.

Through Julie, I learned that Brian was getting married. To a girl from Long Island he had met in his last rehab. My parents were planning the rehearsal dinner. Brian had asked Andy to be his best man and was disappointed when Andy had to turn him down because he was in someone else's wedding. For some moments, I felt vindicated by the irony of this, wondered what my mother thought about this, until it lodged right behind my breastplate, a mass of sadness and regret.

Brian and the girl I thought of as his rehab sweetheart broke up within the month. I wouldn't know what had really happened between them for almost twenty-five years.

In the spring of 1989, Michael dropped me off at a weeklong program for families of addicts and alcoholics. He'd met the founder at an NA convention and was convinced I'd like her.

The family program was connected with a rehab center, and almost all the attendees had a relative or loved one just inside that big rehab building at the top of the hill. Except for the mom whose twenty-something son, a newly recovering addict, died by suicide in a jail after being charged with a DUI. And me. We were housed in a cottage but took our meals at the main facility. There were group discussions, exercises, tearful confessions, angry withdrawals and family trees of alcoholism and addiction and mental-health challenges drawn and displayed as best we could, given the layers of family secrecy. Considering the impact of genetics and epigenetics left most of us feeling set up at first, hopeless. Until the facilitator pointed out it was just like any family medical history, there to show us the risks ahead and how to reduce them, and for many, a confirmation that indeed, they or family members had been set up. Not intentionally. There was no blame or shame, she said. As if we could believe her.

After a long emotional morning, I sat down with my lunch tray at an empty table in the cafeteria. I was soon joined by several people, none of them in my program, all from "the inside." A slightly built Black man sat next to me, said hello in a low but friendly voice, asked me to pass the salt. Isaac chewed his chicken and rice for a few moments before saying, "So, you come in today?"

I shook my head. "No, I'm in the family program. You?"

"I been in here for six weeks, got two more. Who you got in here?"

I shook my head again. "No one. I just needed to do the family program, and Jamie said OK."

"Jamie is good folks. So, who is it?"

"Who is it?"

"Who is it that made you want to come to the family program?"

"Well, my boyfriend is in recovery."

"Hmmm." Isaac buttered a roll and took a bite, white crumbs hanging on his lower lip before he wiped his mouth with his napkin. "He ain't it."

I stared at him for a moment. "No. It's my brother. He's an addict, an alcoholic, has been since he was in high school; he's thirty now." I said this calmly, putting into practice detachment, detachment, detachment. But Isaac was having none of it. By this time, our conversation was a private one, our heads close together, voices low and under the main current of conversation at the table.

"That hurt, don't it," Isaac said.

I looked into his eyes, so dark I couldn't make out the pupils. "Yeah."

"You grievin' him. He gone away. It's like he dead."

I stood then, holding my tray. "Yeah. I gotta get back, Isaac. Maybe I'll see you in here later."

That wasn't the day that grief arrived, of course. I'd kept it waiting outside for years, hosting anger and frustration and unrequited hope instead. That day, I discovered that the grief just wanted to claim its rightful residence, just wanted to be let in, just wanted a place to rest its head.

When I got home, I wrote to my parents, told them about the family program and invited them to my wedding. I sent them an invitation to the small ceremony we planned to have in our backyard. I sent my mother a Mother's Day card, simply saying that I was thinking of her. On Father's Day, I sent my father a letter, asking for some sort of communication. When I didn't get a response to any of this, I didn't know what to do.

So, I did nothing, and the months added up into a year, which stretched to eighteen months. I didn't tell them that, at the last minute, Michael and I decided not to get married, that we felt we weren't ready. I didn't tell them that we decided to live apart to work on our problems. I sent them a Christmas card the following December but didn't tell them that I had finally paid attention to the misgivings I had about my sales career, lucrative but without much purpose. I didn't tell them that I found a job as a community organizer for a pro-choice political organization for one-third the pay, but one hundred times the connection. I didn't tell them any of this. And I didn't tell them that I missed them. Didn't tell them because I was detached, detached, detached.

One morning, in early August of 1990, my Al-Anon sponsor called to say that her brother, also an addict, also older, also once adored, had died after an alcohol binge. I was at work, at the pro-choice organization, where offices were shared and crowded and work relationships intimate.

I hung up the phone and looked at my office mate. "I can hear the footsteps coming to my door."

Inventory

[2007]

A friend emails after reading a draft of this memoir and asks about Brian: How come we never glimpse the conversation or thoughts of this wonderfully articulate and brilliant mind?

Of course, I point out the places where Brian did speak in scenes with my parents, Floyd, Harold, Andy and me. He spoke when I interviewed him for my boxing report in the seventh grade. But I'm stalling. Despite emails, letters, and interviews with friends and acquaintances in which Brian is described as a keen judge of character, as articulate or as a philosopher he didn't often engage in these types of conversations with me, at least not in later years. His brilliance was always in play whether he was teasing us or telling funny stories about kids at school, but it was like air, we breathed it without much consideration, as if it were part of the family's autonomic nervous system.

I search about in my memory for a conversation I had with Brian that might show his adult thoughts, and I feel that old frustration of how distant he kept himself after he reached puberty. I'm sure I've pulled out all the salient quotes from the small collection of his writing that I have, but maybe I missed something. I go through it all again, slowly, creating an inventory that might, taken as a whole, give some insight.

I open the black-and-white composition book he used as a journal for his senior English class. There are twenty-eight pages of writing, scribbling and cartoons. Short scenes of a buccaneer-type character, a convict heading to the gallows and an exhausted man in an easy chair are interspersed with snippets of unrelated dialogue and quotations. There's an assortment of essays with titles such as:

Heroes
Why Are There Stripes on the Sides of Sneakers?
School Is Unnecessary
What's in My Desk Drawer
The Poetry of Smoke
Stoned Logic Argument for the Observance and
    Command of Your Mind

The teacher was pretty generous, throughout the pages making small comments that are encouraging and appreciative and sometimes instructive. I had this same teacher when I was in high school, and I knew that he could be something of a task master. Perhaps he was just glad to have something turned in from Brian. On the last page of entries, he wrote: "Well, Brian, you're a pretty complex character. You have a clear, terse style… there is a hint of stream of consciousness. I really don't know if you like writing or not. I suspect you do but would rather think than write."

My collection also includes loose-leaf pages, folded and tucked inside the composition book. There are eight poems, including one sonnet, two haiku and one semi-haiku:

Humble

School
Ring
Task
Digression
Opinion
Desperation
Farewell to Hazy Days

Brian also penned a short script on the front and back of one piece of lined paper. It's about a fighter, his sweetheart, his manager, and a miscellaneous mobster without apparent motive for his presence. I can't help but think of the vignette from the movie *Pulp Fiction*, which came out almost twenty years later, and see Bruce Willis in the main role. The script consists mostly of stage directions, ten to be exact, and only nine lines of dialogue. Brian offered a choice on the title: "The Frightening Punishment" or "Rags to Riches."

There's a photocopy of the essay Brian wrote for *The Huguenot Herald*, "The Other Side of the Ropes."

In another folder, there are essays Brian wrote while in community college in the early '80s:

*My Impression Upon Returning to the Woods of My
    Childhood*
*My Generation: Society's Effect on the Generation and
    the Generation's Potential Effect on Society*
88 Seconds in Greensboro
*Evaluation of Equal Opportunity in Employment and
    Education*
*Character Portrait: My Impressions and Learnings of
    Floyd Patterson*
an untitled essay on boxing techniques and training

By the time I get to this, I'm feeling fairly satisfied that I have mined everything for the important quotes. Clearly, Brian's humor and wide-ranging mind would be apparent to a reader if not his most personal thoughts. But there is one more thing I could add to the list. It's a three-and-a-half-page letter he wrote while in his last rehabilitation center. I'm sure it's related to Step Four of the Twelve-Step Program: Made a fearless and moral inventory.

I haven't considered sharing this because of the admonition from my mother marked at the top of the page in blue pen: "Brian's letter is for family viewing only." Part of the family rubric where top grades were earned through loyalty and silence. But I am no longer angling to be the perfect student.

To My Disease:

Well, I guess there was a long time there when I was young, that I didn't know you were hanging around. When you first made your appearance, I thought it would be the start of a long and beautiful relationship. But it wasn't in the cards. No. I came to regret it and soon and for the rest of my life.

You see, you first came cloaked in gay party attire and suffused me with confidence, with wit and a warm glow. I was immortal then, as we all were, and you were going to be the oil on the waters of my eternal life. Cajoling, nudging, even driving me to fetes where I knew no one. I suppose I should have known then that you had the wheel. I guess, even if I had, I would have trusted you to get me to the right places.

I'll admit in the beginning, there were good times. Great even, what with the excited blush of our newfound relationship. You wooed me with fancy crystal, clandestine rendezvous filled with intrigue at places I'd never been.

It was terribly sweet, for a while. But it soon turned sour and with each passing day, turned more rancid with the fetid odor of the corpse you were building within me. At first, so sly and silent I wasn't aware. A worm under 6 feet of dirt, busy, unseen, unheard.

The first time I was aware of you is when you clouded my vision so as to lose sight of my dreams and forfeit the sweat and blood invested in my boxing career. In doing so, you pulled the lynch pin that held my identity together. Floundering, I was then subject to the winds of your whims. Amidst the doldrums and gales that were to be my life, you were always there, steady at your task, methodical and effective. You were surgical in your expertise, first removing my self-esteem and sense of direction, all the time keeping me anesthetized, unaware or at least uncaring. From there, I'm sure, it became a routine operation and a costly one at that. I don't believe you would have itemized the bill, so I am taking the liberty.

My esteem.
My direction.
The trust of family and friends.
My health (hepatitis, broken bones, various cuts and
    bruises, stamina, brain damage, etc.).
My faith and the creation of Sins of Omission.
My trust in others.
My emotional capacity.
Thousands of dollars in lawyers' fees, insurance premiums,
    boxing licenses, medical bills, lost jobs, spent money,
    damaged cars and property.
The death of Larry.
The pain and grief of those unfortunate enough to know me.
Time.
Miscellaneous.

I've been making my payments over the years, but now I feel it is time to get off the table though you do protest it, it has simply gone too far. I have come to see the end you have in mind: to take off your rubber gloves and lower your mask to say, "the operation is a success, the patient is dead" as they roll another gurney beneath you.

Get me out of this shroud, give me my clothes. I'm checking out.

I am,
Brian.

Chapter Forty-Three

[1990]

"Brian's dead," Julie said as soon as I picked up the phone, just as she had announced Larry's death thirteen years before.

The conversation was brief: how it happened, when it happened, where it happened, and who was with him. Sammy. I had to call my parents. The moments it took to dial ten digits were too long. As if I needed to catch them before they would leave to go somewhere, as if not reaching them right then meant I never would.

"Dad? It's Janet. Julie called and told me."

"Yeah, yeah, Jan." It was as if my father were telling me the whole story in those syllables, each carrying a hundred times their weight in despair.

"Do you want me to come home, Dad?"

"Gee, Jan." My father's voice got hung up on that old gate he kept locked so tight on his emotions but then squeezed through at half its strength. "Would ya?"

After I got off the phone, before I called Michael, I poured the rest of the bottle of Chablis I'd been working on into the sink, rousted the beer bottles out of the fridge and threw them, unopened, into the trash. This was it, I promised myself. How could it not be?

I flew home with a small carry-on bag and a large stuffed gorilla my workmates gave me to hold on the flight. Michael decided to remain in North Carolina. He now had a full-time job in a drug and alcohol rehab, working Saturdays and overnight shifts. He used this as a reason not to accompany me. We both knew it had more to do with the difficulties of our relationship. I was relieved in a way, though I wished for someone who would be there with me, be there just for me. The flight attendant smiled as she checked the overhead bin and reached over the big black stuffed animal. "Got a kid waiting for you on the other end?"

"No." I smiled back.

I spent the flight wondering what it must have been like for my mother to answer the door and find the visitors she'd dreaded for at least seventeen years. Julie had shared the details as she'd heard them. It was a uniformed cop and a detective, Brad, who grew up just blocks away and was a year younger than Julie. Brian never had high regard for Brad, and they weren't friends. Now Brad had the official duty to notify my parents that their son was dead, give them some of the facts, including that Sammy had been with him when the emergency squad arrived.

Julie and Nora picked me up at the airport and filled me in on the plans for the wake and funeral. When I walked in the door, my mother was just coming down the hall from my parent's bedroom. "Hello, Janet." Her tone was stiff to match her embrace. "Where's Michael? You know he's welcome here."

I shook my head. "He's back in North Carolina... He's not, we didn't get married..." But neither of us really cared about that right then. I just let my answer dribble away and wondered if we would ever heal our estrangement or just shove it into the past. My father came out from where he was sitting in the dining room and hugged me with arms that felt twice as long as they should be.

Later in the evening, I asked my father if Andy had called. He shook his head. I knew it was unlikely Andy had heard the news if he hadn't called the house by then. When his father died of cancer, I sent a card to the address my mother found for me in Albany. Now, it seemed crazy that I would have to call information for his number; I felt as if I should just know it.

My father sat at the dining room table. He fingered the newspaper and smoothed out the placemats again and again. My mother was in bed. With the usual humming of the refrigerator and the clicking of the heat as it adjusted to the cooler fall evening, the rhythm of the house was calming, as if it were unaware of the grief it hosted

Tina answered in a sleepy voice. "Yeah, he's right here." And then as she passed the phone to Andy, she said, "It's Janet Hurley."

"Janet?"

I needed to be brief, knew that my father would be pained just to hear me deliver the news. "I'm calling to tell you that Brian is dead."

"When?"

"Just last night."

"How?"

"It was a drug overdose."

There was silence. Then, "When's the funeral?"

"Saturday, at ten at Pine's Funeral Home. Can you come?"

"Yeah, of course. I'll be there."

"OK." I hung up the phone and felt raw and reassured at the same time.

When I sat back down with my father, he cleared his throat. "We're not telling people that, Jan."

"What?"

"That he died of a drug overdose."

"What are we saying?"

My father shrugged. "That he just … died."

Chapter Forty-Four

For My Brother

You and I
Were close at times
But I never really showed
How much I cared.
Now I'd like to say
That these tears are for you
That they might wash away
The pain from your troubled mind.

– Janet Hurley, 1977

At the wake, I stood next to the coffin and stared at Brian's face. He looked exhausted, first, dead, second. He was heavier than I remembered, and the flesh sagged a bit, gray under the makeup. His hair was still close to the skull, a style he'd chosen for years, as if, once banished, he would never let his curls back into the kingdom. His chin dipped down, giving a sense of resignation. My parents chose casual clothes for him, a sweater with a green and blue stripe against a cream-colored background. In the usual convention, his hands were folded just below his solar plexus, fingers interlaced. I tried to put an envelope between his fingers but they were unyielding. Instead, I slipped the envelope further down into the coffin. Inside was the poem I wrote for him when I was fourteen, the poem I never gave to him.

During the long afternoon and evening hours, we welcomed gray-haired old men and women, younger faces I knew most of my life, coaches who worked with my father, and some men and women I thought maybe were off the street for just these few hours, probably glad not to be in the coffin themselves.

I saw Gino come in. He looked good, dressed in dark pants and a dark jacket with a zipper, his frame as broad and capable as I remembered it from his years of wrestling, his skin dark and vigorous. He passed quickly through the crowd with an energy and purpose that made people step aside to clear a path into the viewing room. He was back in minutes, looking around the room as if confused, then moving to the guest book, which lay on a table near the front door of the funeral parlor. But once there, he didn't even take his hands out of his pockets, instead just looked down at the signatures. Just as I was excusing myself from a conversation to speak with him, he left.

Toward the end of the evening, I looked up from a conversation to see Floyd at the back of the room with his adopted son, Tracy, and another fighter, Bryan, who I knew was Andy's good friend. The three stood in a row, wearing dark blue or black suits, hands clasped in front of them like secret service agents. The suits looked more like strait jackets, not natural for bodies that preferred to move, sweat, be challenged. I was glad Floyd was there, that something had compelled him to come.

I held out my hand to him. "I'm glad you came. Brian would be glad too." I felt sure this was true.

Floyd's voice was low. He didn't look directly at me. "I'm sorry for your loss."

"He was a good man," Bryan said and looked straight at me with eyes nearly as blue as mine. "He was a good man." He nodded, as if confirming it, and a slight blush rose from his jaw line, quite visible against pale skin.

I nodded. "Thank you. Thank you for coming."

My father was suddenly there, taking Floyd's hand in both of his, saying his name in a beseeching way. The two bent their heads together, one pink with a gray crown and the other still thickly covered with the short, black distinctive hair that came to almost a knob in the front. They looked as if they were conspiring, and I stepped away. My father seemed even frailer next to Floyd. I had the distinct feeling that he was begging Floyd to use his fame and star power to right this terrible wrong, to transport us back to when Floyd fostered Brian's dreams. It was only a momentary feeling, because I knew that instead, my father was probably saying what he said to everyone that night, with his Yonkers accent thicker than usual, "This isn't right. This isn't the way it is supposed to be. The son is supposed to bury the father. The son is supposed to bury the father."

My mother didn't acknowledge Floyd at all.

When viewing hours ended at 9:00, my parents departed as soon as was acceptable, leaving Julie, Nora, their boyfriends and me to check in with the funeral home staff before we left. The night was clear. We lingered just outside in the parking lot, under the streetlights. We debated the idea of going for ice cream, reluctant to go back to my parents' house without a chance to talk about who came to the visiting hours and theorize about those that didn't. We needed to share the stories, to pick over the details that were meaningful for a sister but perhaps too hard for a parent to hear.

A small man startled us as he hurried across the parking lot. He crossed the pool of light from the streetlamp, the skin of his bare forearms flashing white and vulnerable. Despite the cool of the night, he was in shorts and a T-shirt. A baseball cap clamped down his curly hair and shadowed his face.

He went directly to the door of the funeral home without acknowledging us and tried to open it. Finding it locked, he took a step back and looked at it as if amazed that he would be refused.

"Open up!" He leaned in with one hand against the door so that he could pound with the other, palm flat, as hard as he could. "Open up!"

Lights flared in one part of the funeral home and then marked the progress of the staff person as he flipped switches on his way to the front. The door opened, and the man in the baseball cap made his case in a low voice. We couldn't hear what he said. It must have been compelling because the attendant stepped back and let the man enter. Lights came on in the viewing room. The five of us just waited and stared at those windows. I remember wanting to respect the privacy of this stranger as he said his goodbye to Brian. I didn't want to follow him, though the thought was there. He could have known my brother from anywhere. What story could he offer?

After some moments, the man was ushered back out into the night and the door closed. We heard the lock snap. One by one, the lights were extinguished, and the man stood still, just outside the threshold, facing us for the first time. As if he was seized by some larger hand, he twirled around and smashed his fist into the side of the funeral home, taking the full impact on his knuckles. His screech was like a valve relieving the pressure that had been building all day.

"Why couldn't he just love himself?" He turned in a circle, and with that momentum he smashed the wall again. "Why couldn't he just love himself?"

He sat down on the front stoop of the funeral parlor and cried into his arms. Julie, Nora and I walked toward him with a hesitation that one might feel upon discovering a wounded dog on the side of the road. He looked up when he felt our presence; his beard stubble glistened in the parking lot light.

He was ageless in the way of someone who has lived on the edge of surviving for a long time. He smelled like tobacco and beer and sweat. I asked, "How did you know Brian?"

"Floyd's. I knew him from Floyd's."

I looked at him closely, but I didn't recognize him. He shook his head. "He was a great boxer." And then, as if to further his credibility he said, "Then we worked together some, driving taxi. That's where I was tonight when I heard. Over at the stand. I came over right away. I couldn't believe it."

I thought about him driving a taxi, full of grief and alcohol. "Why don't you go home and get some sleep and come back tomorrow for the service at ten."

He nodded and pushed himself up to standing. "OK, OK." He walked back across the parking lot, not stumbling, but slowly and with great care for each step. We hadn't even asked his name.

Chapter Forty-Five

I was thinking about Brian and my relationship
with him over the years. As a kid in eighth grade, I
looked up to him, admired him as a fighter. I tried to
emulate him and I believe he had a big impact on
my success as a fighter.

I really got to know Brian when we worked together
on the bus. We spent 6 hours a day talking about
everything from boxing to the meaning of life. It
was during this time that I got to know the real
Brian Hurley. He had deep feelings about life, love,
family, and our discussions were full of meaning and
discovery.

I learned a great deal from Brian. His impact on
my life was extremely positive, and I am grateful for
having the opportunity to know him.

– Andy Schott, note to Bill and Sonia Hurley,
September 15, 1990

The next morning, my father gripped the edge of the coral-colored Formica in our kitchen and struggled for breath. His broad shoulders sloped forward, shuddering with each inhalation. A two-pack-a-day smoker since his army days, he now lived the paradox of being a retired athletic director with emphysema. He leaned on his hands, head down, dressed in a coat and a tie that didn't help his breathing.

"Are you OK, Dad?"

"Yeah, yeah," he said. "I just, you know, they say the worst part is when they close the coffin. I don't think I can do that." He shook his head and used one finger to push up his thick black glasses from where they clung to the end of his nose. His skin, normally an Irish version of fair, was almost gray with grief and lack of oxygen. He swayed then, with just one arm supporting himself, and I put out my own to steady him. We didn't tell him or my mother about the man who came after the viewing hours. We thought it would be just too hard. Now, seeing my father struggle just to breathe, I was glad I didn't tell him. And then it was time to go.

As people gathered at the funeral home for the service, I stood outside. The small man came across the parking lot in almost the same trajectory as the night before. This morning, he wore long pants, a jacket and a white shirt, all barely up to the job. No hat. I could see that he'd taken time to shave, a small piece of tissue pressed on his chin like a white flower with a red center.

I smiled at him. He sidled up to me with a crinkled brown paper bag, opening it to show me the worn jump rope inside. "I wanted to ask you, can I put this at the grave?"

I nodded. "How will you get to the cemetery?"

"I'll take a cab." He smiled shyly at me and went inside.

Andy arrived a few moments later with Tina, their car zipping past me into a parking space. As he stepped out of the car, I wondered if I'd ever seen him wear a suit. And then, he was there. I hugged him, with a rush of intense familiarity with this height and frame, these blue eyes and fair skin, the nose he once good naturedly told a reporter was just a funny nose, never broken in a fight.

"I'm so glad you came," I said.

"Of course," Andy said. "Of course, I came."

My family sat in the front row during the service. My father was a lapsed Irish Catholic, my mother a distant Protestant. The minister, however, was Black, Baptist and southern. He had worked with my brother during one of Brian's more recent periods of employment as a houseparent (read guard) at a juvenile detention facility and had been a good friend to him, had helped him find a way into yet another rehab.

The service itself was brief, and both Julie and I did readings. Hers was from *The Prophet* by Kahlil Gibran. I took mine from my Big Book, from Alcoholics Anonymous, about acceptance.

"Nothing, absolutely nothing, happens in God's world by mistake," I finished in almost a whisper and didn't look up as I sat down again. I knew that no one in my family was really listening to what I read, their ears buzzing with exhaustion, their minds filled with a thousand fragmented thoughts. If they had really listened, they probably would have disagreed. And while I was not so sure about the God part, I thought, on that day at least, that I had some acceptance. But then again, exhaustion and acceptance sometime feel like the same thing.

After the service the family sat on the gray metal folding chairs as people came to express their condolences. I held my father's hand and listened to him breathe.

I didn't see Sammy approach my father until he was right on top of us. He wore a dark suit, but his hair, cut close in a short afro, was uneven. A shred of paper clung to it. He was tall and as thin as he'd been in high school, but his face had deflated from round handsomeness into sallow, tight-skinned sculpture. He bent over my father, put his arms around him and sobbed. "Please, please forgive me," Sammy muttered. My father patted his back.

"Please, please, forgive me."

I stood up, pulled Sammy away and headed him toward the anteroom. He didn't acknowledge me, seemed unaware that his body was being sent in a direction that he might not have chosen for himself.

After he disappeared into the next room, my father said, "Who was that?"

"It was Sammy."

"Jesus." His voice was low, shaking. He coughed then, in that way of emphysema patients, a heaving, unsatisfied cough that I listened to while holding my own breath.

At the cemetery, I found Andy in the few moments before the final graveside service. "Would you do something for me?" I asked.

"What's that?"

"It's about Sammy," I said, and he nodded. "He was with Brian when he died." I shared my worries about his state of mind and that he might again approach my father, shared my fears about my father's frail health. "Could you just stand next to him and keep him out of trouble?"

"Yeah," Andy said. "I can do that."

Reassured, I hurried to take a place next to my father. I slid my hand into his and held it tight. The coffin sat on its metal rods as if on a conveyor belt. It was massed with flower arrangements bearing the cards from Smitty's Body Shop or Dedrick's Pharmacy, from distant friends of mine who had never met Brian, from relatives who hadn't seen him since he was in grade school. It took me a moment to focus as the minister cleared his throat to speak. I tried to listen to him. But I saw the jump rope twined through the arrangements of rust and yellow mums, perky daisy faces, blue irises. And there, nestled in with daylilies and ferns, was a pair of training gloves, creased and worn to a dull maroon-brown.

I stood in the kitchen of my parent's house, handed coffee to one of my parent's friends and watched Andy with my father. My father sat in the brown upholstered swivel chair in the living room. Andy sat almost in front of him, on the low marble coffee table. Their heads were bowed close together. My father talked while Andy rested his chin on his hand and nodded every once in a while. After a few minutes, Andy put his hand on my father's shoulder and handed him something. When he came into the dining room, I made my excuses to the couple in the kitchen and hurried to grab his arm.

"So, tell me what happened with Brian." Andy stood in front of me as I sat on the steps of our front porch and stripped the leaves from the boxwoods as he listened. Then he said, "I didn't have to deal with Sammy, you know. I don't think he was at the cemetery."

We were both quiet for a moment.

"We probably have about ten minutes," I said. "Quick, tell me everything."

He laughed and did his best. He'd finished college. Gotten his master of industrial psychology degree at George Mason University in Virginia. Now he was working as the academic dean at Bryant & Stratton College, married and living in Albany with Tina.

"I saw Brian one day when I was in New Paltz," he said. They were downtown, on Main Street, and in Andy's estimation, Brian looked really bad. But he was glad to see Andy, asked him how he was doing. "I told him I was working at a job that was pretty cool and I was doing well. I told him I was the academic dean," Andy said the word "dean" now with a mocking tone. Brian had nodded with a smile, and Andy gave him one of his business cards.

Now, he shook his head in disbelief. "I was proud of that, but what was I thinking? Brian just looked at it, said, 'Yeah, I'll call ya sometime,' and stuck it in his pocket." Andy sighed. "I was such a jerk. You know? What if I had just sat down right then and there with him? What if I had made a plan to spend some time with him? I felt really bad about that. For a long time." He sighed again. "But I didn't do anything about it. What if I had?"

I thought of all the "what ifs" in my closet. What if I hadn't detached, detached, detached? What if I had called him every month and told him I loved him. Would one have finally gotten in?

I said, "He knew, deep down, that you were his friend."

"Maybe."

I felt a reluctance to let these moments with Andy be finished as we walked back into my parent's house. My connection to Brian through him was as strong as ever. I stopped, with the door open, and he put his hand on my shoulder.

"I'll call you," he said. "We'll talk more, I promise."

After Andy and Tina left, my father pulled an envelope out of his jacket. "Andy wrote this for me and your mother. It's damn nice." Later, I saw my father unfolding that piece of paper time and again, showing it to the guests that lingered, wiping his eyes as they read it, folding it carefully and tucking it back into his breast pocket.

After everyone had left and the kitchen was cleaned up, I went to an open AA meeting in town. I just listened.

The next morning, I lay on the bed in Brian's old basement room, now used for storage. I could hear people moving around upstairs and saw the outline of sun against the high shuttered rectangular window. I couldn't get up, as if drugged by the cellar mustiness. My mind flittered over all the "lasts" until it settled on the memory I'd been staving off, the last time I saw my brother.

It was Christmas eve, 1988. I was up for just a few days of holiday visiting. The phone rang just as Mom, Dad, Julie, her first husband Jim, Nora and I were sitting down at the table to eat. I answered it with dread.

"Jan? Pearl and I had a fight, and she threw my keys out the window, I can't find 'em, Can you come get me?" Brian's voice was thick and careful.

I held the receiver, glanced into the dining room.

"Jan?"

"Yeah." There was just a moment left before some- one would glance up and see my face. Just a moment for the sparkle and shine of my mother's best tableware, just a moment to breathe in the smell of the roast, just a mo- ment more for the great pretense, the not-mentioning, the let's-just-have-a-nice-holiday-meal-ness.

"Yeah," I said to Brian and broke that promise made all those years before: that I would never go after him again. "We'll be right there."

My father and I went together. He searched about in the bushes for the car keys while Brian's girlfriend screamed out of the second-floor apartment window, "Fuck all of ya, just fuckin' go to hell with all a ya."

Brian and I stood close together under a streetlamp. He had on his puffy royal-blue down jacket, which made his close-shorn head look small. He was clean shaven, as if may- be earlier in the day he thought he really would come for Christmas dinner. His ears were red-rimmed with the cold. We stamped our feet on the icy sidewalk to keep the blood in them and hugged ourselves to keep warm. Brian occasionally tried to warm his ungloved hands by cupping them and blowing into them, like he was playing a harmonica to a tune only he could hear. Every couple of moments I reached a hand to steady him.

"She's gonna fuckin' steal the car," he muttered as he watched my father get down to crawl under the bushes, heedless of the snow or the scratchy branches. "Or she'll fuckin' smash it."

I didn't argue. Both things had happened before.

"I'm gonna go up there and talk with her," my father called and stood up, brushing the snow off his knees and shoulders. "I don't know where she could have thrown them."

"Dad," I began my protest. I was afraid of Pearl, a small, angry woman I first met as a smiling classmate in fifth grade. As an adult, she had stabbed her own mother. Charges were never pressed, Brian said, because it was just a really bad day for both women, and they knew it wouldn't happen again. My call had no effect on my father. He disappeared into the foyer of the building. I looked up at Brian and found him watching me. His breath floated between us, a cloud smelling of gin and hastily chewed mint gum.

"What are you doing here?" he asked almost shyly. "It's Christmas Eve. How the fuck are you?" He reached over and rubbed his knuckles on the top of my head, hard enough that I could feel it when he took his hand away. I knew he was drunk and high and full of self-pity for losing his keys and having such a crazy girlfriend. But I took it, that touch, the first one I could remember in years. I looked at him, at eyes that were unfocused, at the smile that remained because of the time delay of alcohol and God knew what else.

"I'm fine," I said. "I'm fine."

My father came out of the apartment house. "She's not answering the door. We just gotta go, Brian. We'll come back tomorrow."

We climbed into the car, Brian in the front passenger seat, me in the back, as always.

No one spoke on the ride home. The car was warm and dark and quiet, filled with the smell of sweat and stale cigarettes and alcohol. Exhalations from the three of us mingled and condensed on the cold glass. Brian leaned forward several times to rub the windshield in front of my father with his forearm. We pulled into the driveway, and the lights from the house shone out onto the snow with innocent invitation. Just before I got out of the car, I reached up to smooth my hair where Brian mussed it. And then, thought better of it.

Chapter Forty-Six

And you were raised by your parents
but you never quite grew
that's the one thing I always held
in common with you.

– Michael Kelsh, singer-songwriter,
"Baby Blue Eyes," Steel Blue Ballads, 1992

When I returned to North Carolina, I told Michael, "You'll have to take care of our relationship right now. I just can't do it."

He tried, the best way he knew how, but I couldn't feel it. I worked twelve-to-fourteen-hour days, adding the commute from my farmhouse on both ends. I let the work schedule prevent me from seeing him all week. On a Saturday night, I would arrive at his tiny house with a couple of beer bottles rolling and clinking on the floorboards of my car. I'd shove them under the seat and put a piece of Big Red gum into my mouth before I knocked. Some nights were good together, but most nights were like crude recycled paper, tiny fragments held together by pressure, but not really adhering, not smooth enough to write something new.

Most nights, when I got home from work, I had a beer, then two, or maybe a glass of wine, then two. Just enough so that my time at home would be totally useless, just enough so that I could fall asleep immediately but not before thinking, that's the last time I'll have anything to drink. It was the same promise I'd made the night I heard that Brian was dead, and I'd broken it the same night I returned from New York and the funeral.

I didn't know how to move around with the grief, wanted to be relieved of all responsibility to anything, even wished that I would get the flu, be able to stay in bed, ignore the phone, everyone.

Finally, in mid-December, I called a friend and asked if I could go with her to an AA meeting.

When the ritual I'd seen a hundred times began, when that white chip was offered to anyone who wanted to stop drinking or using for any reason, I was so nervous I almost missed it. I slowly knocked across the knees of other alcoholics to get out to the aisle. The woman holding the white chip saw me and waited patiently. As I walked toward her, I thought of the program saying, some will die so that others will live. I didn't like the phrase. It seemed too Christian to me, or too militaristic, an assurance that a battle death wasn't meaningless. But as I walked out of the meeting that night, I thought, OK, Brian, you have died, so I will live.

When I told Michael later that evening, he whistled, pulled me onto his lap and said softly, "My little alcoholic." I leaned my cheek against his; both were warm and wet.

Michael went home with me that Christmas. We were all cordial. In a large gesture, my father gave Michael my brother's old, cracked heavy bag and said in a gruff voice, "Thought you might use this." Michael accepted it as if there was nothing he would rather do than go a few rounds though, as far as I knew, he'd never touched a heavy bag in his life.

After the Christmas visit, my parents and I continued to re-establish a relationship that was tender, not tentative. We talked on the phone every few days. I called them when my dog was hit by a car and eventually died, and they consoled me. We never returned to the topic of our estrangement again. We all just moved on. Julie married the following spring, in a simple service including only her, her fiancé and a Unitarian minister. Nora finished another semester of college.

By spring, my relationship with Michael was over. I imagined that if our five-plus years were recorded on an EKG strip, it would have been long and curling with erratic highs and lows. Had the relationship been allowed to completely die, perhaps the anger and sadness wouldn't have taken so long to work through. But it never flatlined, just seemed to run out of paper for recording the all of it. And of course, he gave me the heavy bag. We both knew that it belonged with me.

The summer after Brian died, I visited my parents for a couple of days. I went for long walks through the streets. I had the sense of... silence, a post-bombing sort of silence. I went to AA meetings almost every night and met people who knew Brian, who had sat with him in those very rooms. I wasn't surprised to find people there who I'd known since childhood, a few had even been neighbors.

I called Andy. We went for a walk one evening, he still in his suit from his new job as a trainer for Blue Cross Blue Shield, me in what he called my hippie clothes. We found a large rock to perch on and talked about our jobs, about relationships and about my trip. He confessed that he was success-driven, and when I said, of course, we both laughed. When I asked him if he still kept charts and lists, he reluctantly admitted that he still did, which made us laugh again. He was keeping his distance from the boxing world, he said, in a tone that somehow sounded sure and wistful at the same time. When we talked about Brian, there was humor in many of the stories, and we laughed some more. Then Andy sighed and said, "If we're all here on earth for two blinks, you know, relatively speaking, and Brian was here for just one, isn't that still worth something?"

I felt a relief so strong it felt like my bones were melting. So many people had referred to Brian's life as "a waste." Most of them were well intentioned, I knew. They were just as lost in that forest of "what ifs" as I was. As I drove back to my parent's house, I felt as if Andy had helped me package my sadness for easier traveling, wrapped it up with his listening and care.

My mother had a doctor's appointment on the day I was to leave. She found me outside on the stone patio with the news-paper and a cup of coffee. "Drive safely," she said. "Call us when you get there so we know you're OK." She hugged me, kissed my forehead and left.

A few minutes later, I heard the screen door slide. My fa-ther stepped gingerly onto the stones. He stayed inside most summer days to escape the cloying humidity that saturated his lungs. He pulled out a patio chair from the table and sat down just as timidly, as if he might change his mind at any moment. The day was quite clear; the morning sun felt good with a breeze to offset the heat. My father cleared his throat. "When are you going to leave?"'

I folded the paper and sat up straight. "In an hour maybe."

"How long do you think it will take to drive there?" He'd asked me this the day before. It's what fathers do, talk about drive times and tire maintenance. And after I answered, he nodded and looked away then, toward the back of the proper-ty, where trees buffered the lawn before thickening into what we'd always just called "the woods."

"We never knew if he was going to come from back there."

I followed his gaze. "From back there?"

My father crossed his leg and picked at the trim on his deck shoe. "Yeah, sometimes he'd camp back there when he didn't have anywhere to stay. Close to home but not at home, I guess."

I stayed quiet. My father shook his head. "You never knew if he was going to come over that hill or what he wanted or what condition he'd be in."

I murmured something. Something like, "I know, Dad." But it was probably something less intelligible, just encouraging.

"One time, he came over the hill, and I don't know what he was on. He was really angry about something. I don't know what. We were in the garage, and he suddenly picked up a gas can and poured it, poured the gas all over… all over himself and showed me this lighter he had. Jesus." My father shifted, glanced at me, his eyes watery and squinty in the sun. "We had some bad times, Jan."

Again, I made that noise, that urging murmur.

"You know." My father cleared his throat. "When all of it started happening with Brian, I just couldn't… I just… It was all I could do to just be there for him. I knew you girls were going to be all right. But I thought Brian might die. So, I just had to put everything I had into saving him."

Reunion

[2005]

Andy puts it together. He says that he'd been intending to do this for a long time, get all the guys from the old Huguenot Boxing Club together. But it's my interviews and interest that are the catalyst. I feel good when I hear this, though soon enough the reunion planning takes on a life of its own and has nothing to do with me.

Andy calls Janet Patterson to tell her about the plan. She's very enthusiastic and says she'll be there. Her daughter just happens to be sitting next to her, listening to the conversation, and gets very excited about the idea. She swears she'll help round up some guys. As for Floyd, Janet is more guarded. He has cancer and problems with his memory. Some days are good, some bad. If it's a good day, maybe he can come. Andy calls Longo who is immediately on board and starts to call other fighters from his home in Florida. Then Longo calls Janet Patterson and says he hopes that all the bad blood (whatever it was) between him and Floyd can be water under the bridge. She agrees and says, "We're old now, Jimmy. That stuff doesn't matter anymore."

It's an overcast, surprisingly cool August afternoon. The gathering is sizable, mostly of fighters from the first years at Floyd's gym, including Andy, Longo, Alfie and Sammy. Andy called to invite Sammy after not seeing him for at least fifteen years and is surprised that he actually came. But Sammy's there early and is one of the last to leave.

There isn't really an agenda for the reunion. It's basically a talk and eat and slap each other on the shoulder affair. They do a little ceremonial weigh in. Andy announces each fighter, gives their fight weight, and then each man steps on the bathroom scale Andy brought. There's clapping and laughter as the current weight is announced. Longo does the math to figure out who has the biggest difference in weight. He pronounces Joey Walsh the winner, who fought at 112 pounds and is now, according to Longo, a butterball.

Then Longo gets serious and proposes a toast to the fighters from the club who died. First, he toasts to Bernie Dyer. He's the guy who left the gloves and jump rope at Brian's funeral. I never knew his name until I told Longo the story and he filled me in. Bernie was bipolar, or maybe he was schizophrenic, Longo said. "But such a nice guy. Harmless, you know? But he didn't take his meds." One day, Bernie painted his face blue and held a gun under his chin. According to Longo, the cops didn't really try to talk him out of it, they just kept pushing in. "And then Bernie pulled the trigger."

Now Longo toasts him, doesn't talk about how he died but recalls how Bernie helped him steal a piano from a sorority house at the college back in the seventies. Everyone laughs and raises a glass. Then Longo toasts Brian, asks for a moment of silence, and there is one, a long one, no laughter, and everyone raises a glass.

The reunion lasts three hours, one for every decade since Floyd opened the gym. Toward the end, Floyd's daughter shows up with her boyfriend and without her mother. She makes it in time to be in the photos. And in every frame, there is Sammy.

At the end of the afternoon, Andy talks with him about the night that Brian died. When he calls to tell me Sammy's story, I suddenly have the sense that this is like a set of nesting figures, the kind I loved as a child. If I open Sammy, there will be Brian, open Brian to find Larry. But then, we all have our set of nesting ghosts, and now Sammy is one of mine.

Later, when I see Sammy in the reunion photos, I think of what Isaac said about Brian when I sat with him during lunch at the family program. "It's like he dead." I thought about Brian's letter to his addictions. "You're building a corpse within me." At least Sammy went to the reunion. It meant something to him. And I feel better, like I do when I snap a twig off what I think is a frost casualty in my front garden and see that there is still sap.

Chapter Forty-Seven

The crowd is roaring. The referee pulls you away
and shows you the neutral corner. You turn around
in the corner. 5...6...7 he's not going to get up. God
damn, don't get up, we're through. We have lived.

– Brian Hurley, "The Other Side of the Ropes,"
The Huguenot Herald, New Paltz, New York,
June 23, 1976

Just home from yet another rehab, with the ink still fresh on
the letter he wrote to his disease, Brian was supposed to spend
only a brief day or two in New Paltz, then to head to New
Jersey where a bed was reserved for him at a halfway house.
He told my father he would meet him later in the day for the
three-hour car ride and left the house. He walked downtown
to cash the check he received from the insurance company
that paid for the treatment. I've never been clear on why he
got this check, and it turned out to be the fulcrum of the day.
He walked from the bank right across the street to P&G's and
slid onto a stool at the bar with the cash in his back pocket.

It was late afternoon, and there probably weren't many
people there. Brian went to the pay phone in the back. His
then on-again-off-again girlfriend, Alice, said later she was
surprised to get his call. She was a college student, and I'm
sure she got into their relationship totally unprepared for the
realities of his addiction. When he stole money out of her

purse, she called the police and had him charged, maybe trying a tough love approach. But she couldn't quite stick with
the plan, and their relationship followed a familiar path for
Brian, with some highs and lots of lows. She wanted to get
married, and when he was sober, he wanted to end it. They
hadn't figured out what the halfway house would mean to the
relationship. "I thought you were coming over here before you
went to Jersey," she said when she heard his voice.

"No," Brian said. "Look. I'm down at P&G's."

"P&G's? What are you doin' there?"

Maybe he looked over his shoulder and saw a drink sitting
on the counter. "Look," he said. "I'm gonna party hard. Just
one last time."

"I'll come down there," she said.

"No! I just want to do this by myself. I just wanna party
hard one last time and…" His voice got gentle. "I don't want
you to see me like that. OK?"

What could Alice say? "OK."

Brian went back to his drink. And when it was done, he
probably ordered another and another round for the house.
He sat with his back to the door, so when he felt a hand on his
shoulder, maybe he started as he looked up into Sammy's face.
He slid onto the stool next to Brian as if the effort tired him.
He likely had flecks of white paint riding his close-cropped
hair, paint smears on his hands. A thin white girl sat down
next to Sammy and leaned against him, her face tiny and
blank in the dimness of the bar. The girlfriend, Sarah. "How
ya been?" Sammy asked Brian.

"I've been," Brian said and pulled out his wad of cash to
pay for Sammy and his girlfriend's beers. "What are you up to
these days?"

"I've been working with this guy, painting some houses.
Hey, you see that fight last Friday on HBO? That guy Holy-
field? He's somethin.'" Sammy tilted his beer.

Brian shook his head. "Nah, I was... out of town."

Sammy nodded and said, "Looks like you got some cash to spend."

"Yes, I do."

They checked into the Super 8 Motel at the edge of the New York State Thruway early in the evening with supplies for the night. Some pretzels, chips, beer, a bottle of bourbon, small plastic bags with white powder, a roll of cloth that contained a syringe, needles, spoon, lighter, rubber tubing. Brian took these last items and went into the bathroom to inject a mixture of the heroin and cocaine, which I would later learn is called a speedball. Maybe Sammy turned on the television and sat on the bed with a plastic cup half full of bourbon. And maybe Sarah sat in a chair next to the window and watched the traffic while she waited her turn.

Tiny little sounds must have come from the bathroom: a slight bump as Brian unrolled the cloth, the snap and shhh of the lighter, a clank of the spoon, the thwap of the tubing as it was tied, a tiny click when Brian flicked the plastic side of the hypodermic to get rid of the air bubbles. After a moment of quiet, Sammy would have heard him release the tubing. All these sounds so familiar that Sammy probably only half heard them as he watched the television.

The loud thud made him jump up immediately. At first, Sammy told Andy, he thought the sound came from the door to the room. He moved in that direction even as he realized that it came from the bathroom. He pivoted and, in two steps, reached the door and pushed it hard. It gave easily halfway and then was stopped by Brian's body.

Sammy squeezed in and knelt beside him. "Brian," he shouted. "Brian." No response. "Shit, shit, shit, shit. Sarah. Sarah! Come help me."

For a small girl, she was surprisingly strong. They grabbed Brian under the arms and dragged him across the room to the bed. I can imagine a running commentary: "No, shit, pull up, no, you're dropping him, get his leg, Jesus Christ, Goddamn it."

On the bed, Sammy bent his head to Brian's mouth. He couldn't hear anything. He laid his ear to Brian's heart, then straightened up, put the heels of his hands on Brian's chest and pushed. He opened Brian's mouth and gave a breath in, thought he felt Brian's chest rise with it and returned to the CPR. "Jesus Christ, call the fucking rescue squad," he said to Sarah.

Her hair swung wildly as she looked around the room. "There's no phone."

Sammy looked about him in disbelief. "Then run downstairs to the desk or to a fucking pay phone."

She nodded, grabbed her purse and banged out the door.

He continued the CPR until he realized that Brian's body was resisting him, that he was making no impact at all. Then, he sat next to him. He looked at the man who had patiently worked with him all those years ago at Floyd's gym, who showed him how to throw his jab, who encouraged him when everyone else said he was glove shy and would never get over it. And then, after he stopped going to the gym and got into some trouble, Brian was always an ear for him.

Sammy heard the sirens. Sarah didn't come back, and he figured she took the chance to get out of the way before the police arrived. He knew he should do the same. But this was Brian. He wasn't going to just leave him.

Where did he look while he was waiting? Maybe he looked at Brian's hands, large and white, backs freckled, fingers long, with haggard, dirty nails. How many times had Sammy ducked and parried when these same hands balled into friendly fists for a little mock sparring? Later, when talking with Andy, Sammy said he remembered thinking, You wanted this didn't you, Brian? Out loud he had said, "Why me? Why did you pick me to do this with?"

When the emergency squad and the police arrived, he had one last irrational hope. Maybe that big bruise on Brian's forehead put him in a coma. He must have hit his head on the edge of the sink. Sammy moved away from the bed as the room swarmed with men and women who spoke with calm authority. He let his hope stay with him as he watched the gurney go out the door.

Intercom

[1968]

"It won't be long enough," I say and look down the hall toward my bedroom on the other side of the kitchen.

"Yeah, it will." Brian is ten and I'm six, so his opinion counts more. He kneels in front of me, uncoiling a long phone wire. I squat in the doorway to his room and take the end he offers. He stretches the cord as far as it will go and then uncoils it some more. Scuttling backwards, Brian plays out the line down the three steps into the kitchen, across the linoleum floor and through the door of my bedroom. "I told you it was long enough," he yells and runs back up to his room to hook up his end.

The crude intercom system, a gift from my grandfather, has two small plastic phones attached by a phone wire. Only one of the phones has a dial. The other end is just ready to be rung at any time. There's no question as to who will have the phone with the dial, who will be the caller.

"Go down there." Brian points. "Let's see if it works."

When my little phone rings, I snatch it up, thrilled, even though I can see Brian at the other end of the house talking into his receiver. "Hello, who is it?"

Brian makes a face at me, widening his eyes like a ghoul. "It's Draculaaaaa," he says, contorting his tongue and sticking it out at me. I shriek and hang up.

After we're supposed to be asleep my little phone rings again. "Are you asleep?" Brian whispers.

"No."

"OK." He hangs up. He calls back a few minutes later. "Do you hear the refrigerator running?"

The refrigerator is just outside the door to my room. I pause and listen. "Yeah. I do."

"Then you better get up and go catch it!" He snorts a laugh at me through the wire.

"Shut up." I put the receiver back. The light comes on in the kitchen.

"Brian and Janet, go to sleep. You can play with those phones in the morning," my mother calls out. Neither of us answer.

A few nights later, my little phone rings long after we've gone to bed, a tinkly, jangly sound that makes its way into my sleep and summons images of ice cream trucks. I pick up the receiver without saying anything.

"I had a bad dream," Brian says.

Nightmares always made me sick to my stomach. "Do you have to throw up?"

"No." He hangs up. The click tickles in my ear for a second, and then slides further into my dreams.

Epilogue

[2021]

My mother moved to North Carolina in 2003, a couple of years after my father died of complications from emphysema. It was a brave thing to do, to move out of the Hudson Valley after living there for seventy-six years. She settled in a quaint mountain town about twenty minutes from my family and me, in a condo that overlooked a lake and a park where she walked her dog, and a senior center, where she ate lunch daily. She volunteered at the local museum and library, was active in Democrats on the Move and wrote letters to the local paper to protest injustice. In the early years after her move south, it seemed like she'd found a reasonable facsimile of peace.

But when Floyd Patterson died in 2006, she called as soon as she heard the news on the radio. "They didn't say exactly what he died of, but I hope it was a long and painful death."

I cringed and then sighed. "Well, I think it was."

"That man was a crud. He was just evil. He ruined Brian's life."

"Well, Mom, Brian's addictions ruined his life."

"But you remember what Floyd did!"

"Yeah, I remember," I said. By this time, I had done most of my interviews about that long ago argument in the gym, something I wasn't prepared to share with her. "But he wasn't evil. He did a lot of good things in his life and maybe some things other people didn't like. Like most people. And he and

Brian seemed to work through all of that."

"Well." My mother's annoyance pulsed through the phone. "I think he was a horrible person."

"I know."

I wished she could tie up all of her bitterness and throw it into the lake the next time she walked her dog. By then, I had two small children and had some compassion for her when she pulled out that bundle of blame, wrapped as it was in the very thing she tried to ward off, that any parent might try as hard—even desperately—to prevent.

In 2015, when she was eighty-eight, my mother received a phone call from a young woman who said she was Brian's daughter. It was her mom who had met Brian in that rehab so long ago and gotten pregnant not long after, the one who he'd planned to marry. I never knew that part—about the pregnancy. Didn't know that when Brian showed up drunk or high on a visit, she'd shut the door and refused to let him back into her life. She died a week after her daughter was born healthy, from complications of childbirth. Brian died a little over a year later. His daughter was raised by her maternal grandmother, who kept her father's identify a secret. My niece didn't know the truth until she was twelve and didn't know Brian was dead until an against-all-odds serendipitous connection with Julie some thirteen years later.

There are so many questions that remain unresolved about who knew what when, and my mother's memory yielded no answers before she died at ninety-three. My niece does have a letter from my mom to her mom, dated a couple of weeks before she was born, but my mother didn't remember it. This had all happened during the eighteen-month estrangement between me and my parents, but why did I never hear about this? My wondering, of course, is about Brian. What did Brian know at that time? What did he do or not do? The inventory he wrote at the rehab he attended doesn't mention his girlfriend or the pregnancy. I think about the grief issued from any version of the story Brian knew and carried. That my niece carries to this day.

When I met her, I was struck by her green eyes, so much like Brian's. Her mom was Philippinx, and my niece didn't inherit the Irish tendency to burn bright red in the summer. Her hair is dark, not curly. She is strikingly beautiful. And so smart. I gave her Brian's Big Book from Alcoholics Anonymous, from his last rehab, and a bit of this memoir. She told me that one time, she had gotten into boxing for fitness, had even thought about fighting.

Brian, age 32, at one of his first loves, fishing.

When I started writing this story about my brother, about making my peace with regret, I looked up the word *reckoning*. One of its meanings is *to count one by one*, which is certainly what I did through all the years and, even after writing all of this, still do. Because there is something about those regrets. They have such familiar heft and form. They have tumbled against each other for so long, smoothed by the constant flow of feeling that there was something that I could have done, a power I never exercised. A polished collection, they have settled at the bottom of a murky pool. They anchor me down so that I am not drifting in a vast sea of powerlessness. I can always reach in, feel about, pull one out, let regret divide the immense loss into small manageable touchstones that I can count, one by one, that let me revisit the grace of my reckoning, that keep me focused on all that is at stake in any family.

I also find refuge in old photographs in which I can revisit, one by one, moments of possibility. If I concentrate, that feeling prevails for a second, sometimes two. Recently, I looked at a picture of my brother when he was three or four. His dark hair is buzzed short; he is sitting next to my older sister on the couch, both in footed pajamas. His shoulders are scrunched up as if the very taking of the picture is tickling him, his eyes bright, the fun of it all on his mouth, lips suffused with life, dark and healthy in his pale face. His freckles earnestly claim kin to Pippi Longstocking. The family dog, a beagle, leans against him, looking up at him, ears flopping back as he adores him. And all is as it should be.

Acknowledgments

My Family
This manuscript wouldn't have moved forward at all without the generous spirit of David, my husband since 1992. From taking care of our small children while I traveled to residencies at my MFA program and the Vermont Studio Center to his patience with the hours and distraction from everyday details that writing demands, he has always been a never-questioning cheerleader. My children, Maren and Liam, have grown up with this manuscript always hovering, much as this story and my brother's spirit always will. They are brave, thoughtful people who love each other and their parents fiercely and with humor. I want to be just like them when I grow up and, the universe willing, maybe someday I will.

To my brother's daughter, who so warmly gave me permission to provide a glimpse of her story and its impact, I hope this memoir provides some healing and more understanding with regards to your father. I wish he could have known you.

The Fighters and Trainers
I am indebted, most particularly, to Andy Schott who, from the first email I sent to him about writing this memoir, has been absolutely supportive and invested. He never failed to answer a question, make a connection for me, provide memories and reflections, or read sections for accuracy and authenticity. He gave me permission to tell so much of his story

as it wove in and out of my brother's life and mine and to share excerpts of his letters. In addition to teaching psychology at Hudson Valley Community College, he trains amateur fighters and the occasional pro at his gym, Schott's Boxing, in Albany, New York, which also has a large and devoted boxing-for-fitness clientele.

Jimmy Longo, Alfie Bevier and Tracy Patterson responded to my requests for interviews generously, putting in time and effort at the beginning of this journey and here at the end that I can only attribute to their affection for my brother, for each other and for the bonds built in that barn-turned-into-a-gym while training with Floyd Patterson.

Though I was never able to speak with Sammy at length, I am grateful that he finally told his story to Andy of what happened with my brother on that last night of Brian's life. Sammy died in 2011. He was just fifty. Andy Schott emailed me, and I couldn't help but wonder why I hadn't felt a little tremor in my world when Sammy passed.

Jim Fredericks and his wife, Fanny, created such a warm and welcoming space for me. Jim's storytelling and regret about what happened with my brother's attempt to go pro were invaluable for helping me to envision and understand the impact of what happened. Jim passed away in 2014 at age eighty-nine, and Fanny died in 2020, at ninety-three.

Though I was unable to talk with Floyd or Janet Patterson, I did read Floyd's autobiography *Victory Over Myself*, which surprised me with its honest and vulnerability and gave me more insight into him and all of the challenges he faced. I also read Allan H. Levy's *Floyd Patterson: A Boxer and a Gentleman*, published in 2008, which provided many details about Floyd I hadn't known. (Please refer to the sources section immediately following).

Brian's Friends

Harold Issen and I became friends as I wrote this book. He's an excellent writer, with a sense of the absurd and the poignant. I admire his deep love of family and enjoy our philosophical exchanges. With regards to reading final pages that included him, he said, "No, that's OK. You just tell your truth."

Gino Wigfall opened his home to me with graciousness and honesty and tried hard to facilitate a meeting for me with Sammy, an effort to benefit Sammy as much as me, I know. I called and asked him to read the finished manuscript, and he was equally gracious and supportive. When I thanked him, he said, "Yeah, well, you know, I lived it too."

Many thanks to Jamie Rhein for providing such an invaluable, candid and well written teenage girl's perspective of Brian and giving me permission to use most of it verbatim. She's a writer, too, and was immediately supportive of this project.

My Friends

After more than forty years, my college roommate Gwen and I are still in touch. Though surprised to be included in this manuscript, she supported the pages where she appears with affirmation and encouragement. She asked only for a pseudonym.

Michael Kelsh offered me not only a thoughtful and honest read as my ex-boyfriend and fellow traveler in a clean and sober life, but as an artist. He is still playing his music in Nashville, where he's lived for almost three decades, and has released several albums through the years.

Writing Mentors, Readers, Supporters

Sebastian Matthews, award-winning poet, collage novelist, book artist, creative nonfiction author and educator, is completely responsible for setting me on this path and providing guidance in the early years as the instructor of that 2003 creative non-fiction class.

This was taken up by the inestimable authors and mentors Rachel Manley and Wayne Brown, who were my main advisors in the Lesley University Master of Fine Arts in Creative Writing Program. Rachel, a memoirist, was the most empathic and intuitive MFA advisor I could have hoped for and helped me to swim deep into the waters with her long, provocative responses to my manuscript. Wayne, a novelist, was not the advisor I hoped for but the one that I absolutely needed, providing unflinching rigor, literary perspective and humor. Many thanks to advisor Rachel Kadish, my MFA cohort and other students who read such early and needy drafts.

Glenda Henderson, a wonderful writer and writing group member, has provided support and excellent feedback for almost twenty years. Other members of my writers group iterations, who read early revisions, include Molly Walling, Lisa Yoffee, Maryedith Burrell and Lauri Maerov.

Jim DeFelippi, of Brown Fedora Books, generously gave time, feedback and an offer to publish the *Glove Shy* manuscript on his then-new independent e-publishing website—back before 2010, when I wasn't ready, but neither of us knew it until we were underway and I needed to pull back. Poet Geoff Hewitt, thank you for making that connection with Jim and also reading the early manuscript and providing feedback to me.

So much appreciation to author and editor Ronlyn Domingue for pushing me on structural choices and character development, and to Sekou Coleman, for reading the manuscript as a "representational editor," a role he was game for though I couldn't fully explain it more than to ask him to look for implicit biases that could lead to tropes and harm for the Black characters I wrote about and for Black readers.

Novelist and memoirist Nancy Peacock didn't read this manuscript but has been and remains a writing mentor and friend who has provided support and guidance for my writing since I was in my twenties.

Unsung Heroes

I was aware as I wrote this memoir that so many people who supported me through my difficult years as a teenager and twenty-something, through my brother's death and my own reckoning with substance abuse, didn't appear in these pages or weren't fully acknowledged, though they are very much a part of my story. They include but aren't limited to: Brenda Roach (née Brooker), Jill Goodrich, Dolores Wells, Bob Burkhardt, Kelly Cottrell, Karen Linehan, Debra Karp, James Driggers, Ray Williams, Louise Kessel, Holly Marrow and my Al Anon and AA sponsors and friends (you know who you are).

Finally

Nora Gaskin, owner and publisher of Lystra Books, facilitated this publishing process with a keen eye to detail, a commitment to a profound reader experience, and total respect for the story and author's intent. Unsurprisingly, the copyeditor and book designer she recommended, Kelly Lojk, brought the same care and attention. This was a truly collaborative and supportive experience for me.

Sources

Readers may be interested in the following books, articles and public records that I have read for background or reference and that may directly be cited in these pages.

Alcoholics Anonymous: The Story of How Many Thousands of Men and Women Have Recovered from Alcoholism, 3rd ed. New York: Alcoholics Anonymous World Services, 1976.

"Amateur Fight Show to Feature Brian Hurley." The Daily Freeman (Kingston, NY), May 21, 1976.

Ashe, Arthur R. Jr. *A Hard Road to Glory: The African American Athlete in Boxing.* New York: The New York Times Company, 1988.

Bauer, Lance O. "Predicting Relapse to Alcohol and Drug Abuse via Quantitative Electroencephalography." *Neuropsychopharmacology* 25, September 2001.

Desantis, Al. "Schott Launches Pro Ring Career with a Quick KO." *Times-Herald Record* (Middletown, NY), October 9, 1982.

Early, Gerald Lyn. *The Culture of Bruising: Essays on Prizefighting, Literature and Modern American Cultures.* Hopewell, NJ: Ecco Press, 1994.

"Golden Gloves Entry Begins Today." *Daily News* (New York, NY), January 2, 1974.

Haglund, Yvonne, and Eriksson, Ejnar. "Does Amateur Boxing Lead to Chronic Brain Damage?: A Review of Some Recent Investigations." *American Journal of Sports Medicine* 21, Issue 1, January 1993.

Hall, Wayne Allen. "Hard Knocks." *Hudson Valley* (NY) *Magazine*, January 1978.

Hurley, Brian. "The Other Side of the Ropes." *The Huguenot Herald* (New Paltz, NY), June 23, 1976.

Hurley, Paul. "Titles and Broken Dreams." *Poughkeepsie* (NY) *Journal*, May 16, 1984.

Hurley, Sonia, testimony. Poughkeepsie (NY) Public Hearing Before the Temporary State Commission to Evaluate the Drug Laws, November 8, 1973.

Kelsh, Michael, singer-songwriter. "Baby Blue Eyes." *Steel Blue Ballads*, 1992.

Levy, Alan H. *Floyd Patterson: A Boxer and a Gentleman.* Jefferson, NC, and London: McFarland & Co., 2008.

Lipsyte, Robert. *The Contender.* New York: HarperCollins Publishers, 1987.

Maclean, Norman. *Young Men and Fire.* Chicago: University of Chicago Press, 1992.

McAndrew, Mimi. "Drug Abuse Coordinator Quits Program." *Poughkeepsie* (NY) *Journal*, November 19, 1973.

Nixon, Richard. "The President's Address to the Nation, April 30, 1973." *Weekly Compilation of Presidential Documents* 9, Issues 1–20.

Oates, Joyce Carol. *On Boxing.* New York: Ecco, 2002.

Patterson, Floyd, with Milton Gross. *Victory Over Myself.* New York: Bernard Geis Assoc., 1962.

Schwartz, Mark. "Schott Does His Talking in the Ring." *Middletown* (NY) *Sunday Record*, May 6, 1979.

Tiano, Charles. "Sportside." *The Sunday Freeman* (Kingston, NY), February 8, 1976.

Vespa, Mary. "Ex-Champ Patterson Sells 'Floydburgers' in Sweden and Coaches Boxing at Home." *People Magazine*, March 15, 1976.

JANET HURLEY was born and raised in the Hudson Valley of upstate New York before heading south to the University of North Carolina at Chapel Hill for its undergraduate creative writing program. She has lived in the south ever since, most recently in the Blue Ridge Mountains of western North Carolina, where she and her husband, David Matz, raised their daughter, Maren, and son, Liam.

After receiving an MFA in creative nonfiction from Lesley University in Cambridge, MA, Janet published feature stories and profiles for North Carolina-based magazines *Our State* and *VERVE*. She also ran a small business, True Ink, which provided creative opportunities for young writers. In 2011, she co-founded Asheville Writers in the Schools and Community (AWITSC), a nonprofit committed to racial equity and social change through the power of arts, culture and restorative self-expression. From 2013–2016, she taught creative nonfiction and writing for the media as an adjunct in the undergraduate writing program at Warren Wilson College. The onset of the Covid-19 pandemic forced many transitions, including, fortunately, a refocus on her own writing.

Glove Shy: A Sister's Reckoning is Janet's first book-length publication. She lives in Asheville, North Carolina, with David and their dog, Wilson.

www.ingramcontent.com/pod-product-compliance
Lightning Source LLC
Chambersburg PA
CBHW030353130626
46549CB00004B/1468